New Zealand
as it might have been

New Zealand
as it might have been

Edited by
Stephen Levine

VICTORIA UNIVERSITY PRESS

VICTORIA UNIVERSITY PRESS
Victoria University of Wellington
PO Box 600 Wellington

National Library of New Zealand Cataloguing-in-Publication Data
New Zealand as it might have been / edited by Stephen Levine.
ISBN-13: 978-0-86473-545-4
ISBN-10: 0-86473-545-6
1. New Zealand—History. I. Levine, Stephen I. II. Title.
993—dc 22

Printed by Printlink, Wellington

To Sofi,
my granddaughter,
as a reminder that life sparkles
with infinite possibility

Contents

Illustrations

Introduction

Stephen Levine

This book offers a new and admittedly unusual way of looking at New Zealand history and politics. Other works dedicate themselves to reporting on what happened and why. This book, by contrast, looks at what might have happened and why it did not—and what the consequences might have been if decisive moments in New Zealand's past had turned out somewhat differently.

This, then, is a work which contains fifteen dispatches from the front lines of a history that we never entirely got to experience. Of course, much of the book is true; it is situated in New Zealand— these two islands, as we know them—and its population is as we find it, a mix of the good, the bad and the ugly, humans in all their diverse complexity. The chapters are not altogether fictitious or fanciful: the laws of biology and physics are not suspended, and protagonists are not provided with a dramatic rescue at the most opportune moment.

Although at times playful, and at other times serious, what distinguishes this book is a degree of disciplined creativity, as fifteen authors re-examine key events and decisions in New Zealand's history, sensitive to possibilities that were plausible at the time, circumstances that with only a modest degree of adjustment could well have taken an entirely different turn.

Of course this is, in another sense, an immodest enterprise, tinkering with New Zealand's past (both distant and recent) in order to see how it might have been altered. But the contributors are not time travellers: the only thing being changed as a result of this exercise is our sense of what *could* have happened—and our awareness that, at every moment, there are a range of alternatives to the path that we (both as individuals and as a nation) are wandering down.

This is in some ways a more light-hearted way of learning about New Zealand's past—its politics, its principal personalities, the government's policies and their effects on people. In exploring what might have happened, we rediscover what actually *did* happen, but from a different angle, from the perspective of events that were only 'possibilities' at the time rather than the 'history' that is the face they normally present to us.[1]

It is possible that looking at events in this manner—re-experiencing the tentativeness of choice (with unknowable consequences) that decisions actually were for those who had to make them—can also assist us to acquire a greater recognition of history as a process, rather than a sequence of events, in which outcomes bequeath developments, and in which much is neither planned nor foreseen.

Perhaps—having read some of these fifteen chapters—a reader may feel initially disoriented, like a dreamer waking up to an unfamiliar dawn. The former United Nations secretary general Dag Hammarskjold's posthumously published book, *Markings*,[2] closes with a poem that begins (in translation):

> Is it a new country
> In another world of reality . . .?

But the poem ends more confidently:

> . . . it is the same land.
> And I begin to know the map
> And to get my bearings.

This book has fifteen different New Zealands in it, each one a slightly modified version of the one that we actually inhabit. Finishing the book New Zealand will still be the 'same land' and yet we encounter here a map—or fifteen of them—showing that there was always an alternative terrain. We can get our bearings, but we need to know not only where we have been but where, with luck (either good or ill) and skill (either superb or poor), we might otherwise have ventured.

Which of these various New Zealands would have made for a better country? Which of these would have been significantly worse? How close were we at times to discovering a newer place, something altogether finer, more distinctive and appealing? How near are we today as we stumble, presumably doing the best that we can, towards futures unknowable, some more hopeful, others wearying if not sinister.

If history is not a record of inevitabilities, then of course responsibility has to be fixed. It may be, as some say, that we get the history (and the politics) that we deserve, but that sidesteps the issue. Robert Kennedy used to say that any one of us can 'make a difference' and this is as true in the life of this small country as it is anywhere else. At the same time, history being what it so frequently is—a deeply dispiriting record of stunning ineptitude and obstinacy—we all too often find individuals 'making a difference' by missing opportunities rather than seizing them. As is sometimes said, it is virtually impossible for one person to win a war, but not altogether unlikely for a single mistake to do much to lose one.

The fifteen incidents in New Zealand history and politics re-examined in this book represent key events, each in its own way a significant 'turning point' for this country. The subjects covered could hardly have been more important for understanding New Zealand's development as a nation. Thus the book begins, appropriately, with the Treaty of Waitangi, the subject of two distinct chapters. The first, by historian Giselle Byrnes, investigates what might have happened had the Treaty not been signed at all. In the process she reminds us that this was, in fact, what very nearly happened. This will probably come as a surprise for most readers. There was nothing inevitable about that document, nor about the Treaty signing ceremony at Waitangi. Had the moment passed, and those assembled for the purpose dispersed, what might have happened? How would New Zealand have been changed by the disappearance of that event from our historical experience? In answering that question—to which Dr Byrnes gives rigorous attention, setting out a range of possible consequences—we gain a new perspective on the nature of that formative treaty and its importance for New Zealand society.

The second chapter, likewise, reflects upon the Treaty, dwelling in this case not on the circumstances of its signing but rather on the contents of the document. Janine Hayward's analysis turns upon a part of the Treaty—Article 3, conferring the status of 'British subject' upon Maori—that seldom receives much if any attention. By showing that in some ways the presence of this article was something of a surprise, Dr Hayward's analysis serves as a reminder of the importance of citizenship, and equality, and the actual content of a treaty that is often spoken of in much more abstract terms both by those seeking greater compliance with its provisions and by those uneasy about its contemporary application.

The third chapter—my own—reflects upon the circumstances by which Wellington, a pleasant and charming (if windy) city, came to be New Zealand's capital. This happened so long ago that the city's success in acquiring such a status—crucial to its development—is sometimes taken for granted. But one of the reasons for engaging in historical excavation is to look at a familiar place in an unfamiliar way, and in doing so know it well and truthfully for the first time. A country's choice of its capital city is a far from unimportant act; this chapter takes a new look at what the options were at the time and speculates on what might have happened had one of Wellington's serious competitors, Nelson, been given the nod.

The first section of the book closes with a chapter reflecting upon how New Zealand (and Australia) might have been changed had the two become one. After all, New Zealand participated in some of the discussions surrounding the formation of the Australian federation. The constitution of Australia to this day contains provisions applicable to New Zealand entry into the Commonwealth as a state (equivalent to New South Wales,

Victoria and so on). There is probably no path more important for New Zealand's national sovereignty than this 'path not taken', leaving the country a separate nation, with its own economic, social, political, military, financial and cultural arrangements. It is left to an Australian historian, based at Victoria University, Dr Kathryn M. Hunter, to speculate on what might have happened had New Zealand not chosen to stand apart.

If these decisions—establishing a nation premised on a special relationship with indigenous Maori, embodied in a Treaty; determining upon the location of a national capital; asserting 'separateness' from one's neighbour—are not *all* there is to an independent and distinct New Zealand identity, they are indisputably major, formative events in the country's history, pivotal to its future development. They helped set the course for future events, doing so with such firmness and authority that the possibility that any one of them—indeed, all of them—might not have happened at all, or at least not in the way that they did, may come as something of a shock. These chapters help to make up some of that deficit in our national attention.

The book proceeds chronologically and the chapters presented in the second part touch upon other important aspects of New Zealand's identity. Even reminding ourselves of them shows how substantially New Zealand has changed over the course of its history. Professor Erik Olssen's study takes us back to a period when perceptions about class warfare and trade union power were what politics was largely about. Re-examining two major strikes, and showing the linkages between them, Professor Olssen traces the impact of those strikes on industrial relations and subsequent political party development, offering suggestions about what it might have meant for New Zealand if the first of these strikes, the one at Waihi, had ended differently.

Next to the Treaty of Waitangi, with its annual 'Waitangi Day' commemorations, there is no event in New Zealand's history so powerful as to inspire a yearly renewal of national memory as the events at Gallipoli. Is it possible to conceive of a New Zealand in which the catastrophe at Gallipoli does not take place? Evidently so, for Donald Anderson provides a remarkably fluid account showing how closely Gallipoli depended upon a variety of contingencies. Any number of things could have unsettled that destiny, but what would that have meant for New Zealand's destination as it travelled ever forward towards independent nationhood?

Much the same question is presented by the next chapter, on New Zealand's entry into the Second World War, written by Denis McLean, a distinguished diplomat and former secretary of defence. As one who has had to argue New Zealand's case in a variety of settings, Denis McLean is well placed to consider ways in which New Zealand's emergence as a small state, defiantly distinctive from both Australia and the United Kingdom (to say nothing of the United States), has reshaped its outlook on world affairs. Although New Zealand's entry into World War II was instinctive, it was not inevitable (simply because it happened) and this chapter explores what might have transpired had New Zealand taken its time about participating.

The impact of war on New Zealand was such as to inspire a third chapter on the subject, with well-known New Zealand military historian Dr Ian McGibbon considering New Zealand and the Second World War from another angle. New Zealanders are accustomed to consider the country as enviably secure, distant from conflict, beyond reach of an adversary. That may be how matters seem today, but it has not always been so. How secure New Zealand actually was during the war with Japan is another story—the subject of Dr McGibbon's fascinating chapter.

The final chapter in the second part of this book—which focuses on war and development—looks at the first grand saga of New Zealand's environmental movement, the struggle to 'Save Manapouri'. As elsewhere, an effort to secure for posterity what might be irretrievably lost had ramifications beyond the particular issue at hand. In some ways the battle over a beautiful lake became the launching point for a revolution in the country's consciousness, opening the way to a redefined New Zealand identity in which being 'clean and green' meant at least as much, for many, as being 'rich and developed'. Dr Aaron Fox's subtle treatment of the topic allows us to consider how the country's economic development and cultural character might have been altered had the Manapouri campaign had an altogether different outcome.

These issues—economic development; environmental cons-ciousness; military preparedness and national security—remain on the agenda, as, for that matter, do questions associated with the Treaty of Waitangi and the country's 'race relations'. The six chapters found in the third section of the book see some of these topics re-emerge in politically new settings. (Some issues *do* disappear: joining Australia qualifies as a serious non-starter and it must be conceded that the chances of shifting the capital to Nelson (for good or ill) are now virtually non-existent).

This final section's chapters, contributed by political scientists rather than historians, represent more 'modern times'. Several of them are from the Muldoon era and so we are brought back to the days of 'think big', and the 1981 Springbok tour, and the challenges to Muldoon's leadership, both from within his own party and from the Labour Party. John Wilson's new look at 'think big' seems overdue, an iconoclastic re-examination of projects long dismissed as a byword for discredited policies and an out-of-touch political/economic philosophy. Dr Wilson takes the premises on which the projects were based a bit more seriously, examining the circumstances that brought them into difficulty and a slightly adjusted context in which matters might have worked out more favourably.

Colin James's chapter is a salutary reminder that the coup-that-never-was might not have resolved matters comprehensively after all. Muldoon had a deputy, Brian Talboys, and at the time and in retrospect it seemed that had Talboys taken over (following the prime minister's overthrow by his colleagues) the country might have seen the end of Muldoon's leadership and influence several years earlier than 1984. Colin James's closely reasoned analysis suggests that the ascension of Talboys (the reluctant saviour) might not have resolved matters so definitively after all.

Professor Bob Gregory's chapter combines his once lively passion for rugby with a love of politics. Indeed, it would be an odd book on 'key events' in New Zealand's history that didn't find space *somewhere* for a rugby match. Probably no single New Zealand sporting contest has been as fraught with political consequence as the final test of the 1981 series with South Africa. Why this was so, and what that match meant for New Zealand's political future, is the story that Professor Gregory (who has been telling it off and on to his students for years) agreed to share with readers—including, perhaps, if he encounters it, the man at the centre of events, All Black Allan Hewson.

Professor John Henderson knew David Lange well, having worked with him in the Beehive. As a result, Professor Henderson was an observer of the events that he describes. His chapter— which moves matters away from the Muldoon era into the period of the fourth Labour government—is devoted to the development of New Zealand's antinuclear policy. For years New Zealand's security was predicated on an alliance relationship, first with the United Kingdom and subsequently with the United States (with Australian friendship slotted in alongside). This was a bipartisan fact of New Zealand foreign and defence policy, a topic so completely a part of the national consensus as to be outside of the normal bickering between the National and Labour parties. This effectively ended with the introduction of the antinuclear policy by Labour, eloquently articulated by Prime Minister Lange. Professor Henderson's scenario shows how the critical event— the planned (but aborted) visit by the American naval vessel the USS *Buchanan*—might well have played out differently, with consequences we would still be living with today.

The penultimate chapter, by Jon Johansson, looks at the aftermath of the turbulent fourth Labour government. In its wake, as in reality, Jim Bolger becomes prime minister with Ruth Richardson as his minister of finance. Dr Johansson's scenario revives memories of the Bolger government's first budget—the famously named 'mother of all budgets'[3]—and considers what might have happened if the prime minister, in partnership with his close colleague cabinet minister Bill Birch, had adhered to a slightly different model of leadership, one arguably closer to his genuine inclinations (in terms of policy and process).

Finally, Nigel S. Roberts—familiar to many New Zealanders for his many years' experience as an election-night commentator—has his own turn at constructing a post-election cabinet rather than merely predicting or analysing one. Professor Roberts's scenario—almost wholly reliant on genuine quotations and citations from published works on the 1996 election, New Zealand's first election under MMP—traces the consequences for New Zealand of Winston Peters choosing to go into coalition with Labour (as many had expected, and as indeed occurred following the 2005 election) rather than National. What such a decision might have meant for MMP itself is also explored in Professor Roberts's remarkably well-documented narrative.

None of these fifteen chapters represent the 'last word' on their topic. Instead, each points towards a different way of thinking about New Zealand's history and politics, inviting a deeper and more widespread conversation from others (students and scholars) interested in who we are, how we have been formed, and what alternatives there may have been for us. For what is most distinctive about this book is that it represents the first of its kind.

These sorts of speculations—explorations of alternative possibilities in history and politics—are sometimes labelled 'counterfactuals'. What is a counterfactual? One analyst, Professor Ned Lebow, defines them as '"what if" statements, usually about the past'.[4] Accordingly, each of the chapters in this book has been given a 'what if' title, encapsulating the principal focus of the narrative in a simple and direct question. Professor Lebow's exhaustive review of scholarly and historical counterfactuals sees them as a weapon to 'combat the deeply rooted human propensity to see the future as more contingent than the past'.[5] He also notes how counterfactuals may be 'smuggled into' narratives with no explicit desire to use them, simply as a part of reasoning about the causes and consequences of factual events. This occurs in political environments no less than in scholarly ones, with Lebow describing the Cuban missile crisis of 1962—the event that drove the United States and the Soviet Union closer to nuclear war than at any time in their often tense relationship—as one in which 'counterfactuals drove policy', a characterisation made possible by contemplating the relevant policymakers as figures caught up in a dilemma in which predictions about actions and reactions flowing out of 'what if' scenarios differed from academic exercises only in the magnitude of what was at stake in guessing correctly. For Professor Lebow, counterfactuals, to be useful, have to be *credible*: that is, *plausible*. Professor Geoffrey Hawthorn's study, *Plausible Worlds*, likewise sees counterfactuals as legitimate to the extent that they are factually based rather than wholly fanciful.[6] Hawthorn's approach emphasises that counterfactual assertions are inevitable in history and political science—'Possibilities haunt the human sciences'[7]—with the validity of explanations (causal statements about events) being tested, at least in part, by the examination of alternative possibilities.

British historian T.G. Otte likewise finds 'a strong case for the sparing use' of counterfactual practice as a technique 'to elucidate possible alternative developments'. While emphasising the need for credibility—'good counterfactual history has to explore realistic alternatives, taking into account the prevailing conditions of the time and the character of the decision makers'—he notes that counterfactuals make for 'good fun' while at the same time making 'the reader think'—which is 'what all good history, "factual" or "counterfactual", should be about'.[8]

Of course, it can be difficult to avoid making counterfactual statements: we all have opinions about 'what might have been'. Even New Zealand's own prime minister, Helen Clark, briefly toyed in public with a counterfactual of her own, famously speculating that if Al Gore had been elected US president in November 2000 the war in Iraq would never have taken place—a hypothesis that, though it passed the test of credibility, needed to be somewhat hastily and apologetically withdrawn.

The counterfactuals in this book were each 'tested' at our first-ever New Zealand counterfactuals conference. Held over two days (30 June–1 July 2005) there was one overriding requirement for participation: the topic of a presentation had to be about a decision, incident or event drawn from *New Zealand's* history. The implication was that New Zealand's history had an importance of its own. Counterfactual studies elsewhere have been dedicated to exploring historical phenomena from *other* countries and regions (principally the United States and Europe). The conference—and this book arising out of it—is distinguished from other studies by its unique and exclusive focus on matters particular to New Zealand.

In offering these fifteen scenarios, it is not to be suggested that the topics covered are the *only* ones of overriding importance for the country. Indeed, in the weeks and months following the conference and during the period in which this book was being prepared, other scholars (who had heard of the conference) suggested further topics to explore. I would be surprised if publication of this book did not stimulate a further reworking (from a 'counterfactual' perspective) of events drawn from New Zealand's history. As this book shows, such an exercise, intelligently conducted, can be informative for all concerned—both researcher and reader—and enjoyable at the same time.

As readers will discover, clearly there is no one style by which 'counterfactual' commentary must be conducted. The fifteen chapters represent a range of approaches and in some cases these may be found within a single chapter.

Giselle Byrnes's study of the Treaty of Waitangi is a carefully reasoned analysis, based on historical evidence, closing with some observations on the nature (and value) of counterfactual analysis itself. Janine Hayward's chapter likewise opens with an analytical survey of the topic, before embarking upon what she described at the conference as 'a bit of a romp' with a brief bit of historical fiction. The chapter about Nelson is a similarly high-spirited sprint which takes the form of a unspoken soliloquy by the prime minister, Helen Clark, reflecting on the wonders of her life in the lovely New Zealand capital. Kathryn M. Hunter's chapter offers yet another style, its narrative composed as an altered history of New Zealand and Australia in the aftermath of the union between the two.

There are, in short, many ways of imagining alternatives, of analysing possibilities. The chapters on the Waihi strike, Gallipoli, 'think big', and the failed coup against Prime Minister Muldoon are factually based analyses, expositions of alternative outcomes that reason their way through the relevant historical context. By contrast, the two chapters on the Second World War are in the form of short stories, Denis McLean's light-hearted yet pointed,

21

Ian McGibbon's a gripping piece of drama that would no doubt translate to the screen very effectively.

Aaron Fox's study of the Manapouri issue is presented as an altered history of events in which the line between fact and fancy is not always easily glimpsed. This is also the case in Nigel Roberts's chapter, in which authors cited in his extensive footnotes may be surprised to see the way in which quotations and references from their works provide strong documentary evidence in support of events that never actually occurred.

John Henderson's chapter on the antinuclear dispute with the United States, and the break-up of ANZUS, takes the form of light fiction, all of it premised on only a very slight adjustment to the historical record. Bob Gregory's chapter has two components to it and accordingly offers a good example of the styles of argument available to authors of counterfactuals. The first section of his chapter is a whimsical piece of work—complete with a limerick!— in which a change that might so easily have taken place brings in its wake a completely altered stream of history. The second part of his chapter offers an analysis—complete with a simple chart—of the logical premises lying behind counterfactual analyses such as his own.

Jon Johansson's chapter likewise offers two distinct styles, the first, establishing the factual grounds on which his scenario rests, and the second, presented by way of a fictional narrative which— as distinct from the Nelson chapter where Helen Clark, thinking, is in effect conversing with herself—invents dialogue for Bolger and Birch as a way of moving the scenario forward.

Preceding this diversity of style is an element common to each of the chapters. For the sake of the historical record—and to provide a contextual backdrop for the staged reworkings of New Zealand history—each chapter begins with an opening section (presented in italics) setting forth what actually *did* happen (in some cases briefly, in others at somewhat greater length). The disruption to historical fact in the fifteen 'counterfactuals' is not, in short, 'postmodern'; these scenarios are not in any way a denial of what occurred. They represent, instead, an effort to place before readers accounts of New Zealand's history in which the genuine sequence of events is presented and then undone via a scenario based on alternative probabilities—much the way a jazz musician will play the theme of a work 'straight' before embarking on some creative and personal reinterpretations.

Each chapter opens with a photograph, representative of the text to follow. This was not as straightforward a task as it sounds. What is involved here is the presentation of visual images for events that did not actually take place. Consider, for example, Ian McGibbon's chapter on the Japanese invasion of New Zealand during the Second World War. It is something of a triumph (to which I am further indebted to Dr McGibbon) to have a photograph illustrating an event that did not actually happen.

As noted at the outset, this book starts from the premise that little if any of our history seems foreordained. Our world—our lives as individuals; our existence as participants in a collectivity— is filled with options and opportunities. In some ways our affairs hang by a thread: everything can change in a moment. There are always alternatives open to us, and to others, and it is the task of historians and political commentators, at least in part, to identify these alternatives, to explore what they might have meant (both at the time and subsequently) and why they were not taken, and what those various pathways might yet mean for us today.

It is the task of policymakers and political analysts to do the same thing for options open to us in our own time. Such a task— thinking about the way things might have been and the way things might yet be—is, in fact, a significant and by no means simple exercise. Carried out properly, it transforms our world from a static and predictable place, filled with inevitabilities, into a dynamic environment, one in which at every moment there are unfulfilled possibilities, each possessing unknowable consequences. In this respect everyday life is something of an ongoing 'counterfactual' experiment, and we find out the outcomes day by day, making history as we go.

BEGINNINGS

1

What if the Treaty of Waitangi had not been signed on 6 February 1840?

Giselle Byrnes

When Captain James Cook first visited New Zealand in 1769, he estimated the indigenous Maori population at around 100,000. Contact was sporadic through to the early nineteenth century, with sealers, whalers, traders and then missionaries making semi-permanent homes under the patronage of powerful Maori tribes, eager to trade and engage with the newcomers. In the late 1830s British designs on annexing New Zealand quickened, and in 1840 the Treaty of Waitangi was signed between Maori and the crown. While the British saw this as a treaty of cession, Maori signatories considered it a confirmation of their sovereignty, in exchange for British protection. This vast difference in expectations stemmed from the existence of two versions of the Treaty in different languages which contradicted each other. While the Treaty extended to Maori 'the rights and privileges of British subjects', it effectively absorbed them into the rapidly expanding white settler society. For the next 130 years successive settler governments pursued policies of containment and 'amalgamation', in an attempt to undermine Maori customs, values, and systems of land tenure. Despite the existence of the Treaty, and sustained efforts by Maori to remind the crown of its obligations towards them, it was effectively marginalised in public discourse and largely erased from the collective memory of Pakeha society. In the mid-1970s, however, political protest, fuelled by international calls for the recognition of indigenous rights, led to the establishment of the Waitangi Tribunal, a commission of inquiry empowered to interpret the principles of the Treaty and determine whether contemporary claims from Maori, regarding acts and omissions on the part of the crown, were inconsistent with those principles. For many tribes, virtually every generation has been involved in presenting some form of injustice regarding Treaty breaches to the government of the day.

The Treaty of Waitangi was first signed at Waitangi in the Bay of Islands on 6 February 1840 between Captain William Hobson on behalf of the British crown, and representatives of northern

Maori tribes. While a further fifty-one Treaty signings took place at various sites around New Zealand over the following seven months, British sovereignty was declared over the entire country on the basis of the Waitangi agreement.[1] The story of the signing of the Treaty is now fairly well known. However, it is less well recognised that Hobson had originally scheduled this first Treaty signing for Friday 7 February, having presented the Treaty to the assembled chiefs on Wednesday 4 February. According to contemporary accounts, by the morning of Thursday 6 February, the chiefs had reached the conclusion that the Treaty business should be dealt with immediately so that they might return home: besides, the food provided as hospitality to them had begun to run out.[2] At this point, Hobson was on the *Herald*, moored in the bay, and completely oblivious to this change of events. By mid-morning, there was no indication of life on board, and when a boat was quickly sent for Hobson, he apparently had 'not the least notion' that a crowd had gathered.[3] Alarmed by this turn of events, Hobson agreed to bring forward the day of the signing ceremony.[4] A stickler for proper procedure, he insisted the meeting on 6 February could not be seen as a 'regular public meeting', since formal notification had not been given. Hobson thus suggested that the Friday meeting still be held for the purposes of discussion, but on the Thursday only signatures would be collected. As it happened, bad weather prevented any meeting from taking place on the Friday.[5] The Treaty was duly signed, Maori left, and the rest, as they say, is history.

This chapter engages with a controversial form of historical reasoning, alternate history. Also known as 'counterfactual history' or 'allohistory', alternate history might seem to have no place in the world of rational scholarly methods. Relying as it does on second-guessing and speculation, this 'what if' approach has earned the contempt of many historians. Counterfactual narratives at first appear to be nonsensical: for if these supposed events did *not* happen, then why study them? If certain events did not happen, then why ponder their non-existence? As one commentator has wryly observed: 'No diary can note what would have happened, no newspaper can report what would have happened, indeed, there seem to be no original sources at all to indicate what might have happened.'[6] Statements about what might have happened seem at best speculation, and at worst sheer fancy. By definition, counterfactual thinking is the antithesis of deterministic thinking: the belief that events were bound to unfold in the manner they did and that the world is meant to be as it is. Drawing on the alternate history method, this chapter poses the questions: what might have happened if Hobson had kept to his original plans and not brought the signing of the Treaty a day forward? Quite probably, Maori would have left Waitangi, the Treaty would not have been signed, and Hobson would have returned to Britain empty-handed. The possible course of events that might have followed is considered in terms of notions of sovereignty and current scholarship in the field of comparative history.

There are a number of possible alternate scenarios concerning what might have happened had Hobson not managed to get his act together. First, Maori might have remained in control of New Zealand as autonomous tribes and political entities. Second, the British might have invaded by force rather than use a treaty of cession. Third, New Zealand might have been claimed instead by the French or the Americans: would Maori (and other settlers) have French as their mother tongue, or perhaps speak with a New England accent? And fourth, British colonisation would have proceeded over those areas where British settlers were resident, with Maori retaining their autonomy in other areas. It is also worth noting that in the absence of a treaty, Maori would have no special rights beyond that of common law rights. This chapter argues that, on the basis of contextual and circumstantial evidence, we should discount the first, second and third scenarios, but the last is possible and indeed highly probable.

The first outcome is possibly the most attractive to those who now champion the cause of Maori sovereignty. The existence of Maori as independent tribes and modern polities in their own right might well be the ultimate fantasy of many Maori nationalists. However, as hinted at above, the evidence suggests this situation would have been highly improbable. Why would Maori have been able to escape the web of empire, when its reaches were so vast? Why would they have been immune from colonisation? It is totally against the run of evidence and logic to assume that New Zealand, with its rich natural resources, would have been exempt from some form of external colonisation. After all, there had been successful trading relationships established between Europeans and Maori tribes from the late eighteenth century, and a good deal of missionary activity in the early nineteenth. On the whole, Maori had been eager to engage with Europe, its peoples and its technologies. Perhaps unwittingly, they had helped facilitate, or at least hasten, the processes of colonisation. For example, there is evidence that many tribes had, well before 1840, expressed a desire for British law and order and at the same time engaged in land transactions.[7]

The second scenario is also historically problematic. While there is some debate about *when* the British crown decided to undermine Maori sovereignty, there is ample evidence that the crown did not want to and could simply not afford to invade New Zealand by force. Trading with New Zealand and working the waters around the country was good business that Britain did not want to jeopardise. In addition, the stereotype of Maori as a 'warlike race' still had immense currency in the popular imagination. For Britain, emerging bruised from the Napoleonic wars, a costly campaign on the other side of the globe could not have been sustained. Quite probably, the British forces would have met a formidable enemy in the Maori, who had had access to muskets for at least twenty years. There were diplomatic issues too. The Colonial Office had earlier considered asking Maori for a cession of sovereignty, a voluntary surrender in essence, over certain areas that would be established as part of a crown colony. As Paul McHugh has pointed out, the crown was legally constrained from exerting any sort of power over New Zealand without Maori consent. This, he has posited, rested on three main principles: first, the crown recognised the sovereignty of non-Christian, tribal societies elsewhere; second, the crown usually exercised power over such societies only with the indigenous rulers' consent; and third, these two principles were incorporated into 'colonial law', that part of the common law affecting the governance of colonies.[8]

British colonisation was therefore predicated on Maori consent. As James Belich asks, 'How else could Hobson have hoped to establish a colony with £4000 and a dozen policemen?'[9] So, we can dismiss the option of invasion. Similarly, the third probability, while perhaps appealing, is equally unlikely. While it is true that James Clendon was appointed American consul in 1838 in the Bay of Islands, and the French established the settlement at Akaroa in 1840, there is serious doubt over their ability (or desire) to expand a toehold into something larger. It is worth noting that in the early nineteenth century French Catholic missionaries had settled in northern parts of New Zealand and French traders had married into Maori communities; but the French had never laid formal claim to the sovereignty of New Zealand.

The fourth suggestion, that a limited form of British colonisation could have proceeded, would have been the most likely outcome. The original plans for a British colony included a Maori New Zealand where settlers would be provided for. In fact, the formation of a Maori governing body, a confederation legislating for both Maori and settlers under British protection, was considered as an alternate, but colonial officials later thought the idea impractical.[10] As early as 1837 Hobson had proposed the crown assume power over certain sites in New Zealand, in much the same way that the British had established 'trading factories' in India. Hobson's plan envisaged that an agreement would need to be made with Maori in these areas and the remainder of the country would remain under direct Maori control. Even British Resident James Busby had suggested that a protectorate be declared over the entire country and that the crown simply manage affairs in trust for all residents.[11] Historian Paul Moon has recently argued that the crown never intended to 'rule, preside over, or govern Maori, let alone usurp Maori sovereign right to self rule'.[12] Moreover, he contends that 'the Treaty was intended by the Colonial Office to allow crown rule to apply solely to British settlers in the fledgling colony. Maori sovereignty would accordingly be left unaffected by British rule over British subjects in the country'.[13] After all, only five years earlier the British crown had recognised Maori autonomy in the 1835 Declaration of Independence—or at least the autonomy of those northern tribes who had consented to this agreement. In the absence of a treaty to override or nullify the declaration, there is no reason why the 1835 agreement would not still have been valid; and according to the Maori language version, remains so.

The idea that the British would have annexed only those areas that British settlers had occupied, leaving Maori with their autonomy intact, is borne out by the historical evidence. Despite the vexed issues of authority and sovereignty, both language versions recognised the customary rights of Maori as the aboriginal inhabitants and thus guaranteed to Maori native title rights at British common law. Besides, the instructions from Lord Normanby, secretary of state for the colonies, to Hobson clearly recognised Maori autonomy. Considerable light can be shed on the final terms of the Treaty as settled by Hobson by reference to the instructions under which he was acting. The instructions were clear that the native title rights of Maori were not to be dispensed with for the sake of commercial opportunity:

[T]he increase of national wealth and power promised by the acquisition of New Zealand, would be a most inadequate compensation for the injury which must be inflicted on this Kingdom itself, by embarking in a measure essentially unjust, and but too certainly fraught with calamity to a numerous and inoffensive people, whose title to the soil and to the Sovereignty of New Zealand is indisputable, and has been solemnly recognised by the British Government.[14]

Hobson was thus charged with obtaining 'the free and intelligent consent of the Natives', and the instructions made it clear that he emphasise to Maori they too would benefit from entering this arrangement—and would suffer if they did not. 'You will, therefore frankly and unreservedly explain to the natives, or their chiefs,' the instructions continued, 'the reasons which should urge them to acquiesce in the proposals you will make to them. Especially you will point out to them the dangers to which they may be exposed by the residence amongst them of settlers amenable to no laws or tribunals of their own; and the impossibility of Her Majesty's extending to them any effectual protection unless the Queen be acknowledged as the sovereign of their country . . .'

As noted above, the early plans for a British colony in New Zealand envisaged a 'Maori New Zealand'; but by the time Hobson received Normanby's instructions in August 1839, both the tenor and substance of the plans had significantly shifted. What was now visualised was a 'settler New Zealand' where Maori would be guaranteed a special position. As Orange explains: 'Britain had decided to make a colony in New Zealand—not because of the small settler population of only two thousand people, but to establish authority over the thousands of expected emigrants and to protect the rights and welfare of the Maori people.'[15] By 1839, colonial office officials, while concerned that Britain should be responsible for both Maori and British subjects, accepted that colonisation was an 'inevitable measure'.[16] Clearly, the tide of British colonisation could not be contained forever. Yet we ought to recognise that while the British clearly had designs on settling in New Zealand, there was serious discussion as to how extensive British colonisation should be.

It is important to emphasise that while Maori independence may well have been guaranteed in certain areas, it is a moot point as to how long this autonomy could have been maintained. It is quite possible, given the willingness of many tribes to enter into land transactions (paradoxically as a way of recognising and securing their title to land), that these rights would have been steadily, and perhaps rapidly, eroded. This would have had major implications for the present. For if Maori were themselves the (albeit unwitting) authors of their own demise, rather than victims of deliberate crown actions and inactions, then they would be in a much weaker position today in terms of negotiating restitution for historical injustices. In fact, the status of Maori would be comparable to indigenous peoples in other jurisdictions who are 'without treaty', most notably those in Canada and the United States.

If the imagined scenario outlined above had eventuated, there would have been a number of implications. The most pressing of these is that once we take away the Treaty, there is an immediate emphasis on what Andrew Sharp has called 'legal constitutionalism': that is, the constitutional arrangements we have in New Zealand obtain their force by 'transmission from the crown, not the consent of Maori or the agreement between crown and Maori'.[17] Here the Treaty becomes something of a side issue. This also highlights the legal source of Maori rights, which is not the Treaty, but the statutory or common law means by which these rights have become part of the legal system in New Zealand.[18] Moreover, the absence of the Treaty of Waitangi confers upon the many hundreds of deeds of sale and individual land purchases a new status: that of individual 'treaties'. As Vincent O'Malley has argued, this would make the New Zealand historical experience similar to that of Canada, where there was not one but many 'little treaties', both oral and written. O'Malley, and James Belich before him, suggested that the many hundreds of agreements entered into between Maori and the crown, in the form of land transactions and other agreements, be seen as 'treaties' in their own right.[19] This is because these agreements had a real, rather than symbolic impact on their lives. As O'Malley states: 'The fact that Maori throughout the country have . . . tended to rely on the terms of the Treaty of Waitangi in promoting their grievances against the crown has tended to undermine other, no less significant, though now largely forgotten, undertakings made by the crown at a local level.'[20] In this context, comparisons may also be drawn between New Zealand and the United States, where between 1778 and 1868 there were 367 ratified 'Indian treaties' signed between the US government and indigenous tribes, plus a number that were not ratified by the senate.[21] For some time, historians have been moving away from understanding the Treaty of Waitangi as an exceptional and 'unique' agreement, and have instead emphasised the established but also highly adaptive tradition of treaty making from which it came.[22] This shift of interpretation has also witnessed an increased recognition of what treaties meant to indigenous peoples and the evidence suggests that in few cases was there evidence of mutuality of understanding between both parties. In other words, in New Zealand, Canada and elsewhere, indigenous peoples seem to have had profoundly different expectations of treaties and treatylike agreements: more often than not they saw such agreements as confirming, rather than extinguishing existing rights, although in a new environment.[23]

What then might this mean in a broader intellectual sense? Why construct alternate realities and speculate on what *might have* happened? What is the point of wondering if the Treaty of Waitangi might never have been? This chapter suggests that far from being a flight of fancy, alternate history is a valid form of historical reasoning. There are strong arguments in favour of counterfactual history. First, by focusing on possible (albeit unrealised) scenarios, counterfactual readings convey a sense of contingency and open-endedness about the past. After all, it is human beings, with all their fallibility, who make decisions and bear the consequences of those decisions. Second, those who have defended alternate historical approaches have pointed out that counterfactual reasoning is intimately connected with the idea of causation.[24] Historians employ counterfactual scenarios all the time, in determining the relationships between events, actions, and outcomes: for they must consider both what did, and conversely, what did not happen. The study of history is, after all, not simply the study of *what* happened, but *why*. Counterfactual reasoning is the way in which these conditionals are tested. Alternate history is, therefore, not simply an anachronism or an example of 'bad history', but a part of historical reasoning, and a potentially rich field of historical scholarship.

In recent years numerous examples of alternate history have appeared. These include historical narratives where the Nazis emerge triumphant after the Second World War; where the American Revolution does not eventuate; where Jesus Christ is not crucified; where the South wins the American Civil War; and where the atomic bomb is not dropped on Japan, among others.[25] Counterfactual narratives have also found expression in popular culture as well as in scholarly analyses.[26] It could be argued, for instance, that the myth that 'Elvis lives' is an alternate history given expression in popular culture. Alternate histories also form the basis of science fiction—an entire genre based on 'what if?' suppositions, which continues to enjoy widespread popularity, despite its unashamedly improbable character. In a broader intellectual sense too, the posing of counterfactual questions can be traced back to the beginnings of Western historiography itself.[27] Further, the current political and ideological climate is increasingly hospitable to allohistorical narratives and speculation. The trend towards postmodernist readings of the past has encouraged the rise of alternate histories, with the blurring of boundaries between fact and fiction, and the privileging of 'other' voices. Rosenfeld argues that the gradual discrediting of political ideologies (the death of socialism and the end of the Cold War), coupled with recent trends in scientific thinking, such as chaos theory, has eroded the power of deterministic world views. The products of the information revolution, cyberspace and virtual reality, have also encouraged some to break free from the constraints of 'real history'.[28] Counterfactual reasoning is not necessarily illogical. It is human nature to wonder 'what if?' and to speculate on the possibilities of alternative decisions and their outcomes.

It has also been argued that alternate histories illuminate the evolution of various historical events in the collective memory of any given community: that is, they reveal the history of ideas about the past, as well as tracking attitudinal changes over time.[29] Even full-scale historical narratives, which construct an entire alternative past, can be critically read as a way of grasping the concerns of any society or group, and can be appreciated as 'documents of memory' and ways of charting the evolution of collective memory.[30] The inherent subjectivity of alternate historical narratives means that they may be read as a reflection on the political, economic, cultural (and other) anxieties of any given society. But this does not mean they are isolated. Indeed the primary task of an alternate history might be to express changing views and ideas about the present. By tracing back to see how any given subject has been treated over time, it is possible to learn something of that society's own views of its past. Despite being about the past, alternate histories are distinctly and unashamedly presentist: they 'explore the past less for its own sake than to utilize it instrumentally to comment on the present.'[31] Alternate history and other forms of 'scholarly' history are, therefore, not as distanced or as different from each other as they might appear: for scholarly histories also reflect the historians' immediate sense of the present as well as their intellectual appreciation for the past. This is because historians not only have the task of describing and explaining the past, but also of trying to show what the past means now: making sense of the past necessarily involves confronting the realities of the present.

The value of an alternate historical approach to the past is its interdependence with, and reliance on, the concept of causation. As noted earlier, historians rely on the construction—and the counter-construction—of alternate scenarios, especially in determining the causal relationships between events and outcomes. They map out other possible storylines in order to understand what really did happen. In this way, the search for causes necessarily involves confronting and dealing with alternate options. Alternate history therefore highlights the importance of contingency, choice, and, most especially, human agency in past contexts. If something is identified as a cause of something else, then it stands to reason that had that event not happened, the course of all subsequent events could have been quite different. Causation and counterfactuals are, in this way, two sides of the same coin: causes connect events in history, while counterfactual conditionals are essential in assigning causality. The particular alternate vision of New Zealand's past I have briefly outlined therefore gives profound significance to the Treaty, for it implies that had the Treaty *not* existed, Maori would now have fewer and certainly different rights in redressing the excesses of colonisation and its aftermath. This vision of New Zealand also emphasises the role of British colonisation, however limited or circumscribed by Maori autonomy.

So is alternate history of any use beyond the ivory tower of the university? Does it have any currency in the world outside academe? Alternate historical reasoning continually operates in public discourse and debate, although much of it goes unrecognised.[32] In the public domain, alternate thinking is often motivated by pragmatic agendas: a good deal of political rhetoric, media commentary and policy making works with counterfactual 'what ifs' to address present problems. In terms of historical thinking, counterfactuals are therefore inherently present minded: the past is there to serve the needs of the present. There are other debates around the use of counterfactual reckoning in the field of Treaty scholarship too. Some of this has centred on the work of the Waitangi Tribunal and its use and abuse of historical methods.[33] Other discussions concern the language adopted by the historical Treaty makers. The Maori version of the Treaty of Waitangi records that Maori only ceded 'kawanatanga' (governance) to the British crown: yet many believe that Maori would never have signed if this version had used the term 'mana' instead, a concept intimately known to Maori. In this particular context, a counterfactual or 'what if' approach towards history serves a number of practical purposes. For claimants, alternate history can offer hope of a past that might have been had the crown acted differently. It is also highly likely that those who consider themselves dispossessed by historical and contemporary processes of colonisation will find some comfort in counterfactual scenarios. Maori may, quite justifiably, continue to ask counterfactual questions of the past in the process of working out their future. Within the ambit of New Zealand's history, 'what if' thinking is not the domain of daydreamers, nor is it unrealistically utopian. Put simply, alternate reasoning is fundamental to the way in which we revise and revisit the past.

2

What if Maori had not been made British subjects in 1840?

Janine Hayward

On 6 February 1840, representatives of Her Majesty and rangatira [chiefs] of many Maori hapu [subtribes] signed the Treaty of Waitangi. It consisted of three short articles. Articles 1 and 2 have been the subject of much debate since 1840. The third article, however, is often overlooked. Article 3 of the Maori version of the Treaty of Waitangi is as follows: 'Ka tiakina e te Kuini o Ingarani nga tangata maori katoa o Nu Tirani ka tukua ki a ratou nga tikanga katoa rite tahi ki ana mea ki nga tangata o Ingarani.' This is translated as: 'The Queen will protect [guard] all the Maori people of New Zealand and give them all of the same rights as the people of England.' The English version of the Treaty states: 'In consideration thereof Her Majesty the Queen of England extends to the Natives of New Zealand Her royal protection and imparts to them the Rights and Privileges of British Subjects.' This guarantee is seen today to make Maori and non-Maori equal 'New Zealanders'. As one British representative stated in faltering Maori at the conclusion of the 1840 signing, 'He iwi tahi tatou'—'we are now all one people'.

Why does it matter what happened?

Treaty debate since 1840 has often overlooked Article 3. Admittedly, it does not have the problems of English to Maori translation that have plagued Articles 1 and 2. Also, the breaches of Article 2 of the Treaty led to extensive resource loss by Maori, and this has appropriately been the focus of much discussion and subsequent action. But Article 3 is extraordinary and deserves to be recognised as such. As Claudia Orange notes:

The third article probably presented Williams [the missionary translator] with the least difficulty. The Queen extended her protection to the Maori people and granted them 'all the rights and privileges of British subjects' ('nga tikanga katoa rite tahi ki ana mea ki nga tangata o Ingarani'), a reasonable equivalent of the English. Elsewhere in the British Empire, native races were supposed to enjoy the status of British subjects, although they were not always treated accordingly. What was remarkable in New Zealand was that this was explicitly stated and the expression of humanitarian idealism thus publicised. However, the implications of accepting the 'rights and privileges' of a British subject (that Maori would be subject to British law and committed to certain responsibilities) were not emphasised.[1]

That the British were willing to recognise Maori as British subjects is, in itself, remarkable. The fact that Maori enjoyed 'the rights and privileges of British Subjects' from 1840 has, arguably, had significant flow-on effects in New Zealand's race relations history that have been overlooked, or at least taken for granted.

Article 3 has two provisions that can be somewhat artificially differentiated. The first provision is a repetition of the extension of the Queen's protection to Maori, as set out in the preamble and Article 1. In the second provision, Maori are granted the rights and privileges of British subjects. *But what if this second provision had not been included?* What if the British had offered Maori protection under Article 3, but had made no reference to Maori becoming British subjects? It is interesting to consider how differently events might have unfolded after 1840 under these circumstances.

There are many questions about Article 3 that should rightfully be the subject of further inquiry. Why was the 'British Subjects' provision included in Article 3 at all? What did it mean to British officials at the time? What did Maori understand the provision to mean? And finally, where did the incentive to include this provision in Article 3 come from: Maori or the British? Paul Moon has noted the role and influence of the 1837 House of Commons Select Committee on Aborigines in British Settlements;[2] perhaps some answers to these questions can be found there. However, the purpose of this chapter is not to pursue these questions, but rather to imagine a very different New Zealand. This counterfactual envisages a New Zealand in which Her Majesty offered Maori *protection* in 1840, but *not* the rights and privileges of British subjects. Only the absence of this provision allows speculation regarding its unrecognised importance in New Zealand's factual Treaty history.

But how might it have been possible for Her Majesty to offer Maori protection, but not British rights and privileges? In fact, such an arrangement was achieved in Canada during British settlement and treaty making. The Royal Proclamation 1763 recognised First Nation [Indian] land rights and established the framework within which the British made land transfer treaties with indigenous peoples. Although the Proclamation and treaties refer to the Queen's protection, they do not make First Nations 'British subjects'. Today, in a strict legal sense, First Nations are Canadian citizens, and are generally speaking subject to the same laws as non-indigenous Canadians. But the nature of that citizenship is highly disputed; First Nations argue that they have 'citizenship plus'[3] which gives them different rights to non-aboriginal Canadians. As a consequence of historical events associated with citizenship status, First Nations display ambivalence and resistance to Canadian citizenship because the Canadian government required First Nations to relinquish their 'Indian status' in order to assimilate into Canadian society. From the First Nations' perspective, a defining characteristic of indigenous politics in Canada has been a deep suspicion of the Canadian state and Canadian citizenship. To put it simply, aboriginal and non-aboriginal Canadians are, some would argue, not common members of a shared society with shared citizenship. As a result, unlike New Zealand, Canada's race relations history is more explicitly based on the politics of 'difference', which is expressed through reserved Indian lands, a legislative framework to control Indian lives, and a separate branch of government to administer indigenous peoples who remained outside Canadian citizenship.

Could the exclusion of the rights and privileges provision in Article 3 have led to similar outcomes for Maori as for Canadian First Nations? What practical difference might this have made for Maori in contemporary New Zealand? Obviously there are significant geographical, cultural, political and social differences between New Zealand and Canada to take into account when comparing the cases. But the point here is to consider the possible implications had Maori not been made British subjects in 1840.

What might have happened?
A counterfactual Treaty history

1840–1865: Differentiated citizenship established

By 1839, the British were forced to concede that they must accept some responsibility for the escalating number of British traders, missionaries and settlers in New Zealand. Prompted by Maori calls for protection from lawless traders and dubious private land deals, the British considered their options in the far-flung islands. Maori appeared amenable to the notion of a treaty with the British, particularly following the success of the Northern tribes' 1835 Declaration of Independence assisted by British Consul James Busby. Busby, who had considerable experience with Maori by 1839, also had a very particular vision for the treaty he thought would be acceptable to Maori. Such a treaty would be an extension of the Declaration—Maori would retain their independence while the British would establish government and institutions to bring law and order and offer Maori the protection they called for. But colonies were expensive; Britain's experience in North America encouraged officials to draft a treaty in New Zealand that would limit the costs of taking on the new territory. The more Maori could continue to do for themselves, the better.

In this spirit, the treaty drafted in February 1840 was very brief. Dispute has arisen over the important differences between the English version (which Busby helped to draft) and the Maori translation of the Treaty, the latter of which Maori agreed to and signed. Article 1 of the Treaty established British sovereignty in New Zealand, which Maori understood to be the right to make laws [kawanatanga]. Article 2 of the Treaty guaranteed to Maori their lands and other treasured possessions and resources; again the Maori version indicated a more expansive concept of 'supremacy' over their own lands, expressed through the Maori concept of 'tino rangatiratanga'. The third article of the Treaty assured Maori that the Queen would offer Maori her personal protection. Originally an additional provision in Article 3 also gave Maori 'the Rights and Privileges of British Subjects'. Before the Treaty was translated into Maori, however, Busby advised against including this final provision. He felt it would hold no appeal for Maori who, just five years earlier, had asserted their independence and would see no advantage in compromising that position. The other British officials were easily persuaded by Busby's concerns. After all, the British had not included this provision in their treaties in other colonies; what might be the unforeseen consequences of taking such a humanitarian approach to Native rights? There is in any case no record that Maori opinion was ever sought on the excluded provision, and thus no way of knowing what Maori reaction to it might have been. Instead, the Treaty was signed on 6 February 1840 without reference to Maori becoming British subjects. This marked the beginning of a remarkable history of race relations in New Zealand.

In 1852, the New Zealand Constitution Act began to lay down the foundations of government in New Zealand. At the same time, it established Maori districts, where tikanga Maori [Maori custom and tradition] would be practised and Maori would (with the Queen's protection) exercise their own authority over Maori resident within those districts. The 1852 Act detailed the rights Maori would have in those districts: the right to schooling in their native language, the right to healthcare and to practise traditional healing, and the right to deal with minor offences within their own cultural framework. Significant blocks of Maori customary land were reserved for the districts, although disputes often rose between Maori and settlers about the adequacy of the land set aside for that purpose. Regardless, most Maori were very supportive of the districts; as long as they remained within these districts, Maori were tax exempt and lived largely as they had prior to 1840, with the exception of trade with the settlers. But some Maori were hesitant about the districts. They preferred to gain the full advantage of settler society and technology and saw the districts as a way of keeping Maori marginalised from the advantages associated with settler society. Despite this rift, Maori were united in their suspicion of settler authority in Maori land, and agreed that the districts were important strongholds of Maori independence.

The districts were controversial among the British as well. Some thought it best to keep Maori isolated in rural locations, while others found it abhorrent to their sense of egalitarianism that two sets of rules were emerging in the colony on the basis of race. The greatest resistance to the districts came from settlers who sought access to land for farming and were frustrated that Maori were retaining such significant tracts of land. But again, despite this difference of opinion, all settlers seemed to agree that London was responsible for the expense of maintaining healthcare, education and other services in the Maori districts; they argued strongly that Maori should not become a burden on the emerging settler administration (and its taxpayers).

By 1863, as representative settler government emerged and assumed greater accountability, the pressure mounted on London to relinquish Maori affairs to the developing colonial government. London resisted, fearing that settler pressure on the new govern-ment would jeopardise the Queen's protection of Maori as guaranteed by the Treaty. Resentment that London stayed involved in colonial politics was very strong among settlers. But the decision was extremely important for Maori, who continued to enjoy 'the Queen's protection' against the intrusions of colonial laws until well after 1900.

London's continued control of Maori affairs had a significant impact on the psyche of the young colony, however. Debate often erupted in the House of Representatives, and elsewhere, about the exact status of Maori in New Zealand. Some settlers saw the exclusion of Maori from the developing society as a loss of potential economic development; others expressed relief that Maori were keeping largely to themselves and were not a burden on the taxpayer (as long as London maintained its part of the bargain). But none could agree on the status of Maori: were they New Zealand citizens or not? Had the Treaty created 'one New Zealand'? As pressure mounted among settlers to gain access to Maori land, including the land set aside for the districts, this question was debated more and more passionately. Should Maori be forced to join, and contribute to, settler society?

1865–1900: War with Maori avoided

In the 1860s, as London continued to control Maori affairs (and pay for the health and education needs of Maori in the districts), the colonial institutions of government experienced an upsurge in popularity and national elections became more heavily contested. Maori, who were not enfranchised and were therefore marginal to this process, responded by establishing a Paremata Maori [Maori parliament] that met once a year in various regions (largely in the North Island) to debate issues. High on the list of priorities was the Treaty itself—Maori were aware that the Queen's protection was tenuous and insisted that London retain control of Maori affairs. Relations between the Paremata and the emerging representative government were also widely debated; some Maori thought it best to try to gain access to the halls of settler power and agitate for the franchise, while others preferred the distance and independence of the Maori parliament despite its lack of formal recognition by the settlers.

The emerging representative government was not averse to the notion of extending the vote to Maori; indeed, some encouraged the idea as promoting national identity and stability. But when legislation was passed to that effect, conditions were attached to the franchise that made it unpalatable to Maori; they would have to leave their districts and become taxpayers as 'contributing' members of society. When European women won the right to vote in 1893, the movement to enfranchise Maori reached its peak; unsuccessful at that time, it could never regain the momentum required to convince Maori of the benefits of the vote, given the sacrifices that would have to be made.

Alongside the Maori parliament, the Maori King movement, largely heralding from the King Country, emerged from the 1860s as a force to be reckoned with in terms of resisting land sales, particularly in the Maori districts. The colonial government, under pressure from settlers to acquire more lands and resentful of the large Maori districts which were seemingly unproductive, put considerable pressure on Maori to sell. When this was unsuccessful, the government considered Maori resistance to land sales as rebellion against the crown and threatened to legislate to confiscate Maori land without compensation. Sensing that such a move would escalate into civil war, London intervened to protect Maori interests and to reduce the potential expense for Britain of a colonial war. Motivated by a strong humanitarian and missionary influence within its own parliament, London asserted its role as protector of Maori interests and warned the colonial government that its greed for Maori land would have devastating consequences for the colony. With relations between London and the colony at an all time low, the colonial government backed off its threats and potential civil war was narrowly avoided. The internal pressure on the King movement began to mount, however, and significant land sales were conceded as a compromise. Nevertheless Maori, particularly in the Far North, retained sufficient lands to continue to maintain Maori districts and some measure of independence.

1900–1935: *Enforced assimilation fails*

With the commencement of the First World War, circumstances changed dramatically for Maori. London's attitude to its involvement in the distant colony (at considerable expense to Britain) was radically altered by the immediate political and economic impact of the war. At the same time, the political party system was emerging in New Zealand and the key platform of the popular Liberal party was outrage that continued interference by London in New Zealand's affairs was undermining the development of an egalitarian society. In particular, as MPs agitated to take control of Maori affairs and amend the legislation governing Maori districts (even at an increased cost to the colony), London began to concede that Britain's stake in New Zealand was more trouble than it was worth and that the colony was now sufficiently mature to fend for itself. Most importantly, the humanitarians in the British House of Representatives were fast losing their influence over colonial affairs. On 27 October 1915 New Zealand was granted its independence from Britain, an act of withdrawal by London from Maori affairs that was resisted by Maori with tremendous force. But Maori pleas to its Treaty partner fell on deaf ears. Non-Maori New Zealand recalls this event differently. The 27th of October is celebrated annually as 'New Zealand Day' and is seen as a symbol of the country's independence and nationhood. From that time there began a new era in race relations; the colonial government, now additionally saddled with the maintenance of Maori welfare, set about to systematically reduce the cost of Maori to the taxpaying New Zealander. The policy was to force Maori to assimilate into settler society and to relinquish the package of 'special privileges' associated with the Maori districts.

Almost immediately after the colonial government assumed responsibility for Maori affairs, conditions for Maori in their districts began to deteriorate. The decision to remain in the districts had always been a principled one for Maori, because conditions were often poor as schools and healthcare facilities struggled to meet growing demands. Apparently oblivious to the struggle Maori already endured in the districts, the government exercised its new legislative authority by closing Maori schools, forcing children to travel considerable distances to be schooled in English to speed up their integration into society. Healthcare facilities were also closed, and traditional healing and spiritual practices, long considered uncivilised by many non-Maori, were outlawed. Maori would now also be tried in settler courts of law, and the same rules and laws would apply to all. At the same time, the government created incentives to get Maori out of the districts and into the cities to become fully participating citizens. The key incentive was the right to vote; in exchange for the franchise Maori would relinquish their ties to traditional lands and their tax-free status and engage in paid, taxed employment. Maori also received housing subsidies in so-called 'pepper-potting' of housing set aside for Maori within established communities.

Some European New Zealanders resisted these developments, seeing Maori as unwanted intruders into their communities. Despite Maori retaining a strong suspicion of the settler state and its policies, some Maori did move into the cities. There they found conditions very difficult, with the housing policy in particular largely unsuccessful. It did succeed in driving a wedge into the strong regional character of Maori politics, however, forcing Maori to look nationally to gain the strength required to resist the government's intrusion on their Treaty rights. Although very few Maori took up the franchise under these conditions, a new cleavage emerged in Maori society between those Maori who sought to retain connections with traditional territory at all cost, and those who believed Maori could find a better future in towns and cities, attempting to break into the institutions from which Maori had deliberately distanced themselves. These new young Maori were soon to be drawn to the hope of a better life outside the districts, and the impact of this on Maori society would be felt by subsequent generations.

1935–1960: The slow pull of urbanisation

With the advent of the Second World War, one issue united an otherwise divided Maori society—this was a European war, in which they had no part. Still mindful of Maori resistance to assimilation, the government avoided further tension by not conscripting Maori, and very few Maori volunteered to fight. However, as soldiers left small towns and larger cities, jobs needed to be filled. Maori continued to resist the urban pull in significant numbers, but by the 1960s almost 40 per cent of Maori had become urbanised. Social conditions for those urban Maori were very poor and this deterred a more substantial urban drift; following the failure of 'pepperpotting', Maori housing tended to be in clusters in poor parts of communities, and the Maori families who relocated there were often largely excluded from the non-Maori society surrounding them. Although many Maori were working in paid employment, resentment began to build within non-Maori communities that Maori were an expense to the taxpayer; in this view, it would be better if they remained in Maori districts to minimise conflicts and tensions within communities. The government was aware of the increasing tensions urbanisation was creating. Again the issue of citizenship was raised. Were Maori who lived in cities and paid taxes equal New Zealand citizens, or did the Treaty, which Maori were quick to recall at every opportunity, create some different status for Maori? MPs and commentators demanded clarification of the issue to quell increasing concerns that different laws applied to different races. Maori themselves were less concerned by the concept of differentiated citizenship and took every opportunity to remind the government that under Article 2, Maori had the right to 'tino rangatiratanga' under British protection. They also spoke of the Maori nation, pointing to the Maori districts as the last vestiges of the independence that had been recognised in 1835 and 1840 and which, in the opinion of Maori, had never been ceded or extinguished.

The return of non-Maori soldiers from the war exacerbated tensions between the races. Maori struggled to retain their jobs and eventually found themselves largely replaced in the workforce. Dependent on welfare, they were further marginalised. This antagonised local non-Maori communities. By the 1960s, urban Maori gathered together in significant numbers and were politicised by the unfair treatment they believed they were receiving. Ultimately they took to the streets to protest that they now had no place in New Zealand society. The focus of this urban protest was the right to vote, which had still not been unconditionally extended to Maori. Rejected by the non-Maori populations in towns and cities, and finding that they now had no place in the Maori districts, urban Maori demanded recognition and redress from the government.

1960–1990: Urban Maori protests appeased by settlements

During the 1960s and early 1970s, New Zealand, like other democracies around the world, experienced a tremendous increase in protest and social movements. Supported by the environmental movement in New Zealand, young urban Maori who felt equally displaced both in cities and in their traditional territories began to agitate for recognition by the New Zealand state. Unconvinced that their future lay in pan-Maori initiatives, they wanted unconditional access to voting rights as well as other privileges taken for granted by non-Maori New Zealand citizens. Bolstered by the Black civil rights movement in the United States, urban Maori protested at unprecedented levels and succeeded in embarrassing the government into taking action.

In 1972 the Labour government, which had traditionally been sympathetic to the plight of Maori, extended the franchise to all Maori without requiring them to relinquish their traditional Treaty rights (in particular the right to live in Maori districts). In a strict legal sense, Maori were from this time New Zealand citizens with the same rights and privileges as non-Maori citizens. The transformation in the political landscape was profound and immediate. Urban Maori used the newly created political platform to lobby parties to recognise a history of neglect that had seen Maori treated as second-class citizens (or not as citizens at all) for far too long. Desperate to quell the tide of racial antagonism, the National government elected in 1975 agreed in haste to the outgoing Labour government's policy to establish a commission of inquiry to investigate alleged injustices by the state against Maori. However, the government placed strict terms and limitations on the commission; it would only consider issues arising since London relinquished control of Maori affairs in 1914, and it would only consider land matters—grievances relating to loss of language and culture were considered the responsibility of Maori themselves within their own districts. This meant that many dubious land sales that occurred prior to 1914, as well as legislation that had an adverse impact on the Maori districts, were beyond the commission's reach. Maori protested this limitation, even taking their protest to London to insist that the Queen herself acknowledge some responsibility for this state of affairs, but to no avail.

The commission was of little interest to Maori who still lived in the districts. Instead it was mostly a pressure release for urban Maori, who were landless and struggling to come to terms with their identity in modern society. Two events in the 1980s, however, made the commission important for both groups of Maori. First, the fourth Labour government initiated a period of radical economic reform that hit Maori, urban and rural, equally hard. That government's market-driven economic policies saw unemployment among all Maori reach an all-time high. This time when urban Maori took to the streets in protest they were joined by Maori from the districts, who could see that even their claims of autonomy and independence couldn't protect them from the hardship the government's policies would certainly impose on their communities. The Labour government responded in typically pragmatic fashion in an attempt to negotiate peace; it agreed to grant Maori their long-standing wish to have the commission's jurisdiction extended to include grievances relating to the loss of Maori culture, language and other 'prized possessions' that had been guaranteed the Queen's protection in the Treaty.

By the late 1980s the first of the major settlements resulting from the commission's work began to emerge. Among these was the groundbreaking 'Te Reo Maori' report, in which the commission agreed that the government had failed to protect the Maori language. Financial redress was recommended to allow Maori to establish Maori-speaking schools. The findings encouraged Maori also to seek redress for housing and health, in order to finally assert the independence Maori had formally declared in 1835 and 1840, with British protection but without government interference.

1990–2005: Maori divided over representation

In the early 1990s New Zealand's electoral system became a matter of national debate. A major part of this discussion had to do with the appalling deficiencies in Maori representation in parliament since Maori were enfranchised in 1972. Only two Maori men had made it into parliament; one of them, a Maori Labour MP (1972 to 1975), had been instrumental in establishing the Treaty Commission. The other Maori MP had been elected in 1990 as a National Party representative. Maori were vocal in their distrust of this MP and his policies; while he stood on sufficiently populist platforms to attract general support, he rarely spoke out in favour of Maori policy when given the chance to do so.

The debate about the electoral system seemed not to penetrate deeply into Maori communities, particularly rural communities and the districts. In these regions, support for the Paremata had remained strong, with Maori enrolling on what was called the 'Maori roll' to elect representatives. The Maori parliament remained a major platform for national Maori debate, although support of the Paremata by the various districts had waxed and waned through the years depending on the politics of the time. Nevertheless, it had endured through the century as a protest against Maori exclusion from the franchise and as an expression of Maori independence.

In the 1990s, sparks of interest in the electoral debate were kindled among urban Maori, who felt disenfranchised from both systems. Maori living in the cities wanted to gain representation in parliament. In 1993, the country held a referendum on the electoral system. With increasing dissatisfaction among the general electorate regarding the existing system—quaintly described as first-past-the-post—the single transferable voting system (STV) was chosen by a slim majority for the 1996 election. In Maori communities there continued to be debate over the advantages and disadvantages of Maori being elected to the House of Representatives. Could Maori maintain their independence from within the state's institutions? Some Maori thought so and were excited by the new opportunities STV offered; others were sceptical, however, and some were openly hostile to the prospect of Maori in parliament, seeing it as a compromise to the tino rangatiratanga Maori should be exercising in contemporary New Zealand society.

In early 2003, local Maori took to court a dispute relating to foreshore access via Maori land. The High Court found that title to the foreshore (where it was adjacent to land reserved for Maori districts) was not clear and that title could be tested in the courts. The potential implications of this finding were immediately evident to the government, as the public reacted with fear that Maori would claim exclusive title to large sections of the foreshore. The government responded by passing legislation that vested in the Crown not only the title to the foreshore, but underlying title to the land that had been reserved for Maori districts for Maori to 'enjoy so long as they wished'. The suspicion Maori had harboured against the government quickly turned to outrage. Setting aside divisions created by the parliamentary representation debate, huge numbers of rural and urban Maori united in protest against the government's actions. Those Maori claimed that the government was breaching the Treaty of Waitangi by assuming title to lands that Maori had not ceded to the Crown. They demanded that the government withdraw the legislation and allow Maori their right to let the courts test their title to customary land on a case-by-case basis. The government remained unmoved on the matter, but the effect of the legislation was still being felt as the country prepared itself for a general election in 2005. For many Maori, this was a breaking point; despite their desire to retain and assert independence, they experienced a new determination to seek access to settler power in order to force change and to protect Maori rights in the future.

Although increasing numbers of Maori had been standing as candidates in general electorates since the introduction of STV, by the 2005 general election only two Maori candidates (standing with the Green Party) had been successfully elected. Motivated by the events of 2003, an unprecedented number of Maori candidates stood for election in 2005, and the number of Maori on the general roll increased by over 50 per cent by the time of the election (to an estimated 35 per cent of the eligible Maori population). If these Maori hoped to see race relations debated during the election campaign, they would not have been disappointed. The interest in Maori issues came not from the incumbent Labour Party, but rather from the opposition National Party which ran on a platform of 'one law for all'. The party leader's opening address tackled 'the Maori question' head on, as he looked straight at the camera and asked: 'Are Maori New Zealanders or not?' He tapped into a debate which had been below the surface since 1840, vocalising the concerns of many voters that there were essentially two New Zealands: district Maori and the 'mainstream'. He identified the raft of legislation that had made special provision for Maori in districts since 1914 as he urged the country to unite once and for all under a fairer system. He said, most memorably, that as the country's next prime minister he would strive to declare that we were, finally, one people, which he then repeated in faltering Maori: 'He iwi tahi tatou.'

Although mainstream voters were captured by his language and vision, Maori were appalled at the attack on the final vestiges of their independence. Perhaps motivated by this concern, Maori turned out to vote in the election in higher numbers than ever before. As a result, when Labour was returned to office in 2005 three Maori MPs were also elected to parliament. They vowed to work from within to ensure that Maori independence was not lost, and that differentiated citizenship would become an acceptable reality in New Zealand.

Soon after the election, the Maori MPs faced their first media challenge. Researchers at the University of Otago had uncovered a sensational fact: that Article 3 of the Treaty had once been intended to include Maori as 'British subjects'. The media picked up the story and debate continued to rage about the state of race relations in New Zealand. In response, one of the country's few Maori MPs made a statement, one that seemed to capture the essence of Treaty history in New Zealand:

> Let's imagine for a moment that Maori had become British subjects under Article 3 in 1840. What difference would that have made? It might have led to a much more cohesive colonial society, or at least the tensions would have been hidden or expressed in different ways. And perhaps there would have been advantages for Maori—the districts have been a tough way of life even for those who cherish Maori independence. But citizenship would have come at a great price for us. Maori have special rights here in New Zealand—the Declaration of Independence and the Treaty of Waitangi say so. And those rights have never been relinquished. And they never will be. Yes, we are New Zealanders now, but we are also more than that. We are Maori.

3

What if Nelson had been made the capital of New Zealand?

Stephen Levine

Following the signing of the Treaty of Waitangi Captain Hobson set up his capital in the Bay of Islands, at a site he named Russell (for the then British secretary of state for the colonies, Lord John Russell). By February 1841 he had moved to Auckland, named for 'one of his patrons in the Royal Navy', Lord Auckland. When the British parliament passed the New Zealand Constitution Act on 30 June 1852, a colonial legislature—the General Assembly—was established, which required elections to be held (they were, in October 1853) and a legislative assembly to be convened. Auckland was chosen for the first meeting (on 24 May 1854), but not without competition from Wellington. Difficulties of transportation made Auckland unpopular for many of those elected: the length and discomfort of travel was followed by long periods of separation from family, farms and businesses. In September 1854, only a few months after its historic opening, James FitzGerald (New Zealand's first premier) moved 'that the next session of the General Assembly should be held in a more central position in the colony'. The proposal was defeated, thirteen to eleven, as a result of FitzGerald's failure to consult with colleagues, leading to the absence of many South Island MPs (favourable to a more central location) from the chamber.

The matter was raised again in 1856. On 26 May a resolution declaring that the next meeting of the General Assembly 'should be held in Auckland' was amended (by a vote of eighteen to fifteen), deleting 'Auckland' and substituting 'a more central position'. It was then proposed that the word 'Nelson' should be added to the proposal; this was defeated, twenty to twelve. This was followed by a move to add the word 'Wellington' to the proposal: this was also defeated, twenty-one to twelve. An attempt to leave matters entirely to the governor—to 'such place as His Excellency the Governor may deem most convenient'—was likewise voted down, eighteen to sixteen. The sense of the members—that Auckland, in any event, was unsuitable—was reflected in the final vote of the day, nineteen to fourteen, which left the choice to the governor, but with the understanding that he select 'such more central place as His Excellency may deem most convenient'.

The matter was debated again on 3 July, in response to the

governor's opinion that, if a more central place is preferred, then 'Wellington is the best place for the purpose'. One member conceived the notion that 'the next sitting of the General Assembly should be held at Akaroa', an idea rejected on a twenty-two to one vote. This was followed by an attempt to substitute the word 'Nelson' for Wellington: the decisive vote was nineteen to fourteen against. It was then agreed to meet in Wellington (by a vote of eighteen to fifteen). The following day, however, on 4 July, the legislative council passed a resolution (unanimously) advising the governor that 'great inconvenience and mischief' would result 'from any change being made in the place of meeting of the General Assembly'. Accordingly, on 16 August, the governor, Thomas Gore Browne, sent a message informing members that 'he is aware that it will be impossible to reconcile conflicting interests' and that 'the next session' will therefore be held in Auckland. He proposed a novel formula, however, under which the General Assembly would alternate its meetings between Auckland and Wellington. Despite this, meetings continued to be held in Auckland. In 1862 a proposal for the assembly to be moved to Wellington was defeated by only a single vote.

In 1863, a group of Wellington and Nelson members proposed that the seat of government be moved 'somewhere upon the shores of Cook Strait', with the 'actual site of the capital' to be selected by 'some independent tribunal'—a tribunal 'best formed by Commissioners having no interest in or relations with any part of the colony, and whose high social and intellectual standing should guarantee a full inquiry and an impartial decision'. The result of such an approach to the problem was that New Zealand's parliamentarians left it to commissioners appointed by three of Australia's governors—'the Governors of New South Wales, Victoria and Tasmania'—to decide the site of the New Zealand capital. In 1864 the Australian commissioners—having Wanganui, Wellington, Picton, Port Underwood, Havelock and Nelson as options—recommended Wellington. That settled that: the first meeting of the General Assembly in Wellington took place in July 1865. Auckland's response—a bid to separate the North and South Islands—was defeated, thirty-one to seventeen.

But 'what if' it had succeeded . . .?—perhaps a topic for another, very different counterfactual scenario.[1]

It makes a difference where the capital city of a country is. That is as true for New Zealand as it is for other countries. The choice has consequences. But what those consequences might be—*that* is more difficult to say.

This chapter is one way of looking at the topic—the choice of New Zealand's capital city.

The matter is seen now, today, from the point of view of our current prime minister, the Rt Hon Helen Clark.[2]

Nelson as the capital of New Zealand
—the prime minister's perspective

Helen Clark looked out of her tenth-floor Beehive office at the view below. She had a panoramic view, 360 degrees; from any direction, anywhere she looked, it was a beautiful day.

At the moment she was gazing out towards Cook Strait, the sun glistening off the water. On a day such as this you had the feeling you could just about see the North Island.

In a few minutes Michael Cullen would be coming in to see her. She thought about her deputy prime minister. She smiled. Michael tanned well in the Nelson sun. They all had to be careful about that. Look at Lockwood Smith. Simon Power had to make sure he was regularly stocked with sun block, maximum strength. Ah, it wasn't easy being whip. But that was Simon's problem.

She loved this place. As a student of history—of New Zealand history in particular—she knew that the capital had nearly been Wellington! It was a close run thing! It hardly bears thinking about!

She knew the effect it would have had on her. Instead of her sunny disposition she'd have become grumpy and ill-tempered.

Everyone knew she had a sense of humour. What would have become of her up there?

Wellington! If it had been the capital, the whole future of the country would have been different. Most people wanted to live in Auckland anyway, but with the capital in Wellington it would have been worse. There would never have been more than about 150,000 people there, maybe twice that many if the Hutt Valley were included. Auckland would've had about a million people by now.

And as for the South Island—she laughed—why, there'd be so little activity here they'd have to put a minimum number of seats for the place in the Electoral Act just to guarantee it had adequate representation in parliament!

She wouldn't have lasted so long in Wellington. As it was, they were never going to get her out of here. She'd beaten Shipley, and then English, and in a little while it would be Brash's turn. He was going to be the Michael Howard of New Zealand politics—leader of the Conservatives for one term, and then, with defeat, it'd be 'hit the road, Don'—he'd be out, and he'd never be back.

Not like her. She looked around her Beehive office. She loved it here, at the top. She would be like Ballance, and Seddon, and Massey, and Savage, and Kirk. The only way she was leaving here was in a box.

Mike Munro would be coming in soon. They had a meeting scheduled with the Victoria University vice-chancellor. Some sport! The last time he'd come to see them he'd given her a gift. He wanted $10 million from her and all he'd come in with was a $9 coffee mug. With an extra one, in a box, for Michael Cullen. Could he spare it?

Victoria University. If they'd built that university in Wellington— she smiled at the thought—the main campus would probably be on a hill somewhere, and there'd be other sites scattered all over the city. There wouldn't be enough parking for staff, let alone students. They'd all be blown about, making their way from one lecture to the next.

Nelson as New Zealand's capital. What a lovely city. She

recalled with satisfaction the way it had happened. It was like the Americans. George Washington had been inaugurated in New York the first time, Philadelphia the second. It took them a while to get to their right choice, their true capital, Washington, 'D. C.' —'District of Columbia'. New Zealand had had three capitals as well. They began up in Russell—plenty of sunshine there!—but it was too small, too remote. So they moved to Auckland, but it was too far north in a country as big as this—two great islands— and at a time when it took so long to travel from one part of the country to the next.

So they decided to move the capital to somewhere more central. Auckland didn't like it. Well, what could they do about it? They could threaten to secede—some people did—but that wasn't going to get anywhere.

She had the papers—the record of the parliamentary debate— right here on her desk. That Victoria University intern of hers had come up with them. What a fine programme that is! He was doing a great job for her.

Now—she looked at her papers—here it was, the turning point.

It had been New Zealand's first premier, James FitzGerald, selected in 1854, who had first understood that Auckland would never do. On 15 September he had moved—quote—that 'the next session of the general assembly should be held in a more central place in the colony'. Oh, the Aucklanders had complained, but in the end it was just as it is today. If you have the votes, you win. FitzGerald would have had the votes in 1854 but some of the South Island members opposed to him and his faction had left the chamber rather than vote for his motion and give him the satisfaction of victory.

It was two years later, on 26 May 1856, when, as FitzGerald was himself to say—quote—'the southern provinces were beginning to grow in importance and political energy', that a motion omitting the word 'Auckland' from a resolution pertaining to the 'next sitting of the General Assembly' was able to be carried, by a vote of eighteen to fifteen, followed by a proposal from Henry Sewell, the member for Christchurch, for 'the next session' to 'be held in some such more central place as the Governor shall deem most convenient'. This was approved.

The choice had come down to Wellington or Nelson. The governor, Thomas Gore Brown, had sought more guidance from the General Assembly and so on 3 July the matter was debated again. A Major Greenwood moved that 'Akaroa', of all places, would (in his words) 'be a more convenient situation' than Auckland, but this received only one vote—his own. The members then moved on to the more serious choice before them—Wellington or Nelson.

It was appropriate that the vote took place with Edward Stafford as premier. Stafford had been elected as the member for Nelson in 1855 and he was the pre-eminent parliamentarian and premier of the period—as the historian John Martin puts it—quote— 'the man best able to forge the perennial factions into durable ministries'.[3] Stafford was to serve as premier on three occasions, the first, beginning in Auckland on 2 June 1856—only a month before the fateful vote over which he was to have such influence.

Everyone outside Auckland had agreed that the place was quite unsuitable. All the parliamentary discussion had led to the same conclusion—that, as FitzGerald observed, 'the seat of government should not continue to be in Auckland.' But Wellington or Nelson? In the end, it had been two factors—chance incidents, really—that had made the difference.

Oh, it was true that Nelson was 'the geographic centre of New Zealand'—they had the exact spot there, in a park, with a sign to prove it.

Of course Wellington wasn't far off being the centre; that wasn't the problem with the place.

But there had been two earthquakes in Wellington already since British settlement had begun, one in 1848, the other in 1855. Who in their right mind would shift the capital to a place with the evidence against it so recent, so obvious and so compelling? New Zealanders wanted stability, and that extended to their buildings, to the ground under their feet, as well as to their governments.

Those earthquakes, and the fortuitous presence of Stafford as premier—Stafford, who had been initially cool to the idea of shifting capital from Auckland but had a natural preference for Nelson over Wellington—Stafford, with his leadership; *that* had made all the difference. No wonder Stafford was known as 'New Zealand's first statesman'. He went on to complete that first term of his ensconced in his home town of Nelson, from which he governed New Zealand two further times, in the 1860s and the 1870s.

The formal opening of the General Assembly in Nelson in 1857 led to a move from Aucklanders to separate the colony into two, with the boundary between the proposed two colonies being Cook Strait. The motion—a peaceful attempt at secession, made only four years before the Confederacy chanced its luck in the United States—failed by a nearly two-to-one margin, and that was that.

But the crucial vote, for Nelson over Wellington, had been a close one—nineteen to fourteen. If only three members had changed their minds—and anything was possible in those days when personal animosities rather than party discipline governed how members voted or, indeed, whether they showed up to vote at all—it would all have been different.

'What if *Wellington* had been made the capital of New Zealand?'

It doesn't bear thinking about!

Oh, the economic capital of New Zealand was still up in Auckland. That was never going to change. But at least the South Island wasn't some sort of backwater, a playground just for tourists. If the capital had been in *Wellington*, they probably would have needed some sort of 'regional development' policy for the South Island, and those things never really worked even under Labour. The government couldn't pick winners no matter how hard it tried. They'd end up backing silly ventures—with names like, oh, Matai Industries—that would never get off the ground.

With Nelson as the capital, development was more balanced. Christchurch was a major city, too, and the property values around the southern lakes, and Queenstown, and even Dunedin, were pretty impressive.

She could imagine what it might have been like trying to govern in Wellington. They'd come in to the chamber and sit there, shouting at each other. The wind howling outside and the members howling at one another inside. What a circus! She shook her head. Even calm and easy-going people like herself could lose their head in a place like that. She remembered how good tempered Jim Bolger had been. Here was someone you could sit down and have a drink with. In the chamber he was just as courteous as he could be.

But that was Nelson for you. It brought out the best in you.

She could imagine that, in Wellington, they'd have sat across from each other—neither of them really wanting to be there—and one day they'd become so irritable towards one another he'd probably throw something at her.

She could see the headline in the Nelson paper:

'*Bolger throws pen in parliament*',

'*Clark unharmed*'.

It would be ludicrous. What kind of example would they be setting for the young people of the country?

You didn't have to be an Oprah fan to realise that happy politicians were apt to be able to work together more intelligently—able to produce better laws—than unhappy ones.

Look what happened when Michael Cullen had that 'economic summit' over by Takaka. He'd gone there through the Takaka tunnel—the 'tunnel through the marble mountain', as it was known—it sounded like a ride at Disneyland—he'd gone there with a huge surplus and when he came back he'd agreed to cut taxes: what a finance minister!

That would never have happened in Wellington. When it's that cold, and that windy, you become 'retentive'; you just want to hang on to everything. What was the saying? 'Power corrupts . . . but absolute power makes you feel very warm and comfortable indeed.'

Nelson was a natural for environmental politics. New Zealand had the world's first environmental party—the Values Party—and it was all started by a Victoria University of Nelson political science honours student, Tony Brunt. Well, Values never got into parliament, but it wasn't *their* fault. We took over their policies—why shouldn't we? Here in Nelson we in the Labour Party could be just as pro-environment, pro-sexual freedom, and antinuclear as anyone else.

As usual, it took National longer to catch on, and the rest is history.

Wellington as the capital!

And what would Nelson have been like then, with the capital up in Wellington? There'd probably have been only one road out in any direction—one road east, towards Havelock; one road west, towards Motueka; one road south, towards Lake Rotoiti. There would have been no ferry service. There would have been no railway—well, maybe just one, a ride for children. Instead of being a stop on a 'national railway', there'd probably have been some sort of nonsense—a Nelson 'notional railway', with shipping costs by truck calculated as though the freight were coming in and out by rail.

Instead, what did they have? She thought of the 'bullet trains'—what the Japanese called *shinkansen*—that linked the South Island's main centres with one another. She could get on a train in Nelson and be in Christchurch in an hour, Dunedin in ninety minutes, Invercargill in two hours. The branch line through Arthur's Pass took tourists from Christchurch to the West Coast in forty-five minutes. From Dunedin to Queenstown was half an hour.

The line to Milford Sound brought tourists—New Zealanders and overseas people, from Japan and the United States—in their hundreds of thousands.

Fortunate for her that the bullet trains were so fast, and so reliable. Imagine if she'd tried to drive up to Christchurch that time when she'd been running late. Why, her driver might have had to go racing down the highway at 170 kilometres an hour. What would the media have made of that!

There were high-speed trains linking the North Island cities together as well. In the old days it took twelve hours in a shabby old train to get from Auckland to Wellington. Now it took only two, and then you could get on a ferry across to the capital. That was the problem; that was the delay. No one wanted to spend any time in Wellington. But you had to get from the train station to the ferry terminal, and then there was the ferry journey across Cook Strait to Nelson. It took almost three hours, sometimes longer, depending on the weather. Sometimes you couldn't get across at all! Then there was Wellington airport—closed by fog, swept by wind, you never knew what to expect going into that place.

They needed to finish the job—get the link between the North and South Islands built. She gritted her teeth. She would get it done. Be optimistic! Be determined! [snaps fingers] 'Think Big!'- that was *her* motto . . .

She'd talk further with Koizumi about their building that tunnel underneath Cook Strait. It couldn't be that difficult for the Japanese. They'd done it before, a tunnel like that, connecting their northern island, Hokkaido, with the main island. They'd do it for her. They wanted New Zealand's support for their bid to become a permanent member of the Security Council. Hell, they could move the entire Security Council to Tokyo as far as she was concerned.

She thought about the life she'd been able to lead in Nelson. Her husband wasn't that far away, over at Christchurch. The twins were growing up nicely.

They had that beach house out past Motueka, and it was lucky they'd bought it when they did. Everyone liked living here in Nelson—hippie capital of New Zealand!, where MPs in suits mingled with beach people in sandals—she thought of Mike Ward—where MPs in suits mingled with *MPs* in sandals—a real café society. It was great sitting outside, sipping lattes, soaking up the sunshine. You couldn't do that in Wellington! Then there was the theatre, the film festivals. It was great of Peter Jackson to launch his last *Lord of the Rings* movie here, lovely the way they'd fixed up the Embassy, down on Halifax Street; his film studio over near the Abel Tasman Park was world standard. He'd come a long way from *Bad Taste*, that horror flick where he'd had dead people coming ashore over by Tahuna Beach.

She thought again about the upcoming 150th anniversary of Nelson as New Zealand's capital. She was making a habit of leading these 150th anniversary occasions. There had been the 150th anniversary of the first parliamentary elections—in 2003.

Then there was the 150th anniversary of the meeting of the first parliament—in 2004. Now, once Brash was out of the way, there'd be the 150th anniversary of New Zealand's capital—in 2006—a great occasion.

Imagine if it had been Wellington! No one would even know the anniversary was coming up. How could they plan a celebration anyway? It would have to be indoors. You could never be sure what the weather would be like up there.

'Windy Wellington'! What a stroke of luck that it is! Wasted as a capital, but a goldmine as a source of endless, clean, cheap, non-polluting energy. All those windmills! Imagine if there'd been people there. They'd have all these objections, even from the 'greenies'. Everyone wanted clean power—windmills were as clean as you could get—but no one wanted the source of that power anywhere near them. 'Nimbys'—'not in my backyard'—would have disrupted the whole programme.

As it was, the windmills had crawled across the hills surrounding Wellington, expanding from one hilltop to the next, extending all the way out to Makara. They were a glorious sight, seen all together, spinning wildly.

Those windmills had made New Zealand come that much closer to being truly independent. 'Independence'—it wasn't something you simply declared. It was something you achieved. First, we had established our state—our political institutions—and had gained a nationhood separate from the British and, yes, the Australians.

Then we had achieved economic independence—well, not entirely: we were still a trading nation, but we were no longer dependent on just one market—the British—for our prosperity.

When we broke with the Americans and left ANZUS we made a statement that we would no longer go where some other country—or group of countries—went. We would make up our own mind.

And *now* we were getting closer to achieving *energy* independence. All those windmills! That Clyde dam was the last one we were going to have to build. If it weren't for those windmills—if it weren't for *Wellington*—we'd still be importing oil, prospecting for gas, burning coal, just to keep our homes warm and our factories producing. Wind-power—there was no end to it! We could keep Kyoto and any other agreements the world came up with. Wellington's contribution to the world!

Just think of what Wellington's windmills were doing for the country's energy supplies; power prices; *and* the balance-of-payments! The next step in achieving true independence—ending dependence on imported oil, ending a dependence that consumed so much of the national income of the country . . . We were selling our food—lamb, fish, cheese, fruit—and selling our countryside, through tourism, just to pay for the oil and the petrol to fuel our cars. No, the next step to true sovereignty and independence was to move to hydrogen or electric fuel cell cars. The Japanese had developed them; we would buy them.

We were going to lead the world—again—as we had before, with women's suffrage and the welfare state—not just by being nuclear free, and being 'clean and green', but by being as close to oil free, and coal free, as we could be—being 'cleaner' and 'greener'.

There were plenty of votes to be had in being green. She'd shown Jeanette Fitzsimons once before that she didn't need her. She would do it again.

New Zealand was probably 'greener' than just about any other place on earth. It had started right here, in Nelson, with lakes, and trees, and parks, and beaches all around, always so close.

Nelson as New Zealand's capital! Of course they would be celebrating that anniversary, and in style! It had been an inspired choice! There would be fireworks over the water. There would be . . . no, there wouldn't. For a moment she had been thinking of a brilliant fly-by by the New Zealand air force, until she remembered how she'd gotten rid of it. Well, never mind. She brightened: they'd get something else instead.

Her mind wandered to the sesquicentennial speech she'd like to give. By then she'd have won three straight general elections, an historic accomplishment. She *deserved* to be remembered. She should come up with a speech unlike any that had ever been heard in this country before. Something historic; something memorable;

something appropriate to the occasion. Like Brash at Orewa, only . . . only . . . harmonious and uplifting.

It was too bad New Zealanders didn't appreciate fine words and high rhetoric. She'd said she didn't much go in for it either but here was a chance to excel. David Lange wasn't the only one who could sing with the angels.

She longed to be Lincolnesque. He'd rededicated the United States to its finest ideals—re-wed it to its original purposes—establishing, amid the wreckage of war, the basis for 'a more perfect union'.

She'd like to do the same—*that* would be her legacy—giving this country a firm identity, rooted in the *warmth* of its people and the *union* of its many cultures and nationalities. 'Warmth' and 'union'—fine words to come from Nelson, with its warmth, and the union of New Zealanders, North Island and South, old and young, Maori and non-Maori, native-born and immigrant.

She knew it was fanciful, but Lincoln had his Gettysburg Address; why couldn't she have . . . what would she call it? . . . her—*PAUSE*—Collingwood Address. She would keep it short.

Heather Simpson wouldn't like it. She would try it on Mike Munro—just to see him turn pale.

Let's see—Lincoln began, 'Four score and seven years ago . . .' Right . . . 'Seven score and ten years ago'—yes, 150 years, right—'our forefathers'—well, there's no point in being PC about it, there were no women MPs in those days—'brought forth in these islands a new capital, conceived in Auckland, and built here in Nelson, a capital at the centre of a nation dedicated to the proposition that all our people, all New Zealanders, whatever their origins, are created equal, and are endowed with equal rights, including the right to life, liberty, and the pursuit of happiness, and the right to enjoy their traditions and their inheritance, and to have preserved for future generations the resources—the lands, forests, rivers and seas—of this great country. Now, today, we rededicate this capital to ourselves, the people of New Zealand, who have ultimate sovereignty over this country, and to whom all those in government, and in parliament, are in the end accountable. And so here, even here in New Zealand, in our capital, Nelson, the idea of democracy—of government of the people, by the people, and for the people—remains on trial, an experiment, and so the whole world watches to see if we can live together in peace, as one, preserving our cultures, and our values, and all that is so beautiful here, all that we see around us, so that this vision of warmth and unity shall not perish from the earth.'

She looked again out the window towards the water, the North Island somewhere out there, just past her gaze. It was 10.30am, the start of another beautiful day in paradise. They had predicted a light rain today. Just then, as the prime minister was looking up at the sky, there it was—a rainbow.

She saw it as, in the Bible, it was meant to be seen—as a sign . . . She would tell Mike Munro, and Mike Williams, and Michael Cullen—she was surrounded by Mikes!—she had her 2005 re-election slogan:

'It's morning in New Zealand'.

4

What if New Zealand had joined Australia in 1901?

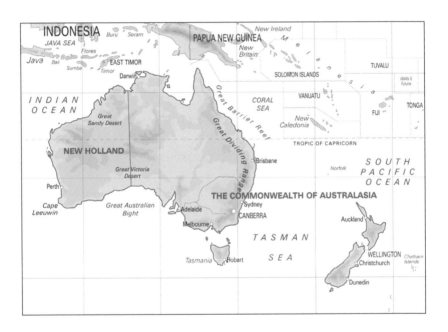

Kathryn M. Hunter

It became clear during the 1890s that New Zealand was not enthusiastic about joining the proposed Commonwealth of Australia. Reasons were various, primarily trade and distance: New Zealand delegate Sir John Hall cited '1200 reasons, the 1200 miles of the Tasman Sea'. There was a late flurry of interest demonstrated most especially by the 1901 Federation Commission, 'inquiring as to the desirability or otherwise of our said Colony federating with the Commonwealth of Australia, and becoming a State',[1] but concerns over Queensland's use of 'coloured' labour and a view that the economic benefits would not outweigh the sacrifice of New Zealand's 'independence as a separate colony' confirmed the decision to remain outside of the federation. That it could be argued the distance from the metropole was larger for Western Australia, and that trade considerations were more significant for Queensland, has led to a consideration of other reasons for New Zealand's decision. Historians have increasingly leaned towards arguments of sentiment, emotion or nascent nationalism as the main reasons for the Australian colonies' agreement and the New Zealand decision to remain outside the commonwealth.

The Australian constitution, drafted in 1900, named New South Wales, Victoria, South Australia, Queensland and Tasmania as the premier states and left open the option for both Western Australia and New Zealand to join at a later stage. Western Australia's relationship with the federation has always been strained. After joining belatedly, the state's first vote to secede from the commonwealth took place in 1933. Prominent Australian historian John Hirst has noted that 'alone of the six states, its allegiance to the Commonwealth cannot be taken for granted'.[2]

What if New Zealand had joined the federation?

It was a hot morning throughout Australasia on 1 January 1901. Well, it was hot everywhere except Hobart, where it was pleasant, and Wellington, where it was a little cool. In Collarenebri, small-town northern New South Wales, the celebrations were to be well under way before the heat of the day settled in. The procession was to be led by the mayor, leader of the local Reform League that had campaigned for federation, who would be followed by the magistrates, councillors, the Collarenebri town band and the local fire brigade. Then would process the Australian Natives Association, who had been against many of the final concessions made to New Zealand, but who were not to be denied public prominence on such an occasion. Members of the trade and labour council, the farmers' union, the licenced victuallers' association, the football team and the friendly societies would swell the ranks of the parade, some vying for the prize for the best decorated vehicle. Penultimately would be the local schoolchildren and finally members of the local Kamilaroi tribe.[3] For the Kamilaroi this was to prove in the future to be a particularly important day, the anniversary of which was worthy of celebration, but at the time there was only half-hearted participation. Their inclusion in the suffrage acts that had formed part of the legislative framework for federation had initially been greeted with some suspicion by the elders. After all, none of the other arrangements that the whitefella had brought to the community had been of particular advantage to them: mission stations where the women had been put to work in the whitefella houses, and the men had been encouraged, and sometimes compelled, to stay on the station even at the height of the kangaroo season had seemed nonsensical to the Kamilaroi. But the whitefella missionaries said they knew best. Now, this whitefella vote was to be given to the blackfellas. The lack of enthusiasm for it was understandable after the missionaries' verve for the Bible. If the vote was anything like that—all promises, prohibitions and singing—then not too many people were interested.

In Kalgoorlie, in Western Australia, the local Aboriginal people who were participating in the procession had been kept overnight in the jail to ensure their presence the next morning; indeed, 'there were second thoughts about including this . . . contingent, and they were removed by rescheduling the annual "blackfellow Christmas treat" to coincide with the street march'.[4] In this colony, this January morning dawned not on a celebration of federation, but on a national day: the second New Holland Day. The Western Australian government, outraged by the deal reached with the New Zealand delegation, had abandoned the federation congress in 1899 to formally constitute itself as a sovereign nation—New Holland—in January 1900. It was the agreement to enfranchise indigenous people that had been the back-breaking straw for the Western Australian delegates. But, as we shall see, it is questionable whether they needed to have been so worried.

The road to federation had been a long and not entirely easy one. The seven colonies of Australasia had often joined together in intercolonial conferences on trade and communications. As early as 1870 intercolonial conferences had been held to promote internal free trade, where unfortunately 'New Zealand's aspirations to preferential trade with the United States irritated Britain and the . . . [other] colonies'.[5] The New Zealand delegates, Captain William Russell and Sir John Hall, attended the first federation conference in 1890, wooed by 'father of federation' and colonial secretary of New South Wales Henry Parkes's appeal to a common heritage, to 'the crimson thread of kinship [that] runs through us all'.[6] Of course this thread of kinship did not run though *all*: the status of indigenous Australians and of Maori, as well as of Chinese and Pacific Islanders in all of the colonies, was to become a sticking point in the negotiations.

The question of the vote for women and for the indigenous peoples of the colonies was hotly debated. New Zealand had enfranchised both white women and Maori in 1893; South Australia had similarly given the vote to their women and to the Aboriginal population in 1894; and Western Australia's white women had gained the vote in 1899. Thus, by the time of the federation conference in 1899, all the white women of the 'free' colonies had the vote and the question was raised by those colonies of women's status as citizens in the new commonwealth.[7] Despite opposition from delegates from Tasmania and Queensland, white women were to be fully enfranchised, and were given the right to stand for office.

In settling the white women's vote, the problem of indigenous votes arose to be met with much the same degree of division, if along slightly different lines. Victoria (whose universal manhood suffrage legislation of 1856 had, technically, included Aboriginal men), New Zealand and New South Wales were willing to concede the Aboriginal vote and the Maori vote; Queensland and Western Australia, with their substantial Aboriginal populations, objected vociferously. New Zealand's motives in supporting the indigenous vote were not entirely noble: they were acutely aware that if the Maori population were not citizens—if they were relegated to official invisibility—the number of New Zealand's seats in the commonwealth's house of representatives (based on population) would be fewer.[8]

The one area that all colonies could agree upon was the need to restrict immigration and to regulate the 'coloured labour' of Queensland. Once federation had occurred, restrictive and punitive immigration acts were introduced almost immediately, curtailing the entry, mobility and rights of 'Asiatics, or aboriginal natives of Africa, or the Islands of the Pacific'. Australasian acts such as the Immigration Restriction Act 1901 and the Invalid and Old Age Pension Act 1908 were designed to restrict and disadvantage the non-white population of Australasia, both the insiders and the outsiders.[9] The New Zealand equivalents of these provisions, introduced just before federation, included the Immigration Restriction Act 1899 which contained the infamous dictation test (a test of fifty words in *any* European language), and the establishment of the Maori councils in 1900, which, according to some parliamentarians, were to begin the process of removing the '"communistic" way of life' that prevented Maori from developing civilised behaviours and values.[10] Manying Ip has argued that in these early years of the twentieth century, the shared idea of an Australasian 'people' coalesced into a notion that defined those who were non-Christian and non-European in culture as 'unassimilable'.[11]

The deals were duly made: South Australia (including the Northern Territory), Queensland, New South Wales, Victoria, Tasmania and New Zealand formed the six states of the new Commonwealth of Australasia. White women, Aboriginal men and women, and Maori women and men were enfranchised. New Holland remained outside the federal structure citing '1800 reasons', being the 1800 miles between Perth and Sydney, why they would not join. In the early years, relations were cordial between the two nations: how could it be otherwise when at the turn of the century, only one third of New Hollanders were 'native born' and nearly one third of the population had been born in Victoria or South Australia? Trade relations were relatively free, migration back and forth across the border (well, into and out of the New Holland ports at any rate) continued, and sporting ties were strong enough that at the 1908 Olympics New Holland and Australasia sent a combined team under the one flag. Legislatively the two nations also remained largely in concert: even in the area of indigenous rights, Queensland's policies remained more closely aligned with New Holland than with the other states in the Commonwealth. Queensland had objected to the indigenous vote, but had economic reasons for joining the federation. Its solution was to enfranchise Aboriginal adults, excluding those receiving charitable aid (effectively excluding those living on missions), and to make enrolling to vote voluntary. Consequently there were very low levels of enrolment and participation among the state's indigenous Murri people.

While the Australasian states' policies governing indigenous people differed, landlessness, poor health and low rates of education characterised these citizens' lives; and persistent notions of races destined for extinction contributed to legislative frameworks that were aimed initially at 'protection' and at 'smoothing the pillow of the dying race'. Over the first two decades of the twentieth century, as it became clear that the indigenous peoples were not fading away, assimilationist policies were increasingly adopted. As Richard Hill has argued, 'the concept of the "dying Maori" then was replaced with that of the "whitening Maori"'.[12] The tensions of assimilation and segregation operated in all states. In New Zealand, the new

80

generation of leaders, including those of the Young Maori Party, 'proclaimed the need for change within Maoridom to counteract the "dangerous hopelessness" of retreat to "primitive" tribalism, which seemingly led to racial extinction'.[13] They aimed for a cultural 'fusion' but maintained the importance of a discernable Maori identity.[14] The integration of indigenous people into democracy through the vote (although there were problems with enrolment) was accompanied by increasing calls for indigenous people to assimilate. To aid this, states began to dismantle the protectionist reserves systems, forcing younger indigenous peoples out into the white community to gain employment.[15] This approach was not uncontested and there were debates in all states and in New Holland. Archibald Meston, Queensland protector of Aborigines at the time of federation, had recommended complete segregation of the Murri people as the only way of protecting them from settler violence and from the destructive forces of venereal disease and alcohol. He rejected the 'doomed race' theory and argued that reserves could easily be self-supporting, and that they would serve also to protect Aboriginal women from white men.[16] In New Holland, Protector Neville similarly determined to protect 'full-blooded' Aboriginal people from white society through segregation although in this he was bitterly opposed by John Forrest, an ardent humanitarian and assimilationist who 'set his face firmly against any schemes to exclude [Aboriginal people] from white society, or to give government officials the power to herd them into reserves'.[17] Forrest was supported by the largely humane recommendations of the 1904 Royal Commission, reporting on the condition of New Holland Aborigines, which recommended stronger regulation of the pastoral industry to reduce the exploitation of indigenous workers. In bringing Aboriginal–white relations more firmly under the rule of law, however, the powers of the chief protector were increased, including creating a legal guardianship of all Aboriginal children in New Holland.[18] The 'dispersal' policies applied to reserves in New South Wales and Victoria mirrored this assimilationist thinking.

In the meantime, the new commonwealth—the Federation of Australasia—needed a new capital city. Locating the seat of government in one of the existing capitals was decided against, with all acknowledging that it would be impossible to choose from among the states' capitals. There were three criteria for the new capital's site that were agreed upon: the first was environmental. The capital had to be in a '"bracing" physical situation. Legislators and public servants might fall asleep in the torpor of a tropical environment. The climate had to be cool rather than warm. And the city had to be on an elevated site.'[19] That ruled out Queensland. The second criterion was security: 'Attack from the air was not a serious concern, but attack from the sea was a real threat. [Australasia's] capital could not be on the coast, subject to enemy bombardment . . .'[20] That ruled out Nelson. And finally,

> the site had to be worthy to be the capital of a great nation. It had to be uncontaminated by industry or previous major urban development. Ample water was essential, to supply the needs of residents and to create 'ornamental waters' for recreation and aesthetic effect. Ideally, it would have some surrounding mountains to provide a grand setting.[21]

That ruled out Upper Hutt, but Queenstown was looking good . . . but no, it was too far from Wellington and Sydney. Finally, after taking everything into account, in 1912 Canberra was chosen as the site of the nation's capital.

These early decades are also where nationalist historians locate the stirrings of national identity and character. The formation of national identity (that most pernicious and contested of ideas) in both New Holland and Australasia came to be formed around three things: a pioneering legend that eulogised itinerant white, male rural workers, and made note of 'useful' women; sport; and, thirdly, what came to be known as the ANHAC legend: an extension, some would say, of the pioneer legend embodied variously in the 'man alone' or the 'Southern man', but in uniform. Russel Ward in *The Australasian Legend* noted of this emergent identity:

According to the myth the 'typical Australasian' is a practical man, rough and ready in his manners and quick to decry any appearance of affectation in others. He is a great improviser [this has its modern equivalents in the 'No. 8 Wire' attitude], ever willing to 'have a go' at anything . . . he is usually taciturn rather than talkative, one who endures stoically rather than one who acts busily. He is a 'hard case', sceptical about the value of religion and of intellectual and cultural pursuits generally. He believes that Jack is not only as good as his master but, at least in principle, probably a good deal better and so he is a great 'knocker' of eminent people unless, as in the case of sporting heroes, they are distinguished by physical prowess . . . he is very hospitable and, above all, will stick to his mates through thick and thin even if he thinks they may be in the wrong.[22]

Much of this emphasis on physical prowess was placed on the disparate codes of football played throughout the region. Rugby union was played in New Zealand, Queensland and New South Wales; Victorian Rules dominated the south-east of the mainland (south of Sydney) and South Australia and was also played in New Holland. Trans-Nullarbor tests between the New Holland Swans and the Australasian Magpies were a constant source of exaggerated national rivalry and political commentary, while State of Origin rugby brought out the worst of provincialism.[23] The truly Trans-Nullarbor game, however, was cricket for much of the twentieth century; New Holland and Australasia were outposts of empire to the last. The Melbourne Cricket Club (formed in 1838) represented the controlling force behind the game until the end of the century with the establishment of the Australasian Cricket Board in 1892. The Western Australia Cricket Association was formed in 1885 and was the forerunner of the New Holland Cricket Association. Sport possibly more so than war was where the true breaks from their beloved England began to occur for the people of New Holland and Australasia. The highly successful 1905 rugby tour of England combined with the political shimmer of the newly minted commonwealth began to fray the crimson ties of kinship, but it was through the 1932–33 Ashes tour (later to become known as the 'Bodyline' tour because of the English bowlers' tactic of bowling directly at the batsman) that the Australasian populace became witness to the fallibility of English manliness and the veneer of English sportsmanship. It was also at this time that netball came to challenge cricket as Australasia's national game. In New Zealand alone in 1932 there were fifteen affiliated associations with 742 teams. This was to grow steadily over the next seventy years to see netball become the largest participation sport in secondary schools, with 200,000 players being represented by Netball New Zealand.[24]

The third stream of national identity, the 'ANHAC legend', was forged in the Dardanelles during World War I. It built on pioneer stereotypes of colonials as 'natural' soldiers of larrikin character. When war broke out in Europe in 1914, both Australasia and New Holland responded to the call. In 1915 the Australasian Imperial Force (AIF) and the New Holland Expeditionary Force were encamped together in Egypt, and communications signallers, finding their nomenclature too cumbersome, created an acronym that was to echo through the annals of history for decades to come: ANHAC—the Australasian & New Holland Army Corps. Serving together under ANHAC bound New Holland and Australasia together with a tie of mythical proportions, but in many senses it was impermanent. There was a darker side to the ANHAC legend as well: ill disciplined and racist, ANHAC soldiers in Egypt particularly were known as much for their riots and destruction of shops as for their exploits on the battlefield.

War also had significant and somewhat unexpected effects on indigenous politics. Billy McPhee's grandfather had been an Afghan camel driver, and his grandmother was of the Arrernte people whose territory included the Alice Springs settlement. Billy's father, the third child of this mixed marriage, had as a young man travelled north-west to Broome with his father, finding work and love in the pearling town. Billy, their first child, was born around 1897 and while still a toddler was denied civil rights by virtue of living on the wrong side of the border and by not being 'substantially of European descent'. In 1915, aged about eighteen years, Billy made the journey south through the deserts, crossed the border and went to his grandmother's people in South Australia.

He enlisted in the AIF early in 1916, Aboriginal Affairs not yet being organised enough to identify him as an illegal immigrant. In 1916, Billy was sent to Egypt for training and then on to France. Having had little education, fellow soldiers wrote home for him, although some postcards with rudimentary messages are believed to have been penned by him. On the Western Front Billy's luck held (or not, depending on your view) until March 1918 when he was wounded and invalided to the Australasian General Hospital No. 3 at Codford. Here he was attended by Dr Peter Buck: it was an acquaintance that would change Billy's life. Buck was descended from Ngati Mutunga, was extremely well educated, and had been a member of the New Zealand parliament before enlisting in the Maori contingent in 1915.[25] Owing to his interest in anthropology Buck befriended the young McPhee, making inquiries into living conditions and customs of the various peoples of Broome and of the Arrernte. Inspired by Buck's politics, upon his return to Alice Springs Billy began making inquiries into the conditions of the indigenous people of New Holland. In 1920 he made the decision to return to the country of his birth to fight for his people's rights. He knew of indigenous soldiers who had fought for the empire, enlisting when New Holland became less stringent about the colour of their recruits, but who were now being denied their rights as returned servicemen. (Ironically, Buck returned to New Zealand to find Apirana Ngata fighting exactly the same exclusions.)[26] Relinquishing his own pension and leaving in the hands of his kin the land he had recently taken up under the soldier settlement scheme, Billy returned to New Holland to take up the cause of returned soldiers and indigenous rights more generally. Inspired by the Maori seats in the New Zealand State parliament and the enfranchisement of the eastern tribes, Billy established the Aborigines Advancement League (AAL) and began petitioning the government.

McPhee found plenty of support among New Holland's Aboriginal population in the north, where the cattle industry dominated the economy and where many clans had rooted themselves firmly within their own country by providing labour for the pastoral industry. Aboriginal culture and white pastoral interests accommodated each other and 'Aboriginal society in the pastoral districts continued to survive and regenerate itself'.[27] Aborigines in the south-west also supported him because they had already begun battling the recalcitrant white administration in an effort to shore up their families. In Beverly, the Anglican rector reported in 1912, 'the aboriginals are howling down at the Reserve because the school is not started . . . two dozen children are roaming the streets and threatening to invade the Government School'.[28] Aboriginal families argued that it was government inaction that prevented their children being educated and yet the government removed their children because of their failure to attend school. They welcomed the message of civil rights.

Billy McPhee also found an unlikely ally in Mary Montgomerie Bennett, 'one of the more unlikely trouble-makers . . . a cultivated, middle-aged widow of artistic tastes . . . the product of an adult life spent almost entirely in good society in England'.[29] Alongside the petitions to government from the AAL, Bennett widely and publicly citicised Aboriginal policy in New Holland, publishing a book in 1930, making frequent public statements, writing for major newspapers under headlines such as 'allegations of slavery', and stimulating women's groups to pressure the government for 'an honourable Aboriginal policy'.[30] Her paper to the British Empire League in June 1933 forced a royal commission into the welfare of Aborigines in New Holland. Its recommendations were not embraced by the government, and indeed, while court procedures improved, the definitions of who was 'Aboriginal' were enlarged to bring a greater number under the 'protection' of the boards.[31]

The interwar period saw seeds of change sown for indigenous people throughout Australasia and New Holland. Based on their participation in the war, Maori in New Zealand, Koories in Victoria and New South Wales, and, particularly, Murris in Queensland also began agitating for more equal treatment. While legally equal before the law, indigenous people of Australasia were poorer, less well educated and sicker than their white counterparts; indigenous land rights were also unresolved in all states.[32] There were a variety of strategies and approaches taken to these problems. In Queensland, the state government was reluctant to act. Queensland had accepted the federation's enfranchisement of indigenous people, but, as noted, the state had made enrolment on the electoral roll voluntary, thereby ensuring a low participation rate among its substantial Murri population. By contrast, while 1930s Maori infant mortality rates were nearly five times that of non-Maori and death rates were ten times higher, systematic efforts to improve health and housing for Maori began during this period.[33] Maori parliamentarians of the 1920s and 1930s, in particular Apirana Ngata, Maui Pomare and Peter Buck, were responsive to the poor conditions in which many Maori were living and the consequent health problems. It was a slow process but over the twenty years to 1955 the reforms resulted in improvements that were nothing short of 'spectacular'.[34] These challenges facing the state government were soon overtaken, however, by Maori urbanisation. According to historian Michael King, '[r]ural depopulation and urbanisation together were to contribute to a subsequent deterioration in race relations'.[35]

The dispossession of indigenous people of their lands, however, was not a question that was going to be solved in the immediate future. In New South Wales at the turn of the century there were a series of escalating pressures on Koorie people and the reserve lands they had managed to retain. The strength of the 'dying race' myth at the turn of the twentieth century saw calls to break up reserves as Aboriginal people 'died out', and there was increasing pressure from small farmers which was supported by legislation such as the Closer Settlement Act 1905 and the introduction of the Soldier Settlement Scheme 1917, both of which divided land into small agricultural parcels for white settlers and their families.[36] These pressures were common across all the states of the Commonwealth. Apirana Ngata and James Carroll both argued that the best way for Maori to save the small percentage of lands they still retained in 1907 was to 'use' their lands—to farm them.[37] But as Richard Hill has noted, 'despite initial hopes for retention, an almost inexorable loss of land . . . continued, with very limited chances of getting even some of it back in any conceivable future'.[38]

In New Holland, Queensland and New South Wales the outbreak

of World War II created an opportunity for the Aboriginal civil and land rights movement: a white labour shortage, especially in pastoral industries, made Aboriginal labour desirable and, indeed, essential. Aboriginal people offered support for the war in return for citizenship, and their labour in return for wages. In response, the New Holland parliament granted full citizenship to Aboriginal adults who could demonstrate to a magistrate that they were 'literate, of industrious habits and good behaviour and completely severed from tribal or communal associations'.[39] It was with the widespread social changes brought about by the revelations of Hitler's death camps, and the establishment of the United Nations after the war, however, that major change began to occur for indigenous people throughout the region. As signatories to the UN declarations on human rights and racial equality, Australasia and New Holland had to rectify the glaring hypocrisies of their own policies. Voting 'irregularities' in Queensland were ironed out in a referendum in 1967; New Holland enfranchised their indigenous people in 1972 after militant and escalating action drew the attention of the world's media; and, in 1997, Tasmania was forced to decriminalise homosexuality to bring the state into line with UN and commonwealth policies.

At the turn of the twenty-first century, relations between New Holland and Australasia were akin to those of siblings forced to share a room: rivalry abounded but many compromises had been reached. There were frameworks in place for Closer Economic Relations and vague murmurings about a common currency. There were spats about ownership of the pavlova—did it originate in the Esplanade Hotel in Perth, or was it brought into being in New Zealand?– but the Finn Brothers were definitely Australasian.[40] The populace, when asked, generally agreed that there were distinctive national characteristics that separated them, but couldn't really name any of them. Indigenous people in all states continued to fight for land rights and against the various other sorts of dispossessions of the colonial period.

Where, then, does our alternate scenario leave us? The very serious questions behind the impudent 'what if . . .?' seem to be: 'would race relations have been any different if New Zealand had been part of Australia's commonwealth?' and 'would the character of Australians and New Zealanders be different if the nation-state had encompassed us all?' To some extent, the answers to these questions are to be found in the enduring strength of regionalism.

This imagined refiguring of the region draws attention to the strength of states' rights and local agendas in Australian politics. Under federation, the states have maintained the lion's share of power—over health, primary and secondary education, land, civil and criminal law—and from 1901–67 indigenous people were considered to have been sufficiently 'taken care of' under state governments.[41] The Australian Constitution was drafted so as not to encroach on the 'established regimes' of the states.[42] There is a system of dual citizenship in which groups have been enfranchised at different times and at different levels, and with varying degrees of efficacy: white women in South Australia and Western Australia in the 1890s, and at the federal level in 1902, but not until 1908 in Victoria; Aboriginal people in South Australia in 1894 (although the Constitution prevented continuing enfranchisement of indigenous people from 1902), and in New South Wales, Victoria, Tasmania, and again in South Australia in 1948; and finally in the commonwealth, and hence in Western Australia and Queensland, in 1967. Similarly, land rights have been dealt with, by and large, in state courts and by local land councils (in the case of the Northern Territory), and now in the state Native Title Tribunals. Daily metropolitan papers, radio and television news coverage are all state-based; sport, with a couple of exceptions, is likewise regionally defined. It is state and local politics that affects people's daily lives: road rules, daylight savings, the quality of state education and the price of private schools, milk and drainage. The things that cross borders are few: taxes, mail, mangoes, tertiary education policy and, every Anzac Day, the prime minister's assertion that there is something intrinsic to being 'Australian'.

An educated guess is that New Zealand, as one of the premier states, would have ensured an even greater degree of autonomy for the states. Indigenous affairs would have remained, very possibly, in state hands: how could it have been otherwise with such a long history of Maori interaction and negotiation with 'the crown' in the shape of the New Zealand government (and, occasionally, with the Queen herself!).

So what, in my alternate scenario, is not true? What did I have to manufacture? Hardly anything. Indigenous people in Australia were not enfranchised at federation, and indeed were deliberately excluded from suffrage at the federal level by the 1902 legislation that enfranchised white women. This exclusion from citizenship extended to the enlistment of Aboriginal men in the Australian Imperial Force during World War I; they were not 'substantially of European origin'. From family histories and other fragments of evidence we do know that approximately 300–400 indigenous Australians served their country despite the legal bar to them doing so. Peter Buck did serve as a medical officer at Codford and perhaps it is only the vicissitudes of coincidence that prevented my 'unidentified Aboriginal soldier' from meeting him. The Finn brothers are, of course, undeniably sons of Aotearoa and no Australian would dare claim otherwise.

WAR AND DEVELOPMENT

5

What if the strikers at Waihi had triumphed?

Erik Olssen

The Waihi strike has enjoyed an enduring status since the appearance of The Tragic Story of the Waihi Strike (1913). The first edition of that book, mainly written by Harry Holland, sold out before being released and has never since been out of print. It was a proclamation, presented as an historical description, portraying a working class distracted from its true mission by apostasy, but being summoned to its task by a united Federation of Labour and, implicitly, its prophet, Holland.

Holland transformed the strike into a myth but distorted it to do so. The Waihi Workers' Union, the only successful industrial union in the country, was dominated by revolutionaries. The Industrial Workers of the World (IWW or the 'Wobblies'), led by J.B. King, were dominant. They called for class war at the point of production, dismissed morality as a bourgeois opiate of the workers, and preached sabotage and violence. Right-wing socialists, led by men such as Tom Walsh (a boilermaker), attacked the IWW with equally vitriolic rage. Holland read these two groups out of his story. The miners actually struck to prevent the engine drivers from seceding, the engine drivers being sick of attacks on skilled craftsmen, the church, the king and the empire. At the time the Waihi Gold Mining Company, which planned to electrify the mine, happily watched the miners walk out on strike.

Somewhat to everyone's astonishment the strike lasted almost six months, sustained by donations from Australian workers. During that time the Liberals lost power to William F. Massey's Reform Party. The new prime minister, together with his new commissioner of police, decided to assist the Waihi Gold Mining Company in reopening the now electrified gold mine. It was the manner of that intervention, and the wanton disregard for the law, that came to define what people understood to be the meaning of the Waihi strike. The role of government in defeating the strike persuaded many 'Red Feds', including revolutionaries such as Holland, that the organised working class needed to unify and build political influence in parliament. Many working-class opponents of the Red Feds and the strikers, shocked by the government's naked use of illegal methods, also decided to bury

94

the hatchet. Most of the country's trade unionists were represented at two great unity conferences in 1913 and agreed, in principle, to affiliate with a new United Federation of Labour and the Social Democratic Party. Before either organisation had established a national presence the 1913 strike erupted.

What if the strikers at Waihi had triumphed?

The outcome might easily have been quite different, in which case the 'moderates' of 1912–13, men like Holland and Michael Joseph Savage, might have been eclipsed. Had that occurred, the leaders of the IWW would have emerged as the dominant figures in the New Zealand labour movement. Had some subsequent events driven the organised working class to seek political influence and power, then the first Labour prime minister might have been an ex-member of the IWW instead of a disciple of Daniel De Leon (who articulated what came to be considered Lenin's position about the importance of a revolutionary political cadre in holding the working class to its true revolutionary destiny). J.B. King, instead of fleeing New Zealand to avoid prosecution for preaching violence and sabotage, might have survived to lead Labour. Had he done so, one can imagine the country's banks being nationalised, New Zealand working closely with the Soviet Union on a range of foreign policy issues, and a series of experiments in workers' control of industry.

Having sketched the scene let me offer a few remarks about the nature of this enterprise. A 'counterfactual' proposition, such as the one with which I am dealing, can be considered a form of comparative enquiry. In identifying the critical variables—time, technologies, the state, and the critical path of events that culminated in the Waihi strike—it is possible to reflect systematically about the possibility that the Waihi strike might have had a different outcome. What I propose to do is offer some reflections about that strike and its consequences before proceeding to examine which of those consequences might *not* have occurred had the strikers won. I will also consider which other consequences might have occurred had the strikers been successful.

Before going any further let me explain why Waihi has been identified for discussion, rather than the great maritime strike of 1913. Many now, having read Olssen on 'The Red Feds', probably agree that the latter strike was much more significant than that at Waihi: indeed, was much more significant than the 1951 waterfront strike.[1] However, I decided on Waihi for two reasons: first, there is very little possibility that the strikers could ever have won in 1913; second, had they won at Waihi, there would have been no strike in 1913.

Let me first review why it is not inherently implausible to imagine the strikers victorious at Waihi. First, it was a sectional strike and geographically confined to one place, Waihi. Although the nearby coal miners at Huntly did attempt to display solidarity by going out on a one-day sympathy strike, by and large other unionists only considered expressing sympathy by providing money. Famously or infamously, most of that money came from unionists in Australia rather than from unionists in New Zealand. Nonetheless that flow of money was sufficient to sustain the strike for the best part of five months, a period vastly longer than the employers ever imagined possible. Second, it is possible to imagine two developments that in all likelihood would have produced a different outcome. First, had Alfred James Mitchell been selected as commissioner of police rather than John Cullen it is possible to imagine that the police would not have supported the Waihi Gold Mining Company's decision to reopen the mine. Had the police force deliberately abstained from intervention, or even protected strikers in their right to picket, it is possible that the strikers would have defeated the company when it tried to reopen the mine. I say this because of what happened in Auckland in 1913, where Mitchell refused to use the police against the strikers and was suspended and then transferred for his pains. Cullen, fiercely anti-union and violently hostile to the 'Red Feds', had no qualms about siding with the company or forcing Mitchell to retire.[2]

Another change is likewise easy to imagine. There was no inevitability about Massey's success in passing a no-confidence motion in the Liberal government in June 1912, more or less the point of time at which the Waihi miners went out on strike. Although the Liberals, unlike Reform, disliked militant unionism, they depended upon the votes of unionists in all of the main towns and in many provincial towns. This electoral dependence had made them ambivalent in their response to militant labour since the 1908 Blackball strike.[3] That ambivalence would undoubtedly have characterised the response of Thomas Mackenzie's Liberal government throughout 1912, just as it had for the previous six months. Moreover the Mackenzie government also depended upon the support of the four Labour MPs elected to the House of Representatives in the 1911 elections. An ambivalent government would not have authorised active police involvement on behalf of the company and would undoubtedly have reined Cullen in rather than giving him a free hand. Under a Liberal government it is hard to imagine the endless arrests of union pickets, not to mention the open support given to the strike-breakers during the strike's last days. (It is not irrelevant to note that the Liberals, now in opposition, fiercely denounced the Massey government and the police for acting illegally.)

There is a third variable that might have changed although this has previously not received much attention. It is not widely known that the company was happy enough to see the union walk out in June 1912 because it wanted to close the mine in order to complete a shift in technology from steam to hydroelectric power. (The company built its power station at Hora Hora, now submerged beneath Lake Karapiro, and the state bought it in 1919.) That shift had been completed by the time the company decided, in November, to reopen the mine. Had there been a Liberal government, or had Mitchell been commissioner of police—or had both of those outcomes occurred—then it is highly likely that the company, having effected the technological changes required to increase productivity, might well have settled with the union in any case. It had done so before and would not have wanted the mine to remain idle one day longer than was necessary.

The 1913 strike

Let me now briefly explain why it is not plausible to imagine a different outcome to the 1913 strike. First, we should remind ourselves that had the Waihi strikers not been defeated in 1912 it is highly unlikely that a strike would have occurred the following year. It is often forgotten that two fuses smouldered throughout 1913, both kept alive by the bitterness occasioned by the manner in which government and police assisted in defeating the strikers at Waihi. That bitterness ran deepest among the ideologically self-conscious (De Leonites, Wobblies and syndicalists, among others). Although the Wellington shipwrights, who usually receive most attention from historians, were not in any way disgruntled because of the defeat of Waihi, their decision to gain some leverage by affiliating with the Wellington watersiders raised the ideological and emotional ante considerably. The Wellington watersiders' union was one of the most ideologically self-conscious and industrially aggressive unions in the country. Their decision to help the little union of craft workers, and to break their agreement with the employers by holding a stop-work meeting to discuss the matter, owed a considerable amount to bitterness arising out of the events of 1912. Had those watersiders not been so keen to assist the shipwrights, there would have been no Wellington strike.

The second and more significant fuse smouldered at the Huntly coal mine. At Huntly the men had been angry since the company blacklisted nine members of the union's executive following a one-day sympathy strike in support of the strikers at Waihi. (On the other side at Huntly was E.W. Allison, one of those Auckland businessmen rabid against unions and socialists, owner of the Devonport Ferry Company, and a key shareholder and director in the Northern Steam Ship Company.) Although the blacklisted executive urged the men back to work while the issue was referred to the Federation of Labour, the men refused. Tom Walsh further embittered the situation by arriving in town to organise an arbitration union for 'scabs'. When the Federation finally suspended strike pay for all but the nine blacklisted members of the executive the men had little choice. At this point Allison's

Taupiri Coal Company repudiated its old agreement with the union on wages and conditions and insisted that these would now be negotiated on an individual basis. Only Walsh's arbitration union would be recognised. The executive remained in town and led the fight, a struggle with its own autonomous history. This second smouldering fuse—the ongoing dispute at Huntly—was, in fact, the key fuse. Without Waihi, this fuse would not have begun smouldering.

Quite coincidentally matters also came to a head when the coal miners again struck at Huntly in October 1913. This was the strike that ignited the country. Auckland's 'coalies' promptly came out for fear that the 'boss class' was importing coal in order to close Huntly. That night Auckland's wharfies voted to join them and thus forced the United Federation of Labour to call out the nation's watersiders. When permanent hands employed by the Auckland Harbour Board began unloading bananas and pineapples from the SS *Tofue*, pickets captured the first trolleys, fights broke out, and Superintendant Mitchell ordered the fruit loaded back on board. Auckland rapidly came to a standstill. The Queen city was paralysed by a general strike. Auckland's *Truth* carried the headline: 'Waihi Being Avenged'.

The rapidity with which those two smouldering fuses ignited the country's largest ever strike transformed two local disputes into a national confrontation with the Employers' Federation and the government. The speed with which Massey, concerned about the loyalty of the police, recruited 'specials' to help maintain law and order is clear proof of the government's commitment to the defeat of revolutionary unionists. 'Massey's Cossacks', as they became known, polarised the nation. His success in persuading the senior naval officer to lend the government HMS *Psyche* and HMS *Pyranus* further inflamed the situation. It was possible to conceive of Auckland being in a state of civil war. Harry Scott Bennett (the great revolutionary orator) wrote to his mother: 'warship guns pointed on the town, armed men everywhere'.

Despite the excitement the outcome was a foregone conclusion, as the United Federation of Labour's executive realised almost at once. It was opposed not only by the Employers' Federation and the government, but quite clearly by the major social classes within New Zealand society as well. It has long been known that farmers throughout the length and breadth of New Zealand were opposed not only to trade unionism, but with particular ferocity to the variants of revolutionary industrial unionism that had flourished since 1908. It was the farmers on their horses, the strike force of Massey's Cossacks, that rode into town to teach the strikers a lesson. As the *New Zealand Herald* reported, 'the whole Waikato was gripped in the fervour of prosecuting a righteous crusade to preserve social order and the butter stocks'. Most of the urban business and professional class also fiercely opposed revolutionary socialism and industrial unionism. Many men from these predominantly urban classes also volunteered to assist the state in maintaining law and order. Many university students also rushed to enlist. In addition, although it has long since been unacceptable to say it very loudly, it is also pertinent to note that the great majority of trade unionists within New Zealand also opposed revolutionary socialism and revolutionary industrial unionism, not to mention the even more extreme views of the Industrial Workers of the World. (Its leader, J.B. King, had fled New Zealand towards the end of the Waihi strike when questions began to be asked in parliament about his advocacy of violence and sabotage.)

Many feared (and some hoped) that a strike on the scale of 1913 might precipitate revolution. Bob Hogg, the revolutionary socialist who edited *New Zealand Truth*, was one of the few revolutionaries in Wellington to realise that the armed crowd of strikers and their supporters, who briefly controlled Wellington's streets before the 'Cossacks' arrived, could easily have marched on parliament and declared 'the socialist republic'. They didn't. Once army units appeared on the streets, and then the 'Cossacks' arrived on horseback, many strikers threw away their firearms.

As that great revolutionary theorist, E.J.B. Allen, later explained in *Labour and Politics*, the preconditions for a revolution simply did not exist in New Zealand in 1913.[4] Moreover the very premises of revolutionary industrial unionism were ill founded in a society characterised by a democratic franchise and representative democratic institutions. The socio-economic preconditions for revolution were absent as well. The country's main business was farming, with family farms dominating that sector. Industry was predominantly small scale and scattered, and (as almost every visiting revolutionary had remarked) New Zealand's workers enjoyed low rates of unemployment, high wages, and high levels of home ownership. As the American revolutionary, Bob Hutchinson, remarked in 1916, even labourers enjoyed a standard of living way beyond the dreams of most workers in the Western world.

In brief, Waihi's striking miners might have won in 1912 but the 1913 strike would then not have occurred; as it was, there was no way the strikers in 1913 could ever have achieved victory. Even had they marched on parliament and declared a socialist republic before the specials arrived, the counterrevolution would have been both prompt and decisive.

Hogg's moment of retrospective regret reflected more his uncertainty about how one might actually complete a revolution—at this time all examples were French and involved capturing the capital—than his intention to do so. He certainly never attempted to lead a crowd on parliament and nor did anybody else. Despite their revolutionary rhetoric, almost all the strikers, like the workers in general, were profoundly democratic.[5] This can be illustrated by recounting the story of Tom Barker.

Barker migrated to New Zealand in 1912—he had a sister in Auckland—and promptly got a job on the privately owned Auckland tramway system. He joined the Auckland branch of the Socialist Party and in 1911–12 he became intensely disaffected both with that party and with the Red Federation of Labour (the inept management of the Auckland general labourers' strike of 1911–12 had sowed the seeds of disaffection among Auckland's revolutionary socialists long before the actual Waihi strike). In Auckland town and its industrial towns, such as Waihi and Huntly, this anger against the Red Federation and the Socialist Party saw the Industrial Workers of the World suddenly flourish—not the De Leonites, who had been expelled in 1905, but 'the Bummery'.)[6] At some point during 1912 Barker joined the IWW. When the Waihi Workers' Union struck, Barker went to Waihi and joined

King. Unlike King he was still there at the end when riots and fighting occurred. This defeat, with the murder of Fred Evans and his subsequent elevation to the ranks of the martyrs of the labour movement, helped galvanise Auckland unionists and stiffened the resolve of the revolutionary cadres.[7]

Barker was in the midst of the fray when the fuse suddenly burst into flame in October 1913. He went down to Wellington but was called back to Auckland when many newspaper boys refused to work. For a brief period the IWW's little paper, *Industrial Unionist*, became the only paper to regularly appear on Auckland's streets. (It had begun as a monthly but now came out three or four times a week.) Barker and his 'Wobbly' mates wrote and printed the paper, then took it into the streets to sell (when they had sold the edition they repaired to a nearby pub to drink the proceeds). One day, as he prepared to go home, a policeman asked him, 'quite courteously, to go to the Police Station with him. . . . At the Police Court the Magistrate was sitting and he told me I was charged with sedition in Wellington. . . . Because the authorities weren't sure how to deal with it they had charged me for the words three times, once under the Justices of the Peace Act, once under the Crimes Act and again under another Act. In fact, the government was as lost on some of these things as we were. It was all brand new . . .'[8]

Here we come to the part of Barker's story that demonstrates conclusively that the leaders of that strike had no clear revolutionary goals and no stomach for bloodshed. The magistrate told Barker he would have to report in four days to the supreme court in Wellington for sentencing. He asked the police to put him in cells and then provide an escort. The police objected 'that being shorthanded and every policeman being needed . . . in Auckland, they couldn't possibly spare anyone. So the Magistrate turned to me and said, "Look, Mr. Barker, if we let you go, on your word of honour, will you take yourself to Wellington?" And that's just what happened.' Barker took himself down to Wellington with Michael Joseph Savage, the key figure in the De Leonite Auckland Socialist Party, on the very train that somebody attempted to blow up. After delivering a rousing speech to the strikers in Post Office

Square, Barker walked down Featherston Street to surrender to the supreme court for judgment. Not surprisingly he had great difficulty persuading either the police or the specials that he was a dangerous subversive required for sentencing. In the end he succeeded in convincing them 'that I was wanted in the Court' and there he was sentenced to jail. The police then escorted him to the jail on The Terrace. (I have no doubt that he would have taken himself there had no police been available.) It was a veritable reunion of old friends, although Barker was the only member of 'the Bummery': Peter Fraser, Bob Semple, a dock worker named George Bailey, Harry Holland, and Tom Young (the secretary of the seamen's union) were all there living in the cells. Big crowds used to come and visit them outside the walls of the prison; the waterside workers' band used to come and play such stirring tunes as the 'Red Flag', the 'International', and famous IWW songs. And these were the leaders of the revolution . . .

The Waihi strike of 1912

Having established the possibility that the strikers might have won at Waihi in 1912 if one or two of the variables had been different, the consequences of a different outcome can now be considered. First, the Waihi Workers' Union, a revolutionary body with revolutionary leaders strongly influenced by the ideology of the IWW, would have become the most influential union within New Zealand. Influential Wobblies such as J.B. King—an outstanding Canadian organiser and orator—would have been armed with considerable authority based on that success, and the IWW almost certainly would have been able to persuade militants, revolutionary socialists, and most industrial unionists elsewhere in the country of the merit of their analysis. Even at the June 1912 conference of the Red Federation, when the issue of Waihi polarised affiliates, the influence of King and the Auckland delegates was sufficient to see the federation adopt the constitution of the IWW. The Wobbly star would have soared into the firmament. Every worker and union leader with a grievance would have noted the outcome. Success, after all, is often the catalyst for ideological conversion.

Second, had the strikers won at Waihi the Red Federation itself would have moved sharply to the left. It would not have been compelled to seek unity with the craft-based trades and labour councils, the various local Labour Parties and Labour representation committees, and progressive groups such as the housewives' unions. Victory at Waihi would have made the reborn Red Federation the most powerful national organisation in the labour movement and one of the most powerful in the country. Although the division within the working class, and particularly within the unionised working class, might have become much deeper, I think that such spectacular success would have converted almost every unionist to the new method and organisation. Opponents of the Red Feds and the IWW, such as William Pierpont Black and Tom Walsh (whose *Voice of Labour* shrilly represented their views), would have become an isolated minority much more quickly than they did. A Red Federation whose constitution and strategy had been vindicated by triumph at Waihi would also have provided dynamic leadership to a union movement that was already one of the largest in the world.

Not only would the federation's success have converted most unionised workers to the new gospel of revolutionary industrial unionism, but Massey's Reform government would probably have hastened the process. Having tasted an unexpected defeat, many in the Reform caucus would have urged their ministry to rescue their friends and allies, New Zealand's puny capitalist class, from the consequences of industrial defeat. Reform's legislative programme for 1913, in short, might have been very similar to the programme that they did actually push through (except that attempts to shore up the arbitration system would have been ineffectual). Such legislation would have hastened the movement of craft unionists, Fabian and Christian Socialists, and other progressives into the new organisation. It might also have precipitated a showdown between the federation and the government, although for reasons that I shall discuss soon I think not.

In these circumstances it seems unlikely that the New Zealand Labour Party (NZLP) would have emerged in 1916. Indeed, it is far more likely that a reborn Socialist Party might have been able to exploit the new situation and constitute itself as the revolutionary elite of the working-class army (which is pretty much what happened in Wellington and some West Coast towns anyway: hence the class-conscious revolutionary rhetoric of such men as Peter Fraser and Robert Semple when they won seats in parliament in 1918). It also seems likely that had significant groups of unionised workers rejected the Red Federation they would have been largely confined to the South Island east of the Southern Alps and its principal towns. In the South Island union labour had enjoyed considerable political influence and civic acceptance since 1890 and that might well have continued, with the Labour parties continuing to work closely with the Liberals. Two working classes might have emerged at that point in time and dual unionism would almost certainly have begun to flourish, as it did in the United States and Canada.

Some may object that regardless of all of this the confrontation between Massey's Reformers and the labour movement would still have occurred; the Federation would still have been smashed; and presumably the actual events that followed the 1913 strike would therefore still have taken place. I think not but agree that the point is arguable. Accordingly, let us first sketch the scenario that ends in confrontation and defeat. If the First World War had still begun in September 1914 and the anti-imperial and antiwar Red Feds— men like Holland—had still been in control of the Red Federation and the *Maoriland Worker*,[9] it is likely that their strenuous opposition to the war, and later to conscription, would have seen the government launch an assault on revolutionary unionism.

We cannot be confident of that, however. Although it is a plausible scenario, two points need to be remembered. First, the anti-imperial and antiwar sentiment in 1914–15 was confined for the most part to a small minority of revolutionaries. Even some of the leading lights, like the author of *Revolutionary Unionism*, E.J.B. Allen, strongly supported the war.[10] Furthermore all the evidence from elsewhere indicates that nationalism trumped socialism. That is why the Second International collapsed. I believe it also explains why the Social Democratic Party (SDP) collapsed in New Zealand. (It was that collapse that persuaded the SDP to seek unity with its enemies and thus form the NZLP.) Most workers, like most New Zealanders, strongly believed in the righteousness of Britain's cause even in September 1914. Germany's ruthless invasion of Belgium only deepened that conviction. Although opposition to conscription was more widespread, not only within the labour movement but among those described as 'non-conformists' in England, that only became an issue when the New Zealand government decided to contribute an entire division to the Allied cause. By then many Red Feds, like most skilled workers, would have accepted the justice of conscription (which came into question only when the voluntary system failed to produce enough volunteers).

The antiwar leaders of the Red Federation would have alienated their own rank and file had they maintained opposition to the war, and so would have moderated their behaviour (as they did in fact). Even had that not happened, however, it is often not realised that the needs of war made the Massey government anxious to avoid industrial conflicts. Even before the formation of a wartime Liberal-Reform national unity government, which gave the Liberals almost equal representation in cabinet, Massey and his able deputy, James Allen, were nervous about the possibility of another massive national strike. Although that nervousness did not always enable the Reform Party to prevent its backbenchers from making inflammatory anti-Labour comments, by and large the government's commitment to industrial peace outweighed whatever residual anti-unionism existed. When the Efficiency Board urged the government to substitute female for male labour across several industries, thus freeing many for military service, it refused point blank. To the disgust of many unionised workers, the government was particularly anxious not to provoke the troublesome coal miners, watersiders and seamen. Had the Red Federation won at Waihi its strength would have made the government even more placatory, so long as it did not oppose the war or, when that time came, conscription.

Had the Massey government *not* ended up at war with the left wing of the Labour movement, as happened in 1912–13, New Zealand would have become a much more divided society in the postwar period. The sort of 'broker state' that existed in embryo thanks to the war would have been much stronger and the position of the union movement within that state would have been much more powerful.[11] It also seems likely had this happened that the Liberals would have disappeared without trace quite quickly, a minority of its adherents identifying with the left, especially in the South Island, while the majority, fearful of revolutionary labour, would have supported the Massey government. The equivalent of the National Party, having formed in the 1920s, would have been dominated by members of Reform. (As it was, of course, when National was actually formed in 1936 Reform's influence was at an all-time low.)

I am not sure what political strategy the Red Federation would have adopted. Reform and National, having formed the wartime National government, would certainly not have been able to persuade the Labour and Socialist MPs to join their coalition. The Red Federation, thanks to its victory at Waihi, would have perhaps forced the Labour and Socialist MPs to form a new Socialist Party, something akin to the SDP, and in the new context that party might have proved effective. It also seems likely that the Communist Party that finally emerged in response to the 1917 Bolshevik Revolution might have been significantly stronger. We cannot dismiss the possibility, however, that New Zealand might have become the last bastion of the IWW and that men such as Tom Barker and J.B. King, who actually became a 'shock worker' in the Soviet Union after fleeing Australia, would have had an ongoing influence in New Zealand. In that case the union movement would have dominated the De Leonite party.

Had this Socialist Party ever won—and the Great Depression would have still given it an unrivalled opportunity—we must contemplate the astonishing possibility that the first Labour prime minister, leading a government well to the left of the 1935 Labour Party (which was in any case well to the left of most Labour parties in the world), would have been a Canadian Wobbly rather than an Australian De Leonite. The debate about republicanism in New Zealand would have begun two generations earlier.

Conclusion

As a final thought, if it seems fanciful to contemplate the possibility that New Zealand's union movement might have been even stronger and more left wing than it actually was for most of the twentieth century—and equally fanciful to think of some equivalent to the Labour Party adopting even more aggressively socialist policies—this reinforces what might be considered the real question to be asked of New Zealand history: how it was that a country dominated by farmers and small towns ever came to have one of the world's most powerful trade union movements and a Labour government—indeed, a radical Labour government at that.

Had the workers won at Waihi then that union movement would have been even more powerful, and more left wing, and New Zealand's first Labour government would have been yet more radical. As noted at the start of this chapter, all the trading banks might have been nationalised, worker-control schemes would have been vigorously encouraged . . . and as for the rest, with everything else it might have done, all that is merely the stuff of dreams.

6

What if New Zealand soldiers had never fought at Gallipoli?

Donald Anderson

On 25 April 1915, the Australian and New Zealand Army Corps (ANZAC) landed at Anzac Cove on the Gallipoli Peninsula. During the following eight months 8556 New Zealanders fought on Gallipoli, with New Zealand casualties numbering 2721 dead and 4752 wounded. Ninety per cent of the casualties occurred in the first four months on the peninsula.[1]

Out of the events and experiences of Gallipoli developed Anzac Day, the ANZAC legend, and the ANZAC experience as a powerful element in the popular national image of both Australia and New Zealand.[2] It can also be argued that the shared experience of ANZAC brought New Zealanders as a whole (then and since) closer to Australia. Asking the question of whether or not the reverse holds true would almost certainly provoke a heated response or heated debate in any bar in Australia. As we are all aware, it is often overlooked in Australia that New Zealand was part of ANZAC.[3]

But the events on Gallipoli may never have taken place had certain events before 1915 turned out differently. This chapter will first explore some of the influential events, both small and large, that led, indirectly or directly, to New Zealand soldiers landing at Gallipoli. Then the chapter will explore what may have happened if New Zealand soldiers had never fought at Gallipoli.

Counterfactual causes— some plausible possibilities

Winston Churchill dies before 1901

The Gallipoli campaign started as a naval operation in which a British and French naval fleet would attempt to pass through the Narrows of the Dardanelles, capture or destroy the Turkish–German fleet, and threaten Constantinople, thereby forcing the surrender of the Turkish government. British leaders hoped that a Turkish surrender would shorten the war as a whole, by opening a supply route to Russia and galvanising the Balkan states into attacking the Central Powers. Naval operations in the Dardanelles commenced on 19 February 1915, but by mid-March the Turkish defences had proven too strong for a naval attack alone. It was only after the loss of six battleships (three sunk, three badly damaged) on 18 March that the British War Council decided that landings on the Gallipoli Peninsula were necessary to the success of the naval strategy to force the surrender of the Ottoman Empire.[4]

One of the main proponents of the Gallipoli strategy was Winston Churchill, the First Lord of the Admiralty. On 25 November 1914, he advocated in the British War Council a joint naval and land invasion of the Gallipoli Peninsula, though he hoped that Greece would join the war on the Allied side and provide 60,000 soldiers to undertake the land invasion. By 5 January 1915 Churchill was arguing that naval action by itself would allow the passage of the Dardanelles, and this strategy was approved by the war council on 13 January. From 16 February, Churchill campaigned in the war council for the commitment of troops to the Gallipoli Peninsula. The land invasion strategy was implemented after the naval setback of 18 March.[5]

Without Churchill's sustained and enthusiastic support for the Gallipoli strategy, the members of the British War Council might have listened to the advice of Arthur James Balfour, former prime minister (1902–05), a member of the war council, and the person who would replace Churchill in May 1915 as the First Lord of the Admiralty. Balfour's advice, given in a letter of 2 January 1915 to Maurice Hankey, secretary of the war council, was that even if a landing on the Gallipoli Peninsula succeeded and the Ottoman Empire surrendered, there was very little chance these events would hasten the end of the war against Germany on the Western Front.[6] Without Churchill's presence in the war council, Balfour might have been able to persuade the other members of the war council not to even attempt an attack on the Gallipoli Peninsula, as the cost in troops, naval vessels, munitions and casualties would be too great when compared to the almost certainly minimal impact of even a successful campaign on the outcome of the war as a whole.

However, Churchill was fortunate that he was still alive in 1914 to be the First Lord of the Admiralty. In late 1895, he accompanied a Spanish military column on its march into the interior of Cuba. During this expedition to locate and defeat Cuban rebels, enemy bullets passed within a foot of Churchill's head.[7] Three years later, on 2 September 1898, Churchill rode as a reporter with the British Light Cavalry Regiment, the Twenty-first Lancers, at the Battle of Omdurman in the Sudan. During the battle, the 400-strong British regiment charged a force of around 2500 infantry and defeated them at a cost of twenty-one killed and another fifty wounded (three Victoria Crosses were awarded), with more than a third of the regiment's horses wounded or killed. Churchill records that at one point during the fighting associated with this charge he was fired upon by the enemy from close range, but that both bullets missed.[8] Though the British casualties for the battle were relatively small, Churchill could have been killed or seriously wounded in the confusion of battle. The Hon H. Howard, a war correspondent for *The Times*, was killed during the battle, and two other war correspondents were wounded.[9]

During the South African War, Churchill fought in numerous battles. On 15 November 1899, Churchill fought in the defence of an armoured train which had been ambushed by the Boers. Though technically a non-combatant as a war correspondent, Churchill was armed with a Mauser pistol and had volunteered his services to the train's commander. Several rail cars had been derailed by Boer artillery, preventing the engine from retreating to safety. Under constant machine-gun and artillery fire from the Boers, Churchill directed the clearing of the line, helped load wounded onto the engine's tender, and then accompanied the engine on the first part of its journey to safety. Churchill then attempted to rally the British troops and was captured.[10]

In January 1900 Churchill was in the thick of the fighting at the battle of Spion Kop. In a letter of late January 1900 he wrote: 'The scenes on Spion Kop were among the strangest and most terrible I have ever witnessed . . . I had five very dangerous days continually under shell and rifle fire and once the feather on my hat was cut through by a bullet.'[11]

The naval strategy succeeds in March 1915

It is widely accepted that the naval attempt to sail through the Narrows of the Dardanelles on 18 March 1915 failed largely because a row of twenty mines eluded the Allied minesweepers. The mines sank three battleships, and a combination of artillery fire and mines badly damaged three more battleships.[12]

If these mines had been found by the Allied minesweepers, or if the Turkish vessel which laid them had been sunk while attempting to lay the mines, it is possible that the Allied naval fleet would have been able to reach Constantinople. If the fleet had forced the surrender of the Ottoman Empire, there would have been no need for an opposed landing at Gallipoli.

The Ottoman Empire never enters the war

When the main body of the New Zealand Expeditionary Force sailed from New Zealand on 16 October 1914, their intended destination was the battlefields of France. The Ottoman Empire's entry into the war on the side of the Central Powers on 5 November 1914 changed the strategic picture, and the New Zealand and Australian troops were disembarked in Egypt to complete their training and if necessary assist in its defence.[13]

The entry of the Ottoman Empire into the war was not inevitable. In August 1914, Enver Pasha was Turkey's practical head of state as the leader of the 'Young Turks'. Enver desired that his country enter the war on the winning side, and he believed that the victor would be the Central Powers. Enver and the German ambassador in Constantinople, Baron von Wangenheim, had already concluded a secret treaty of armed cooperation.[14] Before the 'Young Turk' revolution of 1908 had brought the Committee of Young Turks to power, Enver had served as military attaché in Berlin, where he had acquired definite Germanophile tendencies. Between 1908 and 1914 the Committee of Young Turks increasingly fell under the spell of Enver's immense, if egotistical, personality. German influence in Turkish foreign and military affairs also grew as Enver's power increased.[15] If Enver had died before mid-1914, and especially before the arrival in December 1913 of the German military mission to Turkey led by General Liman von Sanders,[16] perhaps the Ottoman Empire would not have entered the First World War as Germany's ally.

Enver served as a military leader of the resistance to the Italian invasion of Tripolitania (Libya) from late 1911 to October 1912. As a result of his bravery he was promoted to lieutenant colonel and assigned the governorship of Bengazi.[17] Turkish losses during the Libyan campaign numbered 14,000 men.[18] How close Enver came to being one of these casualties is not recorded in English, but it is not impossible to imagine a stray bullet ending his military and political career in 1911 or 1912.[19]

On 23 January 1913, Enver was the leader of a small group of military officers who burst into the Turkish cabinet chamber, forcing Grand Vezir Kamil Pasa to write out his resignation at gunpoint. Nazim Pasa, the minister of war, who confronted the coup d'etat participants at the door of the chamber, was shot and killed.[20] If Nazim Pasa had been carrying a gun, it is possible that Enver would have been killed or wounded in an exchange of gunfire, whatever effect this may have had on the outcome of the coup.

The consequences of no landing at Gallipoli: First blooding on the Western Front

What would have happened had New Zealand soldiers never landed at Gallipoli? To start this exploration, let us hypothesise from a counterfactual scenario where Winston Churchill dies before 1901, where the Ottoman Empire does join the Central Powers, where the naval strategy against Constantinople fails (or is not tried at all), and one where the British war cabinet, without Churchill's influence, chooses not to attempt any landing at Gallipoli. This counterfactual scenario is based on only one plausible, but relatively small, counterfactual event—Churchill's death—and on only one counterfactual outcome arising out of it—no attempted landing at Gallipoli.

Instead of the ANZACs fighting at Gallipoli, it seems most likely that the corps' first deployment would have been to the Western Front. Having abandoned, or having never seriously considered, the 'Gallipoli strategy', the British War Council would have judged the Western Front to be the crucial theatre for victory in the war. The timing and exact location of the deployment is difficult to judge. This would have been influenced by the perceived level of threat of a Turkish invasion of Egypt, and the availability of additional reinforcements from the colonies to 'garrison' Egypt while the better trained soldiers deployed to France.

It is possible that without Turkish troops committed to fighting on the Gallipoli Peninsula, and without the 87,000 Turkish deaths at Gallipoli,[21] that the Ottoman Empire may have chosen to invade Egypt, and that the ANZACs may not have left for France by the time of the Turkish invasion. The Turkish aim would have been to cut off the main supply line from the southern hemisphere British colonies to Great Britain and the Western Front. In this scenario, the first major battle involving ANZAC troops may have taken place in Egypt. But would such a battle have obtained the mythos of Gallipoli for Australia and New Zealand? If the ANZAC casualties had been high and if the campaign had lasted for months, rather than just a few weeks, it seems possible that an Anzac Day may have been instituted on the anniversary of the Turkish invasion. But the counterfactual scenario of the first ANZAC 'blooding' being on the Western Front seems more likely.

Another plausible delay in deployment was that the British War Council may have decided that the ANZACs were not sufficiently well trained or well equipped for the rigours of the Western Front, opting to send them to England for further training and re-equipping. At the war council of 24 February 1915, Prime Minister Asquith had asked whether the Australians and New Zealanders 'were good enough' for an important operation of war. Lord Herbert Kitchener, secretary of state for war, replied 'that they were quite good enough if a cruise in the Sea of Marmara was all that was contemplated'.[22] If not urgently needed for the invasion of Gallipoli, the ANZACs may have trained alongside Lord Kitchener's 'New Armies' of British men who volunteered in 1914. The 'New Armies' spent nearly two years training in

England before deploying to northern France in 1916, in time to participate in the First Battle of the Somme.[23]

Given the severity of fighting on the Western Front and the constant need for new units and reinforcements in this theatre, it seems probable that the ANZACs would have been involved in heavy fighting before July 1916. However, because there are accurate figures for the casualties the ANZACs experienced at the First Battle of the Somme (from 1 July 1916 to 20 November 1916), this battle is a useful tool to consider the consequences if the first ANZAC deployment had been on the Western Front. The First Battle of the Somme provides a concrete comparison to the Gallipoli campaign.

New Zealand and Australian casualty rates for the First Battle of the Somme were considerably higher than for Gallipoli. The New Zealand Division entered the battle on 15 September and fought for twenty-three days. In this period, 7000 men of the New Zealand Division became casualties, with more than 1500 killed.[24] The equivalent figures for the first thirty-seven days of the Gallipoli campaign were over 2600 New Zealand casualties, with 1073 killed. The bloodiest month for New Zealand at Gallipoli was August 1915, with over 3300 casualties, including over 1100 killed.[25]

Had the first ANZAC 'blooding' been on the Western Front, high casualty rates would have provoked the same mix of shock, grief, respect and pride that was the reaction in New Zealand and Australia to the Gallipoli campaign. It seems probable that a day of commemoration would have started on the anniversary of the first day of the battle or on the anniversary of the exact day ANZAC troops entered battle.

If the New Zealand and Australian troops' first battles had been in different areas of northern France, then New Zealand and Australia may have ended up with different dates of commemoration. The first sizeable assault in which Australian soldiers participated on the Western Front was on 5 July 1916 at Fromelles, with 5300 casualties (this one-day battle was not in the Somme area).[26] As noted, the New Zealand Division's first major assault started on 15 September 1916 at the Somme.

Whether or not this counterfactual Anzac Day, or a separate 'New Zealand Division Day', would have taken precedence after 1919 over 11 November—Remembrance Day, the anniversary of the armistice ending the war—is a more difficult matter to decide. Would the fact that New Zealand participation in the campaign on the Western Front lasted two or three years after New Zealand's first experience of serious casualties have given 11 November more significance than this counterfactual Anzac Day or 'New Zealand Division Day'?

It can be argued that Australians and New Zealanders in the 1920s chose to celebrate and commemorate 25 April 1915, rather than simply remember and commemorate on 11 November, in part because the Gallipoli campaign was viewed more favourably by the population than the much longer campaign on the Western Front. In the popular understanding, Gallipoli was a 'coming-of-age' for the Australian and New Zealand nations. The actions of the Australian and New Zealand soldiers at Gallipoli were reported as heroic, and considered by much of the population to be worthwhile, even if not ultimately successful. In contrast, the events on the Western Front were considered to be a slaughterhouse, especially as the conflict dragged on into its third and fourth years, and the wounded who would never be able to fight again slowly made their way back to Australia and New Zealand.[27] By the time arrangements were being made for the first Anzac Day on 25 April 1916, the Gallipoli campaign was over. Would Australians and New Zealanders have continued to support Anzac Day over Remembrance Day if the Gallipoli campaign had dragged on, with ever growing casualty lists, for two or three years?

It is problematic whether an enduring ANZAC legend or mythos would have developed from a first ANZAC deployment on the Western Front. Would the 'slaughterhouse' image have prevailed in the popular imagination concerning the entire campaign on the Western Front, preventing an enduring 'Battle of the Somme' ANZAC legend (for example) from emerging? There can be no definitive answer to this question, not even a counterfactual answer. The need of Australians and New Zealanders to find something positive and meaningful in the events on the Western

Front (and in the war as a whole) may have allowed a 'Battle of the Somme' ANZAC legend to rise above the 'slaughterhouse' image. In such a scenario, the 'Battle of the Somme' Anzac Day would have most likely taken precedence over Remembrance Day. For such a Western Front ANZAC legend to have survived, the legend may have had to have been sustained by its proponents over two or three years of intense and bloody battles. Such an outcome would have been a remarkable achievement by those who wanted the ANZACs fighting on the Western Front to be remembered heroically, and their experiences, wounds and deaths to have significance.

If the Ottoman Empire had never entered the war
or had surrendered in early 1915

A similar series of counterfactual consequences would most likely have followed if the Ottoman Empire had surrendered in early 1915, or had never entered the war at all. In either scenario the ANZACs' first deployment would almost certainly have been to the Western Front. If the Ottoman Empire had never entered the war the ANZACs would have reached France in late 1914, entering the front lines sometime in the first half of 1915. If the Ottoman Empire had surrendered in early 1915 after a successful British and French naval assault on Constantinople, the deployment date of the ANZACs to France would have presumably been before July 1916, and probably sometime in 1915. An immediate deployment in early 1915 seems unlikely, as some ANZAC troops would have been required for occupation duty in areas of the former Ottoman Empire close to Egypt, at least until less well trained 'garrison' troops arrived from Australia, New Zealand or India, to relieve the more battle-ready ANZACs.[28] Even if large areas of the Ottoman Empire had been placed under the control of Russia, as the Turkish leaders feared in 1915, it would have taken months for sufficient numbers of Russian troops to reach the areas closest to Egypt.[29] It also seems likely that the British would have wanted a buffer zone between the Suez Canal and the expanded borders of Russia. For example, at the war council of 10 March 1915 British

Prime Minister Lloyd George wanted Britain to acquire Palestine. Kitchener countered that Palestine 'would be of no value to us whatsoever' and urged the annexation of Alexandretta (on the Mediterranean coast in south-eastern Turkey). Churchill suggested that Palestine could be given to Belgium.[30]

It is also possible, although probably not likely, that with the defeat of the Ottoman Empire, or with Turkey never entering the war, an Allied attack at the 'weak southern flank' of the Central Powers, through the Balkans, would have brought the First World War to a much earlier end. If the defeat of, or negotiated peace with, the Central Powers had happened before July 1916, it is possible that neither Australian nor New Zealand soldiers would have experienced serious casualties at any time during a shortened First World War. In such a scenario, it may have only been in 1942 that the first Anzac Day would be commemorated: a year after the start of Australian and New Zealand involvement in the costly campaigns in Greece and Crete in 1941. Or perhaps a shortened First World War would have prevented the sequence of social developments and events which led to the outbreak of the Second World War, and the Cold War, and there would never have been an Anzac Day of remembrance at all.

Another counterfactual scenario

Australian soldiers fight at Gallipoli but New Zealand soldiers are not involved

It seems unlikely that a counterfactual scenario where Australian soldiers fought at Gallipoli, but New Zealand soldiers did not, could have plausibly occurred, and any sequence of events which would lead to such a situation would probably be pure 'historical fiction'. However, the consequences of such a counterfactual situation are worthy of discussion, because of the intriguing questions these counterfactual consequences raise about Anzac Day, Remembrance Day, and the New Zealand-Australia relationship.

In such a scenario, it seems almost certain that Australia would have instituted its own commemoration day on 25 April, perhaps called 'Gallipoli Day'. This day would have had sufficient meaning to Australians that it would have overshadowed 11 November, Remembrance Day. New Zealand's day of commemoration would not have been 25 April. The special link between New Zealanders and Australia would not have been forged at Gallipoli, and so no such link would permeate the New Zealand–Australia relationship. A link may have been forged subsequently through joint participation in the campaigns in Greece and Crete in 1941, but without Anzac Day it seems unlikely that the bond would have been as strong or as enduring as the one that developed out of the shared (and tragic) experience of Gallipoli.

7

What if New Zealand had not gone to war in 1939?

Denis McLean

When Britain declared war on Nazi Germany on 3 September 1939, New Zealand immediately followed suit. Prime Minister Michael Joseph Savage spoke for virtually the entire nation when he famously declared, 'Where Britain goes, we go. Where Britain stands, we stand.' Relations with Britain dominated New Zealand's political, economic and institutional life and with that went an unquestioned assumption that the global strategic reach of the Royal Navy would be there to guarantee the ultimate security of an isolated imperial acolyte. The volunteers who flocked to the recruiting stations would have seen themselves as signing on in not only a just cause, but a war thoroughly relevant to New Zealand interests. A small country mobilised comprehensively for a war on the other side of the world under overall British strategic direction and command.[1]

In 1941–42 when the Japanese overran South East Asia and captured Singapore, the British were shown to be incapable of providing security for New Zealand. Where Australia immediately looked to the United States for assistance and withdrew its land forces from the Middle East, New Zealand was more reticent. Australia was attacked many times by the Japanese during 1942; territorial New Zealand by contrast was effectively untouched and when United States forces began arriving in great numbers in the country, the sense of threat receded. Although a second division and major air force and naval units were raised for service in the Solomon Islands and further north, New Zealand's war effort continued for the most part to be focused on Europe. Indeed, the decision in 1943 to retain the New Zealand division in the Middle East caused great annoyance in Australia, which expected that New Zealand would share the new priority it attached to the security challenges in Asia and the Pacific. New Zealand and Australia patched up their differences in 1944 and together proclaimed the Canberra or ANZAC Pact, a statement of common regional interests. Their great power allies, Britain and the United States, were not amused by what they saw as presumption on the part of their smaller partners. Neither Australia nor New Zealand were allocated any decisive military role in the final stages of the war against Japan.

122

Although both countries would eagerly signed on to the ANZUS Pact with the United States in 1951, a divergence between the British and Commonwealth connection on the one hand and regional interests in Asia and the Pacific would persist for many years. A full meeting of minds with Australia on shared strategic and security concerns has proved elusive.[2]

New Zealand breaks with its past: From imperial acolyte to regional power

On 5 September 1939 the prime minister appeared from inside parliament buildings and stood at the top of the long granite steps to make an announcement to be broadcast live to a waiting nation. The day before, the people had heard over their large, boxy wireless sets the clipped tones of the British prime minister, Neville Chamberlain. Germany, he declared, had defied a British–French ultimatum and proceeded to invade Poland, and therefore a state of war existed between His Majesty's Government in the United Kingdom and Nazi Germany.

Australia had immediately taken the position that when the king declared war, all his governments throughout the empire were likewise at war. New Zealand, however, with an independent-minded Labour government in power, was determined to make up its own mind on so grave a matter. This was a matter for parliament to decide. The prime minister, who had been in hospital the previous day, roused himself to make the pronouncement which stunned the nation and sent a shock wave around the world.

> With gratitude for the past and confidence in the future, we declare that we no longer range ourselves alongside Britain. Where she goes, we cannot blindly go; where she stands, we do not find cause to stand.
> This war is not our war.
> We are a small, proudly independent nation of the South Pacific. We are a peace-loving people with a history of strong commitment

to multilateral action through the League of Nations. We do not believe in the resolution of international disputes by one country unilaterally taking up arms against another. We believe it is for the League of Nations to mediate between the contending parties and to take collective action.

We live in a benign strategic area. Nevertheless, affinities between the totalitarian powers of Germany and Italy could yet extend to the Pacific to create an axis of evil. A militaristic Japan is already waging war in China. Other peoples' wars in Europe must not distract us from the responsibility to help secure the peace in our own region in the South Pacific.

New Zealand will help the Mother Country in every way it can— through the provision of food aid and humanitarian assistance. Any military role, however, will be limited to the deployment of peacekeeping forces to help bring the warring parties together, and to engineering units to help repair the damage.

New Zealand had broken with its past. One hundred years of staunch identification with Britain and things British had been brusquely discarded. A 'Great Exhibition' had been due to open in a few months time in Wellington to celebrate the centennial of the proclamation of British sovereignty. Now a Labour government, which believed it had an overwhelming mandate for change following two sweeping election victories, was determined to set those British inheritances behind in pursuit of an independent South Pacific nationhood. To this end the old alliance structure of empire had to be renounced. With that came a conviction that the prevailing power system in the world must be challenged. In particular, it was vital that the new weapons of mass destruction, which had been used in aerial bombardment against innocent civilians in Spain, be repudiated by New Zealand.

The New Zealand Aerial Bomb Free Zone and Disarmament Act of 1938 banned the entry into New Zealand ports of any warship carrying such or similar bombs and had been widely supported in the community. Seemingly only a few 'geriatric generals' had been critical. It was in the character of New Zealand, the government believed, to take the lead on such matters—to show the world that concrete steps could be taken, even by a small country, to roll back the menace posed by such weaponry. The major powers had been displeased. They had long operated their navies according to the historic principle of 'neither confirming nor denying' that their ships were carrying weapons of this kind. In a deteriorating international situation they had no wish to give their adversaries an advantage by signalling the presence or absence of bombs on their ships in order to enter New Zealand ports. Nor had they any wish to have the movements of their ships constrained by restrictions of this kind in other countries which might follow suit. Equally they were not about to put the commanders of their ships in the position of being arraigned for interrogation by the New Zealand authorities in terms of the act. The security guarantees to New Zealand implicit in imperial defence arrangements were accordingly withdrawn.

During the previous decade a small isolated nation had suffered severely from the global economic depression. There had been much agitation about the need to protect the country against such pressures in the future by establishing high tariff barriers against imports and building national economic self-reliance. In particular there was resentment at the failure of the City of London to provide loan facilities and capital to help New Zealand weather the economic storm. A gathering isolationism had been matched by a prevailing antimilitarism. The damage and losses inflicted on a small country in the previous world war still caused bitterness. It was widely believed that the blame lay with the incompetence of British commanders, who had not bothered to go forward to see for themselves the conditions in which they had ordered men to fight. The defence vote was whittled down until the armed forces consisted of a handful of about 500 permanent staff and an ill-equipped and grossly under-manned territorial force. Dislike of all things military was so prevalent that members of the armed forces were reluctant to wear their uniforms in the street out of concern for the public abuse they received. In the government itself there were ministers who had been jailed in the previous war for their opposition to conscription; the prime minister himself had at one stage in his career embraced pacifism.

The roots of the decision not to follow Britain into war

accordingly seemed to run deep in the community at large. Nevertheless an astonished nation divided immediately into bitter pro- and antiwar factions. The newly opened British High Commission was besieged with young New Zealanders determined to serve with the British armed forces. There was widespread alarm that New Zealand had let the 'Mother Country' down in her hour of peril. Even within the Labour Party itself, antagonism between the World War I veteran John A. Lee, who had expected to be appointed minister of defence, and the ailing prime minister, Michael Joseph Savage, developed into divisions which threatened the government's majority in the House of Representatives.

Despite wartime shortages of shipping the British government, recognising a crucial source of recruits for its forces, sent transports to New Zealand to carry off the many thousands of volunteers who felt it their duty to serve the empire. There were scenes of great tribulation and distress as these great ships carried off these young men and women, whom many believed represented the flower of the nation's youth, to a war in which New Zealand itself had declared it had no stake. The loss of manpower soon caused economic disruption which threatened to reverse the progress that had been made to escape from the 'great depression'.

On the international front, New Zealand, for so long accustomed to being the favourite son of empire, immediately lost all influence and standing in London. The high commissioner was treated as a pariah and was expressly denied access to the new British prime minister, Winston Churchill. After the fall of France in May 1940, Britain was steeling itself for a life or death struggle as threat of invasion became real. There was neither the time nor the inclination to take any notice of New Zealand's special pleading that it supported the war against fascism in principle but could not do so in practice because of its opposition to the use of military means to solve international disputes. Links were quickly developed with the Republic of Eire, which had also declared its neutrality. But there was little profit there for New Zealand since the Irish were dependent on exactly the same range of agricultural exports as was New Zealand. Australia, of course, stuck by its imperial commitments to Britain and geared up for war. The famous ANZAC bond with New Zealand was not worth much in Canberra. The traditional disdain of Australians for New Zealand was reinforced. Sheep jokes turned nasty as New Zealand's unwillingness to fight for the empire became synonymous with sheeplike behaviour. In December 1939 New Zealand representatives at the League of Nations participated enthusiastically in the decision to expel the Soviet Union from the organisation for its attack on Finland. But this futile gesture was the last act of the League of Nations. The first attempt to establish a world organisation, Woodrow Wilson's dream, foundered under the pressure of global events far beyond the capacity of a multilateral institution to control.

For two years through the successive crises—as Nazi hegemony spread across much of Europe; the Battle of Britain; defeats of British forces in Greece and Crete; the invasion of Russia—New Zealand maintained its position of lonely abstention from the war on the other side of the world. The growing crisis in Asia, however, could not be ignored. As Japanese forces established themselves in the French colonies in Indo-China it became clear that the British base at Singapore, which underpinned the entire British position in the Asia-Pacific region, was at risk. New Zealand had long since taken it for granted that the Royal Navy operating from Singapore would uphold New Zealand's own security—even if by proxy. New Zealand opened talks with Australia and the United States, offering to contribute armed forces in the event of open war in the Pacific. The offer was not rebuffed although serious doubts were expressed about New Zealand's military capabilities. Defence expenditure was steeply increased; military training was begun in earnest.

In December 1941, following the Japanese attack on Pearl Harbor, New Zealand declared war on Japan. As Japanese forces pressed south into New Guinea and the Solomon Islands the threat of direct aggression against New Zealand became very real. Geographic isolation meant nothing in a world war. Serious and strenuous military interaction with Australia led to the formation of combined ANZAC air, sea and ground forces, with integrated command systems working within a unified Pacific war command under the overall direction of the United States. The war in the Pacific was fully shared between the two ANZAC countries. New Zealanders played an equal part in severe fighting in New Guinea as well as in the Solomon Islands. Their reputation was such that the New Zealand division was nominated as part of the massive force preparing for the invasion of Japan in 1945. There was widespread concern about the likely scale of casualties (expected to be massive) from engagement in this operation. Accordingly New Zealanders across the country warmly welcomed the decision to drop two atomic bombs on Japan, thus bringing hostilities in the Pacific to a swift conclusion.

New Zealand emerged from the war with greatly strengthened ties with both Australia and the United States. Australia had overcome its disdain for New Zealand and had begun to see the advantages of securing a close partnership with its stroppy and unpredictable Tasman neighbour. The ANZAC Pact of 1944 became an enduring touchstone for across-the-board collaboration between the two Tasman partners. In future Wellington and Canberra would not deviate from the overriding policy consideration that all decision making must aim to add value to their mutual interests. 'Australasia Inc' was born. Both countries had no hesitation in clambering on board as Washington asserted leadership in the ensuing Cold War against communism. Recollecting that use of the atomic bomb had certainly saved thousands of New Zealand lives in 1945, New Zealand had no qualms about the place of nuclear weapons in the armoury of its great power ally. New Zealanders would henceforth accept the reality of nuclear weaponry and nuclear power. The Second World War cleared away misconceptions about New Zealand's place in the world. New Zealand became a Pacific power alongside, and working closely with, its natural ally and partner, Australia.

Things did not go so well for New Zealand in its dealings with postwar Europe. An impoverished Britain had need of New Zealand agricultural products for a time. Although New Zealand's reputation had slumped, trade with Britain kept up for lack of alternative sources of supply for the British market. Nevertheless Britain was quick to learn the lesson that dependency on external trade in food had made it highly vulnerable to blockade in time of war. Accordingly, agricultural production was stepped up. The National Farmers Union became a force in British politics and New Zealand butter and meat supplies were targeted as inimical to British interests. By the late 1960s, when Britain was campaigning strenuously to join the European Economic Community, New Zealand's vital trading interests in the British market had been seriously compromised. New Zealand had little or no leverage. Memories of the recent war were too strong to give British negotiators any cause to seek special exemptions for New Zealand in their dealings with Europe. New Zealand had few friends. Having been absent when Britain was in crisis, New Zealand was not able to influence Britain to lend support to offset its own developing economic predicament. Glue for the emerging common market was to a large extent provided by agricultural subsidies which pushed food prices up and generated huge surpluses for disposal on the international market. Europe was interested solely in Europe. Those who had fought for Europe—such as Australia— were in a position to plead successfully for concessions. For the rest, including New Zealand, there were to be no favours. The Common Agricultural Policy would simply exclude New Zealand agricultural products from the European market as from the date of British accession to the Brussels Treaty in 1973.

The outcome was devastating for a New Zealand economy still hugely dependent on trade in agricultural products. There were no immediately available alternative outlets. Meat and dairy products had simply to be disposed of at rock-bottom prices or even dumped. At a time of growing world prosperity New Zealand was plunged into depression. The economic and social dislocations were profound. There was massive unrest in the country, accompanied by a sense of bitterness towards those who had ignored reality and tried to isolate New Zealand in the South Pacific rather than recognise that the country had global interests and global responsibilities.

Where was New Zealand to turn? Merger with Australia seemed the only feasible option. And there was widespread support for it, given that the two Tasman countries had proved able to be such constructive regional partners. But how that developed—the story of a prickly pair of neighbours coming to terms with a common destiny—is a tale so well known as hardly to require retelling at the close of this narrative.

8

What if Japan had invaded New Zealand?

Ian McGibbon

New Zealand and Japan were at war from 8 December 1941 to 15 August 1945.[1] During that period the only Japanese forces to venture into New Zealand waters were submarines. One passed through Cook Strait and up the east coast of the North Island, sending a floatplane to reconnoitre both Wellington and Auckland harbours, in March 1942, and there are indications that others may have also operated in New Zealand waters, without doing any damage to New Zealand shipping. German naval vessels in fact made their presence felt in New Zealand waters to a much greater extent than Japanese forces.

The extent of Japanese successes in the first three months of the Pacific war aroused fears in New Zealand that invasion was imminent, especially when Japanese forces captured the Singapore naval base, long regarded as the key to New Zealand's defence, and appeared in the Solomon Islands. But in fact Japan never developed plans to invade New Zealand or Australia. Faced with a shortage of resources while engaged in China, it determined instead to cut off these nations from the United States by capturing New Guinea and the island groups to the north of New Zealand. But a Japanese force heading for Port Moresby in early May 1942 was intercepted by American forces in the Coral Sea and was forced to turn back. A month later at the Battle of Midway, the US navy wrenched the strategic initiative from the Japanese by destroying the core of their naval power, the four aircraft carriers deployed there by the combined fleet and the cream of Japan's naval aviators. From this point the possibility of Japan invading New Zealand became very small indeed.

After the Midway victory New Zealand rapidly became a forward base for American forces operating in the Solomon Islands, where they landed, on Guadalcanal, on 7 August 1942. During the next two years New Zealand experienced a friendly invasion by American troops, some 100,000 of whom would be stationed in the country, in addition to many more naval and air personnel who transited through. Some Japanese also arrived—about 800 prisoners of war from the Solomons, who would be held in a camp near Featherston. When they made a suicidal charge against their guards in February 1943, forty-eight of them were killed *or mortally wounded, along with one New Zealand soldier, the only fatal casualty suffered by New Zealand on its own soil as a result of enemy action during the war. Other New Zealanders died in battle with Japanese forces in the Solomons, where New Zealand deployed elements of all three armed services, and in the final drive on the Japanese homeland in 1945. A handful of New Zealand scientists took part in the Manhattan Project, which produced the atomic bombs that were dropped on Hiroshima and Nagasaki in early August 1945. Together with the Soviet invasion of Manchuria, these blows induced the Japanese to capitulate. New Zealand would later provide an infantry brigade and an air force squadron for the forces that occupied Japan after the surrender.*

Rising Sun in the Land of the Long White Cloud: Japan's invasion of New Zealand 1943–1946

New Zealand went to war in September 1939 with traditional influences to the fore. It would make its contribution to the British effort against Germany by replicating its First World War despatch of an expeditionary force to fight on European battlefields. The 2nd New Zealand Expeditionary Force (2NZEF) left New Zealand in three echelons in 1940 and was eventually concentrated in Egypt. This deployment was made in spite of nagging doubts about the country's security in the Pacific, but the risk seemed bearable. The militaristic Japanese government was deeply embroiled in its undeclared war with China and it had, after all, stood aside from its German ally when war began in Europe with the German invasion of Poland. New Zealand troops took part in the ill-fated expedition to Greece, twice being evacuated by the Royal Navy. After recuperating in Egypt, they went into action against Rommel's forces in North Africa in November 1941.

Even as New Zealander fought German in the Libyan desert a dark cloud had formed over the Pacific. On 8 December 1941 (New Zealand time) New Zealand's worst fears were realised. Japan entered the war, launching a devastating assault on both British and American forces. With their most effective military formation on the other side of the world, New Zealanders watched in horror as Japanese forces advanced into the South Pacific, seizing bases in the Solomon Islands. Fears were soon allayed, however, by signs of an American naval revival, especially when a Japanese invasion force heading for Port Moresby was turned back in the Coral Sea in early May 1942—the first naval battle in which fleets fought each other with aircraft rather than the big gun. A month later, from 4 to 6 June, a major clash between the two fleets near the US-held island of Midway resulted in a heavy defeat for the Japanese, one from which they never recovered.

But what if the crucial battle at Midway had gone the other way? The US navy's victory owed much to American foreknowledge of Japan's plans, thanks to the efforts of American codebreakers. This allowed the US Pacific commander-in-chief, Admiral Chester Nimitz, to ambush the oncoming Japanese, who were unaware of the presence of a dangerous enemy as they approached Midway. But the outcome of the battle also turned on mistakes made by the Japanese commander, who had his air striking force on his carriers being prepared for a strike against Nimitz's force when American torpedo and dive bombers appeared overhead. Although the torpedo bombers were countered, the dive bombers inflicted fatal damage on three of the four Japanese carriers within the space of five minutes (the other was later destroyed as well). Let us assume that the Japanese deduced that their signals traffic was being read, perhaps as a result of careful examination of New Zealand intelligence material seized by a German raider from the *Nankin* and passed to Tokyo.[2] Realising that Nimitz would be preparing to engage them at Midway, they planned to ambush the ambusher.[3] When a Japanese reconnaissance plane spotted one of the two American task forces before slipping away into the clouds, Vice-Admiral Chuichi Nagumo immediately launched his striking force. Appearing over the American task force, Japanese dive bombers set their sights on the two US carriers. Within minutes both were blazing furiously after a series of hits. In the other task force the now solitary US carrier launched a strike on the Japanese carriers, heavily damaging one of them—sunk later by an American submarine as it headed away to the north-west. But Nagumo was now poised for the kill. His remaining aircraft found the surviving US carrier and inflicted fatal blows on it as well. With the US carrier force destroyed, there was nothing to prevent the Japanese fleet attacking Midway Island. Bombing raids quickly reduced the defences, and naval gunfire added to the destruction, including shells from the eighteen-inch guns of the giant battleship *Yamato*, on which the commander-in-chief of the combined fleet, Admiral Isoroku Yamamoto, flew his flag. To save themselves, the remnants of the US fleet had no choice but to hastily retreat towards Hawaii.

The scale of the Japanese victory appalled New Zealanders. Not only had the British fleet been disposed of in the region; the main elements of the US fleet that had survived the Pearl Harbor attack had also now succumbed. The strategic implications were starkly apparent: the Pacific would be a Japanese lake for at least two years, probably longer. A reversal of the situation would depend on the naval building programme that they knew the Americans would set in motion. But ships cannot be produced overnight. In Wellington the service chiefs immediately revised their forecast of the likely time and scale of attack on New Zealand. Before the Midway debacle, they had maintained that the danger of invasion was not immediate, because of the threat to Japanese actions posed by American seapower and Japan's other priorities—and postwar examination of Japanese records would reveal the essential validity of their advice at this time.

Discussion in Tokyo in early 1942 on Japan's appropriate course of action in light of the huge success of its initial onslaught had prompted heated controversy between army and navy representatives. The former, conscious of the size of Japan's commitment in China, pleaded a lack of divisions when some in the navy called for an immediate invasion of Australia. In the end, a compromise emerged: Japan would cut off Australia and New Zealand from the United States while preparing for a showdown with the US fleet to decide the issue of sea command in the Pacific. The first step in this plan had been the capture of

Port Moresby; the seizure of the Fijian and Samoan groups would follow.[4] Although the reverse in the Coral Sea in May 1942 stopped Japan in its tracks, the second part of the compromise plan had succeeded beyond Japanese expectations at Midway. With Japan now enjoying complete freedom of action in the Pacific, the New Zealand chiefs of staff warned that invasion might come within weeks, and on a scale far above that previously predicted. At the same time, they predicted that such an attack was unlikely until after Fiji had been taken. The vital importance of this island group to New Zealand's security was reflected in the more than 8000 of its troops that were already manning its defences (the first having gone there in 1940).

New Zealand did not in fact face an immediate threat of invasion. The Japanese victory at Midway had opened up glittering strategic possibilities. In particular Yamamoto perceived the advantage of moving Japan's intended defensive perimeter eastward to encompass the Hawaiian islands. With this group under Japanese control, Japan's hold on the Pacific would be more secure, and an American comeback that much more difficult. New Zealanders witnessed a Japanese island-hopping campaign towards Hawaii, starting with Midway and Palmyra Island and ending with a landing on Hawaii Island. A major base at Hilo provided the springboard for the assault on Oahu, which had in the meantime been heavily attacked by carrier-borne aircraft. The invasion of Oahu was a bloody affair, but highly motivated and determined Japanese infantry eventually prevailed. Once Oahu was in Japanese hands, Japanese engineers immediately began restoring the facilities at Pearl Harbor. To further cement Japan's hold on the Pacific Yamamoto looked to knock the Panama Canal out of commission. A raiding force succeeded in damaging two of the locks. The loss of the use of this waterway greatly complicated the American response to the Pacific war situation.

Even as these operations proceeded Japanese strategists returned to the vexing question of what to do next in a situation now vastly different to that existing in early 1942. The one area remaining in the western Pacific from which an American comeback could be made was that encompassing Australia, New Zealand and the islands groups to their north. By neutralising these areas Japan would remove a potential base area for an American counter-offensive, using South African and other African ports. The discussions followed a similar pattern to those in early 1942, with the navy and army at loggerheads. Still deeply engaged in China, the latter continued to insist that there were insufficient divisions to spare for the invasion of such a large country as Australia. Another army–navy compromise emerged. Japan would invade New Zealand and take such of its territory as would allow the establishment of a major base there. This would provide a means of dominating the populated south-eastern part of Australia, whose naval and air forces were far too weak to resist raids and incursions. As a first step, the plans foiled at the Battle of the Coral Sea would be carried out.

Japan's initial target was Fiji. With complete command of the seas in the Pacific, it was able to despatch a powerful task force to the area without the possibility of a Coral Sea-like intervention by the US navy. The New Zealand and American forces on the island put up some resistance, but the overwhelming airpower and naval gunfire advantage enjoyed by the Japanese quickly turned the tide in their favour. Most of the Allied troops on the island surrendered after a week's fighting. Japanese units based on Fiji then moved into the Tasman in strength, quickly making all sea movement very dangerous.

These events had immense consequences for New Zealand politically, economically and strategically. Post-Midway was a period of recrimination and controversy over the nature of New Zealand's war effort, which had left New Zealand denuded of its best trained troops in a time of crisis. When Japan had entered the war, the United Kingdom (UK) had asked Australia if it could redeploy two of the three Australian divisions in the Middle East to the Far East.[5] As these formations were en route, the situation deteriorated to such an extent that Australia insisted on them being landed in Australia (rather than Burma, as proposed by the British prime minister, Winston Churchill). These divisions now formed the basis of Australian home defence, along with a US division that had arrived there in mid-1942. By the time this redeployment was completed, and it became possible to bring home 2NZEF, the situation was such that any movement of troops across the Indian Ocean had become too dangerous to contemplate. The division was in effect trapped in North Africa, because a redeployment through the Mediterranean (and thence round the Cape of Good Hope to New Zealand) was equally ruled out by the threat posed by German and Italian airpower.

Many in New Zealand recognised the impracticability of redeploying the division, and were relieved by the arrival, shortly after the Japanese victory at Midway, of a US Marine division, while other American troops had bolstered the garrison in Fiji. Nonetheless, Prime Minister Peter Fraser came under increasing attack for the predicament New Zealand now found itself in, threatened at home with its best trained men on the other side of the world. This pressure resulted in a successful vote of no confidence in the government. The existing war administration collapsed amidst vociferous demands for the formation of a coalition government. With Walter Nash in Washington, Robert Semple came to the fore, his position improved by his reputation for innovation—exemplified by the improvised tank that now bore his name, which had boosted morale among the public while not adding one iota to New Zealand's defence capacity. John A. Lee, who had previously advocated a home defence strategy, gained in influence, the crisis overshadowing his differences with the Labour Party that had led to his expulsion in 1940. Semple emerged as the prime minister in a coalition ministry that included Lee as well as members of the National Party.

The government faced a major crisis long before any Japanese troops set foot in New Zealand. The New Zealand economy was almost exclusively devoted to supplying the UK with foodstuffs. The loss at Midway initially led to a redirection of New Zealand trade. With the Panama route ruled out, New Zealand merchant ships made their way across the southern Pacific to Cape Horn or used the safer route westward to the Cape of Good Hope. While this traffic continued for months after the Midway defeat, it ceased once Japanese naval forces moved into the Tasman in strength. The capture of Fiji put New Zealand under siege in a way never experienced before. With the cutting off of New Zealand's overseas trade, drastic regulation of the economy became necessary. Food supplies were more plentiful (leading to a relaxation of some rationing introduced earlier in the year), but distribution within the country presented major problems. With all available petrol now reserved for military purposes (and no prospect of getting any more), horses and carts became ubiquitous on New Zealand roads. Feeding the populations of the main cities became much more difficult. All farm produce was now commandeered by the state. The government tried desperately to overcome problems introduced by the drying up of the flow of money into the country.

Militarily New Zealand's position in late 1942 was bleak. Within the country there were three weak divisions, whose ranks were filled by men who had been called up early in January and kept in uniform despite the major problems this caused on farms in the spring. The only bright spot was the US Marine division, which was well trained and keen to get to grips with the Japanese. The number of troops available to defend such a large country was inadequate. Some support was provided by men of the Home Guard, many with combat experience in the First World War; but the state of their equipment and training meant that little reliance could be placed on them against an enemy able to deploy an array of modern weapons, including tanks. Heavy guns guarded the ports, but delays in providing planned 9.2-inch guns left Wellington vulnerable to a well-armed enemy.

More worrying than the state of the military forces, however, was the equipment situation. New Zealand tried during 1942 to secure some modern aircraft for home defence—to no avail. Taking a realistic view of the prospects of defending New Zealand against full-scale attack, the joint chiefs of staff in Washington decided that available resources should be devoted to higher priority areas. Moreover, following the loss of Hawaii, American opinion had demanded a major strengthening of defences on the western mainland coast of the US, soaking up available materiel. New Zealand faced a powerful enemy with no more than a squadron of Hudson bombers and an assortment of converted training aircraft, including Tiger Moths. Having seen at Singapore in December 1941 the impossibility of successfully meeting the Japanese Zero with antiquated aircraft, their pilots were resigned to their early demise. If the equipment problem was disastrous, it was matched by the logistic problems confronting New Zealand. There were substantial reserves of artillery ammunition in the country— about 1700 rounds per field gun and 1000 per medium gun[6]—but modern weapons have an insatiable appetite for ammunition. New Zealand had no means of manufacturing artillery shells. Nor could it rely on Australia, which was stretched to capacity meeting its own needs. Once the Tasman was effectively closed to sea traffic, New Zealand had to rely on what it already had in its ammo dumps.

All these problems were exposed when the Japanese landed in New Zealand early in 1943. The main concentrations of New Zealand forces were in the northern part of the North Island, on the assumption that the Japanese would attack the nearest point to Fiji. But Japan's primary objective was to secure a base to blockade the coast of Australia, and Wellington fitted the bill perfectly. Not only was it the site of a magnificent harbour; it was also well placed to dominate the two main New Zealand islands.

Wellingtonians received their first indication that their city was a target when Japanese shells began falling on the coast defences at Makara and the Miramar peninsula. Standing off to the west, out of range of the Wellington six-inch guns, a powerful Japanese fleet brought its firepower to bear, using small spotter planes to indicate fall of shot. This shelling continued all day, steadily reducing the positions. Periodically the guns would fall silent as Japanese carrier-borne dive bomber squadrons arrived and added to the destruction. An attempt by New Zealand's Hudson bombers to get through to the Japanese fleet proved disastrous; all but two were shot down by Zeros long before they reached the ships. Only one managed to unload its bombs, but scored no more than a near miss on a cruiser. By nightfall New Zealand's air force offensive strength had gone, and all the six-inch guns at Wellington had been destroyed, several by direct hits by eighteen-inch shells. Rather than sacrifice them in a quixotic attack on the far superior

Japanese fleet, the authorities had ordered New Zealand's two cruisers, *Achilles* and *Leander*, to make off to the east; by heading far to the south they would eventually find refuge in Melbourne harbour, where *Leander* would later be sunk in a Japanese raid.

During the day, reports had begun coming in that before dawn Japanese forces had landed north and south of Napier. The battle did not last long, despite the courageous efforts of several small units in the vicinity and the sacrifice of some home guardsmen who were more valiant than sensible as they tried to counter-attack the much better armed enemy. Pillboxes on the Napier foreshore disappeared under a deluge of fire, and the Japanese pincers faced little opposition as they rapidly moved inland and linked up west of the city. Accompanying these forces, a small unit had sped into the bay and seized positions just west of the port, from where they disrupted attempts to destroy the facilities. All that could be done by the defenders was to sink a coastal lighter against one of the wharfs. By nightfall Japanese units had advanced into the city and occupied the port.

Within days the Japanese began landing large quantities of supplies and more men. An armoured regiment bolstered their strength. A powerful Japanese column pressed south against limited opposition. Most New Zealand units retreated to the south; those that stood were overwhelmed. By the time Japanese soldiers marched through the main street of Dannevirke, they were facing only minimal resistance. Racing through the Wairarapa, they eventually reached Lake Ferry. Behind them came Japanese engineer units, who were soon rapidly restoring the railway line and building airfields in the Masterton area.

Even as the Japanese occupied the east coast, other Japanese units were landing in the Foxton area. Although they were able to get ashore without difficulty, they came under increasing pressure as they encountered one of the US Marine division's regiments (the other two were deployed in the Auckland area). The Americans counter-attacked with reckless bravery, but Japanese airpower soon began to make its impact felt. As the marines, and New Zealand units supporting them, fell back towards Wellington, Japanese units occupied Palmerston North and quickly made contact with their compatriots on the other side of the range. Engineers began repairing the road through the Manawatu gorge.

It remained for the Japanese to complete the capture of Wellington. This they did by steaming into the harbour in force at dawn on 28 March 1943, after minesweepers had undertaken the perilous task of ensuring that the main channel was free of mines. While the Japanese carriers and battleships lay off to the south, a powerful squadron of cruisers and destroyers took up station opposite the largely undamaged city centre. Although there had been plans for the government to vacate the capital, these had been left too late. Japanese forces blocked the land route to the north, and an attempt to get ministers out by air had failed when the flying boat sent for them from the South Island was intercepted by Japanese fighters and downed before it reached the city.

Some of the capital's defenders fired on the cruisers with rifles and machine guns, without visible effect. When a group of gunners tried to bring a field gun into action on Pipitea Point, a well-placed salvo from two of the cruisers obliterated them. A curious quiet then descended on the harbour as one of the cruisers crept up to Queen's Wharf. Soon afterwards Japanese marines began landing. Moving quickly along Jervois and Lambton Quays, they surrounded parliament buildings. From the time the Japanese warships had appeared in the harbour, black smoke could be seen billowing from the courtyard of the Defence HQ building, indicating that classified files were being hastily burnt—a necessary action that would complicate historians' later efforts to piece together New Zealand's response to the Japanese invasion.

With most of the New Zealand/American forces in the area holding the lines in the Rimutuka and Pukerua Bay areas, there were few forces in the city itself. By noon Japanese marines held all the key points in the downtown city; during the afternoon they captured ten of the fourteen members of the cabinet. The rest had taken to the hills, where two more were later captured. But two, Adam Hamilton and Dan Sullivan, would eventually manage to evade the Japanese altogether. With thirty-nine other members of parliament who had remained out of Japanese hands, they would form the basis of an interim government established in Auckland with a certain amount of constitutional licence and considerable difficulty (because eighteen of the MPs were cut off in the South Island). Hamilton became interim prime minister. The captured ministers spent the rest of the war in captivity on Somes Island.[7]

With the capture of Wellington, the Japanese commander, General Hyakutake Haruyoshi, had achieved his primary objective. He had his base, from which to operate against Australia, and it was secured by possession of the hinterland.[8] There was little incentive to occupy the rest of the country, for New Zealand contained few resources of immediate use to the Japanese war effort. The New Zealand and American forces still undefeated in the northern part of the North Island and in the South Island offered little threat to the Japanese position, given their lack of air support and supplies. Japanese forces therefore stood firm on a line running roughly from New Plymouth–Turangi–Wairoa, while Japanese air forces ranged over the Auckland area, destroying power stations and other facilities. To demonstrate the impotence of the forces in this area, Japanese warships demolished the coast defences, using the same tactics that had been so effective in Wellington. Lieutenant General Harold Barrowclough, who had been given the field command of all forces in the dominion, deployed them in defensive positions in the Taupo area. Few were under any illusion that the Japanese could be prevented from taking over the whole of the country—if they so desired. The government would spend most of the next two years desperately trying to cope with the problems of feeding the population of Auckland and other centres, including many refugees from the occupied area to the south.

Meanwhile, in Wellington, the New Zealand and American troops holding the lines north of the city had fought on for a few days after the fall of the city, but with Japanese both in front of and behind them they soon perceived the situation as hopeless. Following their surrender, they were held at a prisoner-of-war camp established near Featherston.[9] Within the Japanese occupied area, Haruyoshi established a military administration, and soon acted brutally to impose Japanese control. Not everybody within the occupied area had accepted the situation. Bands of determined men took to the hills, their ardour to engage the Japanese in battle overriding their recognition that such action was bound to bring down heavy retribution on the population under Japanese control. A decree by the Japanese commander made plain what would happen: for every Japanese soldier killed fifty New Zealand hostages would be summarily executed. This brutal threat led to numerous atrocities, as guerrilla groups attacked isolated Japanese posts or convoys. On 26 June 1943 five Japanese soldiers were killed in an ambush near Waipukurau; in reprisal Japanese troops executed 250 people plucked from the streets or dragged from their homes in the town and threw them into a mass grave. Shannon suffered an even worse fate when snipers killed two Japanese soldiers passing through the town on 7 August: Japanese troops surrounded the town before dawn the next day and proceeded to kill every man, woman and child they could find before setting ablaze every building. (With the town never rebuilt, the ruins remain a moving memorial to the 448 people who died in the worst atrocity committed on New Zealand soil.)[10] The ruthlessness of the Japanese approach gave reason for pause among the insurgent groups, and they were soon ordered by Barrowclough, in contact with them by radio, to cease all offensive operations. Attempts by Australian officers landed by submarine to sustain the insurgency failed. Men remained in the hills in sullen defiance, but they largely refrained from launching attacks, biding their time instead in the hope of a change in the situation.

The Japanese treated the New Zealanders under their control with contempt. Much anger was caused by their importation of a number of South East Asian 'comfort woman', and even more when New Zealand women were forced into this role as well, albeit in small numbers. Most New Zealanders tried to keep their distance from the Japanese garrisons, though inevitably some fraternisation did take place. Despite the unlikely circumstances, some relationships even developed between Japanese soldiers and New Zealand women. This would lead in due course to twenty-three war brides going to Japan after the war.[11]

New Zealand's only hope of salvation lay in the course of events elsewhere—and in particular the return of the United States to the offensive. The American response to the Japanese victories in the Pacific was to expand its naval building programme tenfold and to begin preparations for a counter-stroke through the North Pacific. Huge resources were thrown into building a massive highway north through British Columbia to Alaska—a remarkable engineering feat. At the same time American and British scientists pressed ahead with the weapon that would ultimately bring about Japan's demise. Tested in July 1945, the atom bomb was quickly recognised as a decisive weapon—if it could be delivered. The highest priority was given to the development of a long-range bomber capable of carrying the bombs from Alaskan airfields to the Japanese mainland. By August 1946 the US had created a stock of twelve bombs, and it was six of these that devastated Hiroshima, Kobe, Osaka and three other cities, causing nearly a million deaths, on the night of the sixth. The US broadcast a demand for Japan's surrender; Tokyo, it was made clear, would be the next target. This settled it: the Emperor called on his people 'to endure the unendurable'. And American desire for revenge would ensure that the occupation, which lasted until 1959, would be in fact barely endurable.

The Japanese troops in New Zealand laid down their arms on 15 August 1946. Because Haruyoshi had committed hari kari, it was his deputy who handed his sword to Barrowclough, who had arrived in the capital aboard *Achilles*. The cruiser had made a quick dash across the Tasman to collect him from Auckland. Two hundred Japanese soldiers were held as possible war criminals; trials during 1947 would result in 113 of them being executed. The rest of the Japanese troops were repatriated within two months, after being kept well separated from a vengeful public. Their ships passed those of the 2NZEF which was at last able to return to New Zealand; though steadily weakened by a lack of reinforcements to replace men killed or severely wounded, it had helped defeat the Germans in the Mediterranean before being deployed to India to join General Slim's Fourteenth Army in Burma. New Zealand's long ordeal, which had cost it 5500 lives, was over. In the end the New Zealanders had been liberated by the success of Allied arms in far distant theatres. But the ramifications of New Zealand's partial occupation by a hated enemy would continue to resonate in

New Zealand society and politics for the next half century. When the Japanese government sought, in 1996, to establish a monument to Japanese soldiers who had died on New Zealand soil, it caused such an outcry that the request was quickly withdrawn.

9

What if the Manapouri power project had never been constructed?

Aaron Fox

The 700 megawatt (MW) Manapouri hydroelectric power project was constructed between 1963 and 1971 to supply continuous high-load power to an aluminium smelter located at Tiwai Point, Bluff, which first produced aluminium in 1971.[1] The Manapouri project represented a number of firsts for New Zealand—our first integrated electro-industrial project, our first significant exposure to transnational and multinational corporations, and, by 1970, our first national environmental campaign.

Many consider that environmentalism in New Zealand commenced with the national campaign to 'Save Manapouri' which ran from 1969 to 1972.[2] The campaign was in response to a proposal to raise Lake Manapouri by 8.2 metres, so as to permit greater efficiencies in the operation of the Manapouri power station, inundating the lake's islands and shoreline in the process. The campaign united a disparate range of pressure groups and individuals throughout New Zealand, prompting in 1970 what was at the time the largest petition (with 264,907 signatures, equating to almost 10 per cent of the New Zealand population) ever delivered to parliament. The Save Manapouri Campaign prompted a cabinet committee report and a commission of inquiry, and exerted national political leverage during the 1972 general election. The Labour Party pledged not to raise the levels of the lakes and, once in power, the government created an independent body, the Guardians of Lakes Manapouri and Te Anau, to oversee management of the lake levels.

It could also be argued that the campaign to save Lake Manapouri was part of a longer tradition of conservation and scenery preservation campaigning, which evolved into a domestic environmental movement in the 1970s in step with the emergence of an international environmental consciousness. Even in the absence of the Manapouri debate, therefore, it is conceivable that another large-scale industrial development could have provided the catalyst for a national environmental movement during the course of the 1970s.

Manapouri—the power project that never was

The greatest tragedy in the history of electro-industrialisation in New Zealand was that the vast hydroelectric potential of Lakes Manapouri and Te Anau, located in the Fiordland wilderness, was never able to be developed. The combined water resources of the two lakes, diverted by means of a tunnel down some 177 metres, could have powered an integrated industrial complex based on the new electro-chemical or electro-metallurgical processes of the second industrial revolution. Instead, the lakes were preserved in their natural state, unknown to the majority of New Zealanders except as icons of the nation's natural beauty.

Nevertheless, the quest for economic independence and industrial self-sufficiency engendered, within both government and business circles, an enduring faith in the benefits of electro-industrial development. The example of other developed nations had demonstrated that the application of American industrial technology and the exploitation of cheap sources of energy could result in high levels of industrial production.[3] The prospect of a New Zealand 'white gold rush', based on electricity and electro-metals such as aluminium, tantalised generations of politicians and government officials throughout the twentieth century.

While a Manapouri power project could never be realised, the increasingly desperate quest for a cost-effective source of power for electro-industrial purposes led the Muldoon government to a bold solution in the late 1970s. So bold a solution, in fact, that its construction united pressure groups and concerned individuals alike in New Zealand's first national environmental movement in opposition to the scheme.

Engineers versus nature

The potential of the Fiordland area to generate thousands of watts of electricity was first recognised in 1903 by two engineers charged by the government with surveying the nation's hydroelectric resources. In their 1904 report they noted the elevation of the lakes above sea level, and that electricity could thus be generated by means of tunnels whereby water would be diverted from either or both of the lakes westwards to George or Doubtful Sound, and there used to turn turbines. The cost per unit of power promised to be very competitive, and ideally suited to one of the new electro-industrial processes then being developed overseas for the production of aluminium, nitrogenous fertilisers, or carbide.[4]

However, aside from the natural beauty of the lakes, what most impressed the engineers as they sailed across Lake Manapouri was the earthquake which rocked the area, tossing the small vessel like a cork, and causing the surrounding forest to sway and, in places, slip and slump into the lake. Later geological surveys revealed that Fiordland is riven by numerous fault lines, and confirmed what the engineers had understood even in 1903—that the hydroelectric potential of the region can never be realised, as the geography and geology of the area form a natural barrier to major engineering works.

Fiordland National Park

Unsuited to any electro-industrial development—or, indeed, to any commercial enterprise—it was, instead, the natural beauty of the lakes, fiords and mountains which determined the best economic use for the area, and the Fiordland National Park was gazetted in 1905.[5] Historians of our National Parks system have reflected that, unlike other national parks, Fiordland was notable for never being the focus of any nationwide controversy or protest. The remote, isolated wilderness remained known only to the most adventurous or hardy tourists and explorers.[6]

Without a large, easily accessible attraction, tourist operations on Lakes Manapouri and Te Anau remained small-scale affairs. The notable exception was, of course, Milford Sound, where a tourist industry was stimulated by the construction of the Milford Road. The rest of the park, however, lacked the necessary infrastructure of access roads or walking tracks for much of the twentieth century. Indeed, a system of major walking tracks in the Fiordland National Park was not developed until the 1970s, in conjunction with the creation of the national walkway system.

Henceforth, new tracks over steep terrain such as the Wilmot Pass opened up the western fiords to a fresh generation of intrepid trampers.

Indigenous electro-industrialisation

The possibility that New Zealand's extensive lake and river systems could be harnessed in the quest for indigenous electro-industrial development captured the imagination of engineers and entrepreneurs throughout the twentieth century. In a nation dependent upon the export of primary produce to Great Britain for its economic well being, the importation into New Zealand of some of the new fully integrated electro-industrial processes which had been developed with great success in the United Kingdom, Europe and the United States was an extremely attractive proposition.[7]

In the words of the Irish playwright George Bernard Shaw, who visited New Zealand in 1934:

> You have no business to let New Zealand remain dependent on what you amusingly call the Home market, or any other overseas market. The real home market for New Zealand is the North Island plus the South . . . Keep your wool on your own backs; harness your own water power; get your fertilising nitrates from your own air; develop your own manufactures and eat your own food; and you can snap your fingers at Britain's follies.[8]

Poverty and progress

In truth, the government possessed neither the financial nor the technical resources to construct hydroelectric schemes large enough to supply the rapacious power demands of nitrogenous fertiliser plants or aluminium smelters. For much of the century, the preoccupation of the departments of public works and state hydroelectricity remained the construction of an integrated national system of generation and distribution to meet the growing demands of urban and rural consumers.[9]

With no block of surplus power available for electro-industrial purposes, localised initiatives for the production of nitrates or aluminium with electricity from South Island rivers such as the Waitaki or the Waiau were never realised. Attempts by local entrepreneurs to attract Commonwealth or American electro-industrial corporations to New Zealand were similarly unsuccessful.[10] Lacking the necessary raw materials or bulk supplies of electricity, the country offered little incentive for foreign companies to bring their operations to New Zealand. As one American businessman observed, 'You guys sure as hell need us more than we need you!'

'White gold' or South Seas bubble?

Aluminium, the wonder light metal of the twentieth century, assumed a strategic significance during the Second World War as a vital component in military technology.[11] It remained an essential strategic material throughout the Cold War, and aluminium production in the United States more than tripled between 1948 and 1958.[12] In New Zealand, therefore, proponents of electro-industrialisation as the key to untold national economic benefits remained undaunted. Many, such as cabinet minister Ralph Hanan, looked longingly at overseas countries where the application of American industrial technology and the exploitation of cheap sources of energy had resulted in high levels of industrial production.[13]

In the New Zealand context, the prospect of electro-industrialisation became the ultimate national 'get rich quick scheme', a 'white gold rush' based on electricity and aluminium. Hanan extolled the virtues of the South Island's hydroelectric resources, which he argued could be quickly developed for the purpose of industrial production such as base metals, fertilisers and primary materials. These products could then be exported to nations in the 'East', raising living standards in these countries and thereby enhancing New Zealand's national security.[14] New Zealand's white gold fever was further fuelled by events across the Tasman, when a vast bauxite deposit was discovered at Weipa in Northern Queensland in 1955,[15] and profitably brought into production, first in Papua New Guinea in the 1960s, and later in Japan.

Hanan's views were mirrored within official government circles where William (Bill) Sutch, the secretary of industries and commerce, promoted economic, and especially industrial, self-sufficiency. Two large industrial projects commenced in the mid-1950s—an oil refinery at Marsden Point, and the production of steel from the iron sands of the North Island—offered limited self-sufficiency in the petroleum and steel industries.[16] The prospect of fully integrated electro-industrialisation in New Zealand, however, remained an unrealised national dream throughout the 1950s and 1960s.

The resource debate—Exploitation versus preservation

The debate in government circles concerning indigenous electro-industrial development, or rather the marked lack thereof, was matched from the 1950s onwards by a growing debate concerning the utilisation of the nation's natural resources at the expense of the scenic beauty of New Zealand's landscapes.

The scenery preservation debate reached its peak in 1959, in response to the government's construction of a hydroelectric scheme at the picturesque Aratiatia Rapids on the Waikato River. University academics, the professional tourist industry, and nature preservation groups such as the Forest and Bird Protection Society were united in protest. The Save Aratiatia campaign prompted a petition to parliament, a one-day, government-sponsored conference on scenery preservation in Wellington, and the formation of the Scenery Preservation Society, an association of scientists, engineers and citizens concerned with the protection of scenic beauties from the huge dams required for hydroelectric generation.[17] Professor John Salmon of the department of biology at Victoria University of Wellington encapsulated the exploitation versus preservation debate in his 1960 publication of *Heritage Destroyed: The crisis in scenery preservation in New Zealand*. Salmon highlighted the dangers of a 'materialistic outlook' regarding the nation's natural resources, arguing for the preservation of the 'aesthetic and beautiful' in the New Zealand landscape.[18]

It was ironic, therefore, that the relative success of the Save Aratiatia campaign and the scenery preservation lobby in at least partially 'saving' the Aratiatia Rapids also marked the end of any national debate on scenery preservation. Calls by the campaigners for the creation of an independent government body to advise the government on nature preservation matters were answered by the creation of the Nature Conservation Council in 1962.[19] However, the campaigners' faith that advice from an independent government organisation could counteract any plans by government departments which involved drastic alterations to the face of nature was soon proven to be naïve.

While the council's status as an advisory body meant that it could criticise large-scale developments, it lacked the legislative power to halt or even alter them. For the general public, however, the work of the council provided sufficient reassurance that the development of the nation's natural resources by the state would not be to the detriment of natural scenery. Thus it was that the general public continued to delight at the spectacle of large-scale hydroelectric projects such as Benmore, content in the knowledge that such developments, and any associated loss of scenic beauty spots, were clearly in the national interest. And at Aratiatia, while the hydroelectric station was completed, a compromise was reached whereby the rapids were permitted to run twice daily, at set times, when the spillway gates were lifted.[20]

Certainly debate and protest about scenery preservation continued, but the campaigns were notably localised affairs, as, for instance, when the damming of rivers and the inundation of land prompted protest by locals and recreational users who were directly affected. Indeed, commentators on the political scene in New Zealand in the late 1960s have noted the absence of scenery preservation or conservation issues from amongst the many popular national protest movements which characterised the period. Even the protestors themselves realised that conservation issues had little impact on the national political scene, while the professional conservation debate remained restricted to official government and academic circles.

The growing crisis—Energy, industry and the economy

What most marked the history of New Zealand in the early 1970s was the change in the country's economic fortunes. In 1973, Britain's entry into the European Economic Community, the first of the international oil shocks, and a steep decline in the levels of the commodity prices of principal primary exports all served to threaten New Zealand's economic survival. The Marshall administration, which had narrowly retained power at the 1972 general election, maintained a calm and measured façade while attempting to negotiate continued access to the British market. Behind the scenes, however, cabinet ministers and officials cast about for a solution to the growing economic crisis.

Electricity planners had long concluded that, once the nation's hydro, thermal and geothermal resources had all been exploited for the generation of electricity, the logical next step was to construct nuclear power stations.[21] Initial approaches to the American-based Bechtel Corporation and the Atomic Power division of the Westinghouse Electric Corporation in 1974 indicated that a 1000-megawatt nuclear power station could be constructed close to Auckland, and that the station could produce sufficient continuous high-load power to supply one or more electro-metallurgical plants.[22] Further negotiations revealed that both the Kaiser Aluminium and Chemical Corporation and the Reynolds Aluminium Corporation of the United States would consider the establishment of one or more aluminium smelters in the event that the nuclear station was constructed, with bulk supplies of electricity made available by the government at competitive rates.

Negotiations between the government and US companies were conducted in absolute secrecy. While the Marshall administration had withstood concerted campaigns opposing New Zealand's involvement in the Vietnam war and French nuclear testing in the Pacific, it considered that the premature announcement of the American nuclear-aluminium proposal would prompt a level of anti-American protest which might deter the companies from coming to New Zealand. Within government circles at least, it was felt that nothing should be permitted to jeopardise the chance to establish an integrated electro-metallurgical industrial complex, with the prospect of employing upwards of 2000 workers and the generation of significant government revenue. So long had politicians and officials been wedded to the concept of electro-industrialisation that little attempt was made at a cost–benefit analysis; the prospect of indigenous electro-industrial production was in itself ample return for the projected costs to the government of constructing the nuclear power station.[23]

Thinking globally, acting locally

The influence in New Zealand of global developments in the 1970s was not confined to economic matters. The growth of the international environmental movement provided a new, global context for the various conservation campaigns being waged at local level in different places around the country.[24] Now when local conservation groups spoke out against a power scheme proposed for a particular river, or lobbied their councillors about the effects of a local industry on neighbourhood air quality, the global language of the 'environment' and 'environmentalism' was available, a new lexicon that tapped into a growing national consciousness, putting disparate, local events into a much wider, even global, context. Environmentalism proved to be a unifying influence amongst conservation lobby groups, as campaigners came to realise that a greater common cause—the survival of the planet—was at stake. As this new perspective on the importance of the local in the context of the national and international environment became more prevalent in New Zealand in the 1970s, environmental campaigners were able to tap into it, and the environmental movement became an increasingly powerful political force.[25]

Associated with the global spread of environmental consciousness was a growing disquiet in the West with government policies as well as a distrust in the processes of government, and with the scientists and engineers who spoke in the government's cause. Here in New Zealand, this disquiet contributed towards a growing dissatisfaction with the Marshall administration's handling of the national economic crisis, contributing directly to the election of the Rowling government in 1975.

Thinking biggest of all—The Rutherford option

The Rowling administration proved to be short-lived, however, and in 1978 it was replaced by a National government led by Robert Muldoon. Muldoon had engineered a landslide victory by promising economic recovery and growth based on government-sponsored, large-scale economic developments.[26] With slogans such as 'bigger is best' and 'thinking big', Muldoon considered that the country had been well primed for what was his first significant announcement as prime minister—the plans for the construction of the Sir Ernest Rutherford Nuclear Power Station near Auckland, to supply power to at least two aluminium smelters, with an estimated workforce of more than 2000.

'Kiss your children goodbye'

It came as a considerable shock to Muldoon and his government, therefore, when the announcement of the Rutherford Nuclear Power Station sparked a coordinated national environmental campaign against the prospect of nuclear power generation in New Zealand, creatively entitled 'Kiss your children goodbye'.[27] The timing of the announcement, just weeks before the Three Mile Island nuclear disaster in the United States, was later acknowledged by Muldoon to have been 'unfortunate'.[28] However, timing alone could not explain the rapid development of a national protest movement which soon united New Zealanders across generational, gender and political lines in opposition to the prospect of nuclear power generation.

Clearly, here was the birth of something truly big—a national environmental movement—and the beginning of a battle for something even bigger—the future survival of New Zealand. But whether New Zealand's survival would be determined by participation in the developing global economy, or by the outcome of the global environmental debate, remained to be seen.

ELECTIONS AND POLITICS

10

What if Muldoon's 'think big' energy projects had succeeded?

John Wilson

'Think big' was a term used to describe a range of large-scale, capital intensive, energy-related projects undertaken in the late 1970s by the New Zealand government. Promoted by prominent members of the National Party then in government (Sir Robert Muldoon and Bill Birch), the liquid fuels components of the projects were intended to reduce the escalating foreign exchange burden being imposed on New Zealand by rising oil prices as a consequence of the Iranian revolution of 1979. This was to be achieved both by substituting indigenous sources of liquid fuels for imported oil and by providing a number of export products derived from natural gas (such as methanol and ammonia urea). Critical to the economic success of the liquid fuels, 'think big' projects, however, was the assumption that oil prices would not only remain at or near the highs being seen by the late 1970s, but that they would keep on rising thereafter. Instead, the price of oil collapsed dramatically from its peak in 1980 of about $US80 a barrel (in 2004 dollars) to under $US30 a barrel by the mid-1980s.

As a result, the financial viability of the state-sponsored projects collapsed. New Zealand's debt position became unsustainable as a result of the massive borrowings required to finance the 'think big' projects. This resulted in the incoming 1984 Labour government immediately devaluing the New Zealand dollar and beginning a process of selling off the state-owned energy projects. The state also withdrew from energy planning, and even energy policy, by abolishing its Ministry of Energy. The debt incurred by the 'think big' projects also bolstered the neoliberal rationale for the selling of other state assets—such as banks, railways and airlines. Where privatisation was not feasible, other sectors of the economy were restructured through corporatisation and deregulation.

The headline in the *Herald Sun* proclaims '"Think big" on energy independence.' '"Think big" and address our nation's current energy needs,' pleads a speaker in a parliamentary debate on energy legislation. 'If you want energy, "Think big",' argues the *Times Online*.[1] Surprisingly, these quotes are not taken from New Zealand's era of 'think big' energy projects (1975–85)— they are from international papers in 2004 and 2005. In no small part, this is because the price of oil appears to be headed back to levels last seen in the 1970s, placing energy security back on the political agenda for many nations around the world. 'What if' questions are beginning to be asked once again about the state of the planet's oil and gas resources.

This paper takes a counterfactual approach to the political and economic consequences arising from the failure of New Zealand's 'think big' energy projects initiated in the late 1970s. Counterfactuals are seen as playing an important role in the efforts of political scientists to assess causal hypotheses.[2] The counterfactual strategy is one that introduces changes to key events—ones that did not actually take place—in order to make credible arguments about what would have happened if they had. These arguments must still adhere to the general principles or regularities in effect, but can be supported by reference to the historical set of facts relevant to the counterfactual scenario.

The counterfactual scenario developed in this chapter assesses the possible impacts from a sustained oil price at, or close to, the peaks actually experienced in 1979–80. Under this scenario, it is suggested that the economic viability of the 'think big' projects would have been assured, and that the political rationale for a substantial role for the state in energy and economic management would have been retained. Consequently, New Zealand's economic and political direction would not have been guided by the neoliberal approach so much in evidence today.

The chapter begins by outlining the rationale for the energy projects variously grouped under the rubric 'think big', followed by an assessment of their contribution to the neoliberal turn in New Zealand's economic and political life once those projects failed as the oil price collapsed. The chapter then outlines a plausible counterfactual scenario in which the oil price stays up instead of collapsing, followed by an assessment of the consequences for New Zealand had this been the case. The chapter concludes by arguing that the counterfactual strategy is a useful approach for exploring the sensitivity of the historical evolution of events to factors whose significance is otherwise difficult to assess.

The 'think big' rationale

The Iranian revolution of 1979 had a dramatic and sudden impact on world oil prices. As that country's oil industry became paralysed, removing 5.7 million barrels per day of oil production from world supply, the Organization of the Petroleum Exporting Countries (OPEC) raised oil prices from a nominal US$12 a barrel to $19 a barrel. In the latter part of 1979 the price was pushed further to $24 per barrel following the taking of Western hostages by Iran, the cessation of Iranian oil imports to the United States, and the cancelling by Iran of all oil contracts with US oil companies. Accounting for inflation, this means that the oil price breached $80 per barrel in today's terms—an all-time high.

New Zealand, like many oil importing countries, was faced with actual shortages. In response, New Zealand's National government first banned weekend sales of gasoline and then introduced 'carless days' whereby private motorists were required to refrain from using their car on a day of the week that they nominated. But while these measures incurred some inconvenience for the private motorist, the real impact was felt in the economic sector. The substantial increase in the oil price contributed to the continuing worsening of the country's terms of trade. The cost of oil was the major component of New Zealand's balance of payments deficit, and its rising price was also fuelling rapid inflation and rising unemployment.

By the end of the 1970s the Ministry of Energy was projecting oil prices to keep on increasing—by over half by the mid-1980s, and to nearly double in real terms by the year 2000. These projections were justified by a number of credible assumptions concerning ongoing political stability in oil-producing regions, increasing worldwide demand for oil, and oil depletion.

Firstly, continued instability in the Middle East—involving further Islamic revolutions or terrorist activities—could easily have continued to disrupt oil supplies. The taking of hostages from the US embassy in Tehran in late 1979 only fuelled such fears. The New Zealand Ministry of Energy considered that the 'possibility of sabotage to large clusters of oil producing facilities in the Gulf poses added uncertainties to future oil supply'.[3]

Secondly, New Zealand energy analysts argued that the rate at which the world was currently using natural gas and oil implied that it was almost inevitable that they would be virtually depleted on a world scale by the mid-twenty-first century.[4] The most recent estimates suggest there are thirty years of oil left if demand continues to increase at its historic average of 2 per cent, or forty years if one believes that world oil consumption will not exceed that experienced in 2005. This appears unlikely given that two economic powerhouses, China and India, are primarily driving the growth in oil demand. Nevertheless, estimates that oil would be totally depleted by 2050 have remained virtually unchanged since 1979.

In terms of price rises, it is not the final depletion point that is of concern, but rather the point at which half the total oil has been produced. At such a moment we 'are not so much faced with an energy shortage, rather a reorganisation of our energy supply system to meet the new era in which oil is no longer cheap'.[5] There would therefore be considerable potential for further increases in the price of oil in a world market, which is likely to have smaller working margins available for demand fluctuations. As ongoing terrorism and weather events have shown, when production cannot be increased to maintain a surplus buffer over consumption, small disruptions in supply can result in rapid price escalation.

This final point—expressed in 2005 as the 'end of cheap oil' or 'peak oil'—is critical to the expected price of oil because it references an actual date at which half of the planet's finite oil reserves will have been used. As table 10.1 shows, by 1981 predictions for 'peak oil' ranged between 1996 and 2005, with New Zealand analysts thinking it 'certain that world crude oil production will reach its peak before the turn of the century'.[6] Interestingly, Shell's 1979 estimate of 2005 as the date of 'peak oil' has yet to be ruled out, and it neatly overlaps current oil peak

Table 10.1 Historical estimates for 'peak oil'

Date of Forecast	Source	Forecast Date of Conventional Peak	Assumed Ultimate
1972	ESSO	2000	2100 Gb
1972	Report for the UN Conference on Human Environment	2000	2500 Gb
1976	UK Department of Energy	2000	n/a
1977	Hubbert	1996	2000 Gb
1977	Ehrlich et al	2000	1900 Gb
1979	Shell	2005	n/a
1979	BP	1985(non-com munist world	n/a
1981	World Bank	2000	1900 Gb

Source: Roger Bentley, department of cybernetics, University of Reading: http://www.oildepletion.org/roger/Key_topics/Past_forecasts/Past_forecasts.htm - table

predictions ranging from 2005 to 2032, with most estimating 2015 or so.[7] Chevron, the second-largest American oil company, believes that 'peak oil' is essentially here: 'the era of easy oil is over.'[8]

During the late 1970s New Zealand had vast and undeveloped gas reserves from the Maui gas field, which had to be used under the 'take or pay' contract signed by the previous Labour government to develop the field. In 1978 the government had urged officials to search for a 'bold solution' for the use of Maui gas, and in particular to reduce New Zealand's reliance on imported fuels.[9] To this end the Liquid Fuels Trust Board (LFTB), established that same year, commissioned a number of studies into petrochemical options. In September 1979 the minister of energy stated that the government was allocating more than 60 per cent of the Maui gas field as a substitute for oil imports in 'a response to the likelihood of continuing tightness in world oil supply and the prospect of escalating imported oil prices'.[10] In October the LFTB recommended several options that included: a synthetic petrol plant at Motonui; a complementary expansion of the Marsden Point oil refinery; a stand-alone plant to produce methanol for export; and the production of compressed natural gas (CNG) and liquid petroleum gas (LPG) as alternative transport fuels. In endorsing the LFTB's proposals, the government aimed to ensure that New Zealand became 50 per cent self-sufficient in transport fuels by 1987, saving an estimated half a billion dollars annually in foreign exchange earnings. Thus, under the leadership of the prime minister, Robert Muldoon, and his energy minister, Bill Birch, the 'think big' energy strategy was born. The last of the government's energy projects was signed up just three months out from the 1981 election and its 'think big' energy projects were a central plank in the campaign.

'Think big' was an umbrella term used to describe a range of large-scale, capital-intensive, state-led and state-underwritten energy-related projects. The liquid fuels project components of 'think big'—the main focus in this chapter—were intended to reduce the escalating foreign exchange burden being imposed on New Zealand by rising oil prices. This would be achieved by substituting indigenous sources of liquid fuels for imported oil and by providing a number of export products derived from natural gas, such as methanol and ammonia urea. Although not the focus here, other 'think big' projects (such as the construction of the Clyde dam, whose surplus electricity would be used in a second aluminium smelter) were designed to widen New Zealand's industrial base, provide employment, and spur economic growth.

Of course the 'think big' strategy as a whole, and individual projects within it, attracted enormous criticism on various economic, technical, environmental, political and constitutional grounds. Many projects were said, among other things, to lack good information; lack independent or neutral technical advice; have been initiated without proper public debate; and to have been managed without adequate standards of transparency and accountability.[11] Indeed, the National Development Act 1979 was passed precisely to overcome the normal planning procedures by 'fast tracking' the planning consents needed for the 'think big' projects, such as the synthetic petrol plant at Motonui. This latter project, for example, was described at the time as a 'highly centralised, technocratic, growth-oriented, anti-ecological and militarily vulnerable response to the fuel problem'.[12]

The liquid fuels projects were recognised to carry substantial financial risks. Firstly, the projects' financial viability rested on assuming that the international price of oil would not only remain at or close to the highs being seen by the late 1970s, but that it would keep on rising thereafter. Secondly, the 'think big' projects had an initial projected capital cost in excess of three billion dollars that would require enormous levels of overseas borrowing. Because the projects were large and in some cases dependent on unproven technology, they were also subject to high cost overruns leading to a further deterioration in New Zealand's external deficit. The final risk in terms of the energy projects' centrepiece—the Motonui synthetic gas to methanol plant—was uncertainty surrounding the ongoing world demand for methanol, and hence its export price. As the *Economist* noted:

> Who will bear the cost if, in the years ahead, the Motonui plant proves to have been a costly and inefficient exercise in import substitution—the international banks or the New Zealand taxpayer? (*Economist*, 12 June 1982)

As it turned out it was the latter—the oil price collapsed dramatically from its peak in 1980 of about $US80 a barrel in 2004 dollars, to under $US30 a barrel by the mid-1980s (see figure 10.1). However, the Motonui synfuel plant's break-even price was US$70 a barrel after accounting for depreciation and debt servicing. By the time the plant finally opened in 1985, synthetic petrol being made there cost seventy-six cents per litre, while petrol bought on the international market cost forty-one cents per litre.[13] Taxpayers lost more than $2.1 billion on the synfuel plant alone.[14]

The economics of other 'think big' projects collapsed as well. The ammonia urea plant at Kapuni in South Taranaki cost $97 million (in 1983 dollars) to build. It was sold to Fletcher Challenge for $500,000 in the late 1980s, after the price of ammonia had slumped dramatically. The ammonia urea plant at Waitara went 35 per cent over budget to build and then lost $18.7 million a year until 1987. The government-underwritten expansion of the

Figure 10.1: Historic oil price trend in 2004 dollars

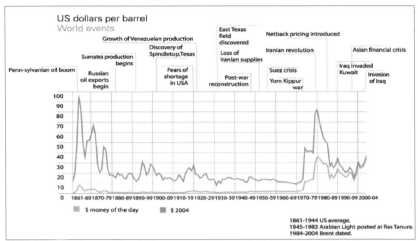

Source: BP 2005, *Statistical Review of World Energy 2005*, 14 June 2005:
http://www.bp.com/genericsection.do?categoryId=92&contentId=7005893

Marsden Point oil refinery cost more than $2.1 billion—three times the original estimate of $714 million. Later a Labour government had to repay $2.05 billion in loans taken out for the expansion.

In 1988 the New Zealand Treasury calculated that the 'think big' projects accounted for 20 per cent of all public debt and that the country was at that stage $1.3 billion poorer because of them. Not until 1993/94 was New Zealand able to achieve its first financial surplus since 1977, and it was not until 2005 that net public debt, as a proportion of GDP, was able to be reduced to 7.7 per cent (see figure 10.2). It had been more than twenty-five years since the country's net public debt had dropped below 10 per cent—in 1978, before the overseas borrowings for the 'think big' projects had begun.

The enormous fiscal and monetary consequences of the 'think big' projects contributed significantly to the adoption of a neoliberal view about the appropriate role of the state in the economy. The gigantic proportion of public debt forced the incoming 1984 Labour government to begin selling some of the country's state-owned energy projects. This then bolstered its claim that much

Figure 10.2: New Zealand's net public debt as a share of GDP

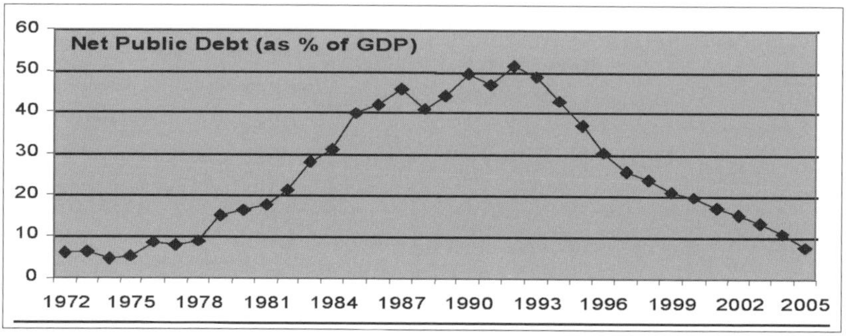

Source: Data Series: Government Debt, New Zealand Parliamentary Library, 2005

of the reason it was choosing to sell other state assets—such as banks, railways and airlines—was to reduce the debt incurred by its National Party predecessor's 'think big' projects. Where privatisation was not feasible, corporatisation and deregulation prevailed, restructuring vast sectors of the New Zealand economy. Within the energy sector itself, the state withdrew from energy planning, and even from energy policy, by abolishing its Ministry of Energy.

'Think big' as it might have been

> Some actions that seemed to be inappropriate may have been desirable if the problem had not been shortlived. For example, synthetic fuel initiatives may have looked prescient had oil prices not collapsed in the mid-1980s.[15]

The above quote is in fact an example of a counterfactual—actions and policies now seen as inappropriate do so only because the problem was short-lived; a change to that context produces a different assessment. This chapter similarly argues by way of counterfactual reasoning that a significant cause of the failure of the liquid fuels components of 'think big'—as well as the impetus for the radical neoliberal shift in New Zealand politics—was the collapse in the oil price in the mid-1980s. In order to assess just how critical that collapse was to the economic failure of the 'think big' projects and New Zealand's subsequent economic and political trajectory, we can counterfactually assume that the oil price had remained at, or even risen beyond, the levels seen in 1980. What then of the implications or consequences had those assumptions been fulfilled in 1985 rather than, as it now appears, in 2005–06?

An oil price at the higher levels that had been projected in 1979, would have had both economic and political consequences. At the economic level, the viability of the liquid fuels projects aimed at substitution and export markets would have been assured. The foreign exchange savings would have reached $2.5 billion by 1990, allowing an estimated 410,000 jobs to be created.[16] Continuing economic growth would then have sustained the debt servicing on the projects, averting the dramatic and pivotal balance of payments crisis that arose in 1984.

Such economic success would undoubtedly have influenced the political arena. At the electoral level, for example, the consequences of the successful achievement of the 'think big' projects could have generated quite different outcomes in the 1984, and possibly 1987, elections. Flushed with economic success, and with the divisiveness of the 1981 Springbok tour behind him, Muldoon may well have won again in 1984. But regardless of a Labour or National win in those elections, the impact of 'think big' success would have confirmed the desirability of an active role for the state in energy markets and energy planning—and conceivably an interventionist role in other policy areas as well. We could well imagine a slight rewording of these remarks from Roger Kerr of the Business Roundtable:

> The whole 'think big' fiasco and the notion that we needed a Ministry of Energy stemmed from the idea that energy was so special that governments needed to intervene comprehensively in energy markets. We preferred the absurd spectacle of carless days to efficient prices for energy.[17]

171

With a different outcome for the 'think big' projects based on improved price performance, he might instead had had this to say:

> The whole 'think big' success and the notion that we needed a Ministry of Energy stemmed from the idea that energy was so special that governments needed to intervene comprehensively in energy markets. We preferred the spectacle of carless days to absurd, but efficient, prices for energy.

Under the second scenario, we would indeed regard energy as 'special'. We would reject the idea that the free market could deliver 'efficient prices for energy' and we would undoubtedly see a vital role for government intervention in energy markets (and elsewhere).

On the first point, consumers and producers would today be much more aware just how special oil is in their social and economic lives. Oil provides the large energy surplus that powers the critical sectors of our economy, including transportation but extending to other activities as well. Oil provides the chemical feed stocks to make pesticides and fertilisers, essential for industrialised agriculture; it powers the global fishing fleets; and it underpins our modern lifestyles. With cheap oil, people can live far from work and a small fraction of the work force can feed those that produce society's goods and services. Without cheap oil enabling international trade, globalisation's ability to move millions of people out of poverty would be severely curtailed. If the oil price had stayed up as expected, US Vice President Dick Cheney would not have had to remind us just how special oil was:

> Oil is unique in that it is so strategic in nature. We are not talking about soapflakes or leisurewear here. Energy is truly fundamental to the world's economy. The [1991] Gulf War was a reflection of that reality. The degree of government involvement also makes oil a unique commodity. This is true in both the overwhelming control of oil resources by national oil companies and governments as well as in the consuming nations where oil products are heavily taxed and regulated. It is the basic, fundamental building block of the world's economy. It is unlike any other commodity.[18]

Had the oil price stayed up, we would today realise that no 'free market' in oil actually exists, since free markets depend on competition, transparency of information, and true cost pricing. None of these conditions exist today in an oil world dominated by an OPEC cartel that for more than three decades—from the 1970s onwards—has imposed a quota system to keep some product off the market and, by doing so, manipulate energy prices. Furthermore, OPEC countries do not release details about how much oil they extract, or how much oil they have left, and they do not permit audits by outsiders. The markets' ability to anticipate the timing and rate of oil decline is severely compromised by this lack of transparency. Efficient energy prices are also unlikely to be achieved in a market that fails to price the economic consequences of oil use—road infrastructure costs, accident costs, environmental costs—and that consequently distorts consumers' ability to make rational choices from among alternatives.

The 1979 view of the market was that price signals were important, but it was unlikely that they would lead to liquid fuels being produced when they were needed at a price that could be afforded.[19] Today, the soaring cost of marine diesel is forcing up to half of Nelson's 60-strong inshore fishing fleet to stay in port at any one time.[20] Yet it is not just New Zealand's fishing industry that is threatened by rapidly escalating prices—our agricultural products for export depend on oil-based fertilisers and pesticides, on mechanised farming, and on cheap oil to get them to our international markets. As a commentator in the *Wall Street Journal* suggests, an overriding focus on efficiency can lead to suboptimal outcomes:

> The totality of impacts may force policy makers to rely heavily on the precautionary principle, which compares the costs of being correct to those of being incorrect. We know that oil production will peak within our lifetime, we think market prices may not anticipate this peak and we know that not having alternatives in place at the time of the peak will have tremendous economic and social consequences. So, if society does too much now, as opposed to later, there will be some loss of efficiency. But if society does too

little now, as opposed to later, the effects could be disastrous. Under these conditions, doing too little now in the name of efficiency will appear in hindsight as rearranging deck chairs on the Titanic.[21]

A high and increasing price of oil would today justify the continued intervention of the state in energy markets—and possibly in other sectors of the economy as well. It would mean that New Zealand would still own oil, gas and coal producers, such as Petrocorp and Coalcorp. The state would have remained active in oil and gas exploration, with a good chance that substantial reserves of oil or gas would have been discovered at some point over the 25-year period since 1980. The suggestion that oil explorers should wait until 2004, before beneficial changes to the royalties and tax regime would be made, would have been seen as doing too little, too late to encourage a substantial exploration programme.

In addition, energy markets would not be deregulated to the extent they are today. We would not have electricity companies generating excessive profits for their shareholders, instead of affordable and reliable power for their consumers. We would be unlikely now to be facing power cuts, because the state would have no compunction about requiring generators to provide enough reserve capacity in the event that low lake levels occur more frequently than a deregulated market appears able to foresee.

Today New Zealand would also have a ministry of energy and not just a minister. This would mean that the state would be actively engaged in energy policy and planning—able, for example, to devise a national energy strategy, or mandatory fuel-efficiency standards for cars (as proposed by the Green Party). Devising such policies, standards and strategies would also see a legitimate role for public discussion and debate, rather than (as at present) a policy area dominated by business and industry interests.

A final consequence of a high oil price is that the liquid fuels projects, had they been successful, would have provided New Zealand with a bridge—from the oil age to the post-carbon age. In 1979, Maui gas was seen as precisely that, a bridge to the use of renewable energy sources and the development of new energy technologies—biomass, wind, solar and coal.

Exploitation of the Maui gas field will dominate energy development until the mid-1990s at which stage alternative sources and technologies may have to provide an increasing share of the market. Continued evaluation and proving of alternative technologies and sources for liquid fuels will have reached the stage where favourable options can be developed to supplement the Maui gas resource.[22]

Had that bridge eventuated—had the economics of using Maui gas succeeded—we would today have made the transition to renewable energy sources and alternative technologies that was seen as inevitable in 1979. If that transition had been made in New Zealand, and perhaps worldwide, the alternative energy sources—wind, biomass, clean coal, solar—in use today would be technologically advanced, efficient and sustainable. In turn, we would have limited our emissions of carbon dioxide and may well have mitigated or delayed the impacts of climate change. The frequency or intensity of heat waves in Europe, of flooding in Bangladesh, and of hurricanes in the southern United States might well have been diminished.

Instead, we have yet to make the necessary transition to renewables, and we are faced with a climate changing at a rate unprecedented in the history of human civilisation. Nor do we now have a bridge—Maui gas—to enable that transition to proceed in a relatively painless and orderly fashion which allows time for the New Zealand economy to adjust.

Conclusion

Of more concern, perhaps, is that the re-emergence in 2005 of headlines exhorting us to 'think big' could only have appeared in the *international* press. The legacy of that philosophy (and slogan) in New Zealand—major economic burdens and a discredited view of the role of the state in energy markets and planning—means that the words 'think big' are used almost as a joke in this country, a shorthand for failure. Yet this legacy is an impediment to the type of thinking that will be required to address the upcoming third— and final—oil shock. As recent headlines suggest, New Zealand,

and indeed the world, is again facing a similar set of constraints to those experienced in 1979. Regardless of the exact year, the implications of 'peak oil' resemble the impacts experienced by the world economy in the previous two oil crises. Accompanying rising energy prices will be inflation, unemployment and low economic growth—leading to the search for alternate forms of liquid transport fuels, with limited time available for such a transition to occur without serious societal upheaval. Given such high stakes, it is little wonder that the energy planners of the 1970s, using a set of credible assumptions, attempted to make oil price projections.

The depletion of global oil fields and the lack of technological alternatives in transport fuels also raise questions about the relative ability of states and market forces to usher in a post-petroleum world. New Zealand failed with 'think big' to appreciate the importance of market forces. In the New Zealand of today, however, the risks are neatly reversed —New Zealand risks getting it wrong again with a belief that market forces are the only things that matter. What if this time around 'think big' is exactly the sort of thinking that New Zealand needs?

Finally, it is apparent that many social and economic commentators employ counterfactual reasoning, if only implicitly, to support their arguments. But the use of counterfactuals in social science needs to be made more explicit. It is a viable strategy to employ when the number of case studies is limited or when the significance of single causal factors needs to be assessed. As the counterfactual approach developed here suggests, the implications of the future price and availability of oil mean that we should all, today, be thinking big.

11

What if Brian Talboys had said 'yes' to the plotters in 1980?

Colin James

In October 1980 Deputy Prime Minister Brian Talboys decided against challenging Prime Minister Sir Robert Muldoon for the prime ministership. He had been assured by a group of four 'colonels'[1] in the cabinet that a majority of MPs was prepared to vote for him when Muldoon returned from a seven-week overseas trip. Nevertheless, he decided against a challenge and instead announced he would retire from politics at the election the following year. The coup collapsed for want of a candidate. Muldoon remained prime minister until he lost a general election in July 1984 amidst a financial and currency crisis that reflected serious distortions in the economy.

The Labour government which replaced him in 1984 at this crisis point was like no other in New Zealand's political history. It was traditional Labour in its attention to, and expansion of spending on, health, education, housing and Maori, and it was modern social democratic in its willingness to address indigenous and other human rights issues and constitutional reform. But it junked its traditional protectionist, high-taxing, heavily regulatory approach to economic management in favour of radical and rapid deprotection, deregulation, state asset privatisation, state sector reform along private sector principles, and tax reform to flatten income tax rates and increase indirect taxes. The direction of the economic reforms was similar to contemporary changes in other Anglo–Celtic countries, but it was deeper and swifter than in those countries and more economically and socially disruptive than in most. New Zealand became an internationally famous and notorious case study in application of the Chicago and Virginia schools' economic analyses, and their related 'classical liberal' and 'new public management' theories.[2]

What if Talboys had said yes in 1980 and the majority in his favour had held?[3]

The simple answer is that Talboys, being much less forceful and charismatic than Muldoon, would have lost the election in November 1981. The Labour government which took office then would have been headed by the 1974–75 prime minister, Sir Wallace ('Bill') Rowling, an orthodox[4] economist who would have resisted Treasury advice to liberalise the economy. Rowling would have been tossed on the same economic tides that eventually engulfed Muldoon and would have lost the next election, in 1984, bringing to power a younger-generation National government predisposed to economic liberalisation, though moderate and gently paced compared with the post-1984 Labour government that took power. The late 1980s would have been a time of reform, not radicalism.

This neat and tidy snapshot blurs on closer inspection.

Muldoon in power . . .

That a coup had even been contemplated was remarkable, verging on astonishing. Muldoon had come into office in 1975 a hero in the National Party and to many voters, replacing a twenty-three-seat Labour majority with a twenty-three-seat National advantage in a parliament of eighty-seven—an 8.4 per cent two-party swing. This gave him a mystique of power and invincibility, which he underlined in office by projecting a macho image, mercilessly attacking and, when he felt particularly aggrieved or determined, destroying those who crossed him. Even senior business leaders were afraid to challenge him. A visiting journalist in 1984, Padraic McGuinness, editor of the *Australian Financial Review*, was to describe an 'economy of fear'.

Liberals either left the party or retreated into inactivity or, if they were contemplating politics, chose the Labour party instead; traditional conservatives also found Muldoon's style discomforting. By 1980 this attrition was well advanced. Into the space in the party rank and file came people of a type Muldoon dubbed 'the ordinary bloke', people who a decade earlier, before Labour set out down its 'identity politics' path, might have been expected to vote Labour.[5] This group, colloquially referred to as 'Rob's mob', formed Muldoon's lodestar constituency. It was composed largely of middle-aged males. 'Ordinary blokes' were socially conservative, discomforted by feminists, Maori agitators and the social liberals who had begun to disturb the social order in the 1970s. They were culturally conservative—framing the national identity essentially as British. And they valued economic security very highly. Muldoon was instinctively in tune with them and they with him. His populist brand of orthodox economics and social and cultural conservatism was much to their liking.

By October 1980, however, Muldoon's mystique had been eroded by a series of electoral reverses. In February 1978, amidst faltering economic growth and farmer uproar over a generous wage deal Muldoon had made with meat processing plant workers over the heads of the companies, National lost a by-election in the previously safe rural seat of Rangitikei to Bruce Beetham, leader of a minor party, Social Credit. Then at the election in November that year National won fewer votes than Labour, remaining in power only by dint of quirks in the electoral system.

Worse was to come. On 6 September 1980 Social Credit's deputy leader, Garry Knapp, won the previously safe mortgage-belt Auckland seat of East Coast Bays, vacant when Muldoon had decided to post its incumbent, Air Commodore Frank Gill, to Washington as ambassador. During the by-election campaign Muldoon announced a rise in fares on the Auckland harbour bridge, over which commuters to jobs in downtown Auckland from East Coast Bays had to travel. Though his announcement at that sensitive time was arguably a rare oversight on Muldoon's part, it was widely thought in the party to have been timed deliberately so as to sabotage the campaign of National's candidate, Don Brash, later to become party leader (also in unusual circumstances), whose market-liberal economics Muldoon openly despised. Muldoon's conduct in this event was the immediate trigger for the coup ferment.

Underlying the stirrings in the party was an ideological shift at odds with Muldoon's directive, command-economy policy approach as minister of finance, a post he held concomitantly with that of prime minister. The new monetarist theories had arrived in New Zealand in the late 1970s and were exciting interest among National Party activists and others under a 'more-market' rubric, a phrase taken from a monograph published in 1978 by Ian McLean, an agricultural economist. McLean became a National MP in the 1978 election and joined forces with a band of other newcomers to promote a moderate version of the new theories within the party caucus. These market-liberals[6] had some small successes in limiting Muldoon's recourse to regulation and his bid for a freer hand on tax. The new mood found expression at party conferences in 1979, through resolutions debated and often passed. A rebellion was afoot.

Nevertheless enough of Muldoon's 1975 mystique remained to underline the second part of the opening question—'and the majority [for Talboys] had held'. For the coup to succeed, not only did Talboys have to say yes and then actively campaign (by contrast with his initial passive agreement to serve if drafted) but the majority for him had to be maintained. This is doubtful.

First, though his maiden speech in 1958 led the then Labour prime minister, Sir Walter Nash, to call him a potential prime minister, Talboys lacked the steel and ambition most prime ministers need to get the top job. His passive response to the plotters and his retirement from politics in 1981 bear witness to this. In real life it would have been out of character for him to challenge Muldoon.

Second, Barry Gustafson's account[7] puts the committed vote for Talboys at only twenty-six in a caucus of fifty MPs (though anecdotes at the time suggested it was higher, no one suggested it was a large majority). A realistic challenge usually requires a higher margin to accommodate some erosion of support.[8] Muldoon was both adept and ruthless at the numbers game. He would have applied pressure to the less committed Talboys backers and appealed to his supporters outside parliament and in the wider public to add pressure—as in fact he did, both before and after he returned from overseas, even though by then the coup was crumbling. Muldoon campaigned both privately among MPs (drawing on loyal ministers such as Duncan MacIntyre, who became deputy prime minister in Talboys's place four months later, to reinforce his message) and publicly, through a television interview in which he portrayed himself as in charge and unfairly criticised.

It is also important to consider how Muldoon would have conducted himself if he had been ejected from the leadership. After he was ousted as leader of the opposition by 'colonel' Jim McLay in late 1984 following National's defeat at the July 'snap' election, he waged war on McLay from the back benches and was partly instrumental in McLay's own ouster in March 1986 by Jim Bolger. If Talboys had ousted Muldoon in 1980 Muldoon would likely have refused a cabinet post and gone glowering to the back benches, from whence he would have offered highly reportable observations on Talboys's policies and provided a rallying point for dissidents. Even if he had not overtly criticised the Talboys leadership, he would not have supported it and that would have counted with the electorate, which habitually punishes disunity.

Muldoon's departure would have disappointed his 'ordinary bloke' constituency. Talboys, relatively liberal (judged by the standards of the day and the fact that he was in a conservative party), was not their sort of man, although Talboys might have held some of the liberal vote which was deserting National in reaction to the 'Rob's mob' phenomenon. Lacking Muldoon's strong man populism, Talboys would have lost 'Rob's mob' and in a close election—as 1981 was—that would almost certainly have been enough to cost National the election.

Most notably, Talboys would not have emulated Muldoon's tough stance on the tour by the South African Springbok rugby team in the winter of 1981. Though he would have allowed the tour to proceed—with Muldoon in power he had defended that course—it is doubtful that he would have done as Muldoon did, insisting that the tour continue against police advice after protesters had invaded the pitch, forcing the abandonment of the first game in Hamilton. This jut-jawed decision by Muldoon pitched two squads of riot police against protesters twice a week in ugly scenes throughout the winter. The tour and the civil unrest split families and friends and heightened racial tension: many Maori interpreted the tour and the government's defence of it as implicit endorsement of apartheid and therefore as disrespectful to Maori or worse. Muldoon played the strong leader on the side of the rugby-loving 'ordinary bloke' and against intellectuals and liberals. It may have been a significant factor in Muldoon's narrow win in the 1981 election.

Indeed, the logic of Muldoon's personality, coupled with resentment at Talboys for supplanting him, suggests that he would have constantly and vociferously urged a tough stance towards the tour from the back benches. That would have won him kudos with rugby lovers and might well have convinced many in the National Party that he could have won the 1981 election when Talboys couldn't.

Talboys also would not have been able to emulate Muldoon's other main election gambit as the mastermind and architect of recovery. Muldoon backed Bill Birch's 'think big' programme of heavy industrial investment, which involved the state in expensive guarantees, subsidies or investment in projects to expand the New Zealand Steel plant, build a natural gas-to-gasoline plant at New Plymouth, electrify the North Island main trunk railway line, and construct a new aluminium smelter at Aramoana at the Otago Harbour heads. While few actually voted on 'think big' in the election, it absorbed much of the campaigning focus and so veiled the message of the opposition parties.

So Talboys would almost certainly have lost the 1981 election.[9] His leadership would not have long survived that defeat. Would one of the coup 'colonels' (Jim Bolger, George Gair, Jim McLay and Derek Quigley) have succeeded? Or would Muldoon have been able to cast himself as the leader who would have won the election, thus reclaiming the leadership?

If the first, we return to the short scenario given at the outset of this chapter: a Rowling-led Labour government struggling with an unruly economy against a National Party arguing for more-market economic policies as a way out of the difficulties and gathering widening support from influential interest groups arguing the same cause. National would also have been willing and able to promote younger MPs to senior roles. The party would not have faced (as it did in actual history) a Bob Jones-led New Zealand Party promoting market-liberal polices, gathering up voters exasperated with Muldoon's economic controls; instead those forces would have been largely contained within its own ranks and on its voting ledger.

A Labour win in 1981 would have brought the party into office without its having completed its own transition from the Rowling generation to the younger breed of politician, increasingly open to market thinking. Making deep transitions of that sort while in office is seldom possible. Given the personalities involved and the bad chemistry between Rowling and David Lange, Labour's deputy leader since November 1979, trying to do so would have generated considerable tension and hamstrung the government.

National would have been well placed to win the 1984 election, provided that Muldoon—who would most certainly not have retired from parliament—didn't get in the way. But that is a very large proviso and would have depended on somehow managing to find a front-bench role for Muldoon that was not in economic policy and to which he would cheerfully consent. This would have required him to play second or third fiddle to the very people who had deposed him in 1980 and is well nigh inconceivable.

In fact quite the opposite is the case: Muldoon would have coveted and actively sought the leadership after the 1981 defeat.[10] Probably he would have regained it, for the reasons given above. Once back in the saddle, Muldoon would have considered that he had a new personal mandate, which would in his mind have doubled as vindication of his pre-1980 leadership style and policies. He would have felt a debt to 'Rob's mob' which, if he remained true to his earlier convictions, he would have interpreted in terms of economic security and social and cultural conservatism. On this reading, a post-1984 Muldoon government would have picked up where it left off in 1980, with the late 1980s a time of policy paralysis.

But would it have? There are two alternative scenarios: first, that Rowling's economic management might have eased some of the pressures Muldoon failed to address or alleviate, leaving Labour in power in 1984; or second, that Muldoon might have begun to edge down a market-liberal route.

Rowling in power . . .

Following the 1981 election Muldoon became more rigid: more autocratic, more 'personal' in his rule, more confirmed in his prejudices, and less open to alternative policy options, particularly on economic management issues. In 1982 he imposed his 'freeze', with its extraordinary controls on wages, prices, rents, interest rates and even directors' fees. The result was to greatly worsen the fiscal, currency and balance of payments distortions in the New Zealand economy, brought about by a one-third fall in the terms of trade between the mid-1960s and mid-1970s. He bequeathed to his successor an economy in near crisis which left the Lange–Douglas government with no option but to liberalise (though, of course, there were options about how fast, how broadly, and how deeply to move). Muldoon's course post-1981 was to drive harder and more blindly up a cul de sac.

A Rowling cabinet between 1981 and 1984 would have been unlikely to have gone all the way up that path. Rowling himself and his contemporaries (such as Bob Tizard, who had been deputy prime minister and finance minister in 1974–75 when Rowling was prime minister) were orthodox in their approach to economic policy, so it is a fair bet that they would have set the tone. They almost certainly would have continued to borrow and run fiscal deficits. But a Rowling cabinet would likely have heeded the Treasury urgings not to impose a Muldoon-style freeze. It would likely have devalued the currency. Moreover, it is just possible that Rowling would have moved somewhat down a market-liberal route, thus easing some of the distortions that Muldoon compounded, in which case the mid-1984 financial–currency crisis would not have developed.

Might this have been enough to head off National in 1984, whether led by Muldoon or by one of the 'colonels'? Probably not, for two reasons. First, as noted, there were tensions in a Labour Party in transition, with a sizeable proportion of the caucus having at best limited faith in Rowling. He had nearly been ousted by Lange, virtually a parliamentary novice, in December 1980. The second reason lies in the social–liberal and Treaty of Waitangi agendas a Rowling cabinet would likely have followed. Rowling himself was relatively conservative on those matters: his demotion of Labour MP Matiu Rata in late 1979 led to the formation of the Mana Motuhake Party which challenged Labour for its hitherto secure Maori vote; and he was ill at ease with the rising feminist tide within his party, as evidenced in a vigorous women's council, and the emergence of the likes of Ann Hercus, Helen Clark and Margaret Wilson close to the apex of the party council, with Hercus and Clark entering parliament in 1978 and 1981 respectively. Nevertheless, Rowling's cabinet would have made some concessions to those rising forces. Muldoon would have exploited this on the hustings as un-Kiwi, rallying conservatives. There was also a strong peace agenda which would have led a willing Rowling to a nuclear ships ban. And Rowling would have kept New Zealand out of the Falklands war. Muldoon, who by contrast offered a frigate to Britain, would have attacked that, too, again with effect among conservatives. A voting majority for a more independent foreign policy, and an antinuclear stance that would separate New Zealand from its traditional allies, did not emerge until the late 1980s, when a Labour government with a large majority in parliament had long enough in office to build a majority around those ideas through firm leadership and voters' habituation to them as a new status quo. In 1984, however, Muldoon would have been able to cast himself as the champion of the 'ordinary bloke', the firm hand at the economic rudder ripped untimely away by treasonous National liberals in 1980. This would have had strong appeal in a time of continuing economic uncertainty and disorienting social change.

We can probably say with reasonable confidence therefore that there would have been a National government post-1984 and that, on balance, it would probably have been led by Muldoon. But would it have been a Muldoon less rigidly opposed to economic and social liberalisation?

This brings us to the second alternative scenario to a business-as-usual command-economy Muldoon.

A *new Muldoon* . . .

In opposition, National MPs would have been unconstrained by the disciplines of government which conspire to constrain MPs and ministers from expressing dissent or challenging the autocrat. So the market-liberals in the caucus, who after 1981 would have been a majority (at least in respect of the milder forms of market-liberalism), would have wanted a commitment to market-liberalisation in economic policy.

It is just possible that Muldoon might have gone along with that, though, if so, only up to a point well short of the Treasury prescription. As prime minister and minister of finance after 1975 Muldoon did initiate or permit some mild deregulation of the financial, meat processing and transport industries, and in the 1979 budget he instituted a process of industry reviews predicated on reducing protection for intermediate goods over time. All this was tentative and hesitant, but it did set some sort of precedent. Moreover, a Talboys cabinet in 1981 would likely have taken a mildly liberalising economic policy line: the four 'colonels', one of whom would most likely have been finance minister, were all either market-liberals or at least less command-economy minded than Muldoon, and would have insisted on a more-market line consistent with the Treasury's insistent advice. So it is just possible that, with a strengthening market-liberal sentiment post-1981 on his front and back benches, Muldoon might in opposition between 1981 and 1984 have developed a greater willingness to go some way down that route.

In any case, it is highly likely that part of the price extracted by MPs for Muldoon's return to the leadership post-1981 would have been his agreement to appoint someone else as shadow finance minister in opposition—his dual command of the leadership and the Treasury had been a focal point of criticisms at the time of the abortive 1980 coup. Almost anyone who would have been acceptable to the caucus in that role would have been to some extent—and possibly to a considerable extent—open to market-liberal ideas and policies. Moreover, Muldoon's older supporters were retiring and being replaced by market-liberals: Jim McLay replaced MacIntyre as deputy prime minister in March 1984.

Finally, while the top leadership of a 1981–84 Rowling cabinet would have been orthodox in economic management, the cabinet would also have included some of the younger MPs (such as David Caygill and Geoffrey Palmer) who had entered parliament in 1978–79 and who were less locked into the traditional Labour mould of economic thinking—Palmer had done some economics while studying at Chicago University, for example, and thus been influenced by the promarket thinking there (later, as deputy prime minister, he was to describe the market reforms as 'orthodox'). What role Roger Douglas would have played in a 1981–84 Rowling cabinet is uncertain, since he and Rowling did not get on. But to the extent that Douglas did play a role, he too would have been one of the liberalisers, though not the radical in 1981 that he was to become post-1984. Thus there may well have been some modest economic liberalisation between 1981 and 1984, though it is hard to see much headway being made by a Rowling Labour government on achieving fiscal balance.

In summary, between 1980 and 1984—first under a Talboys cabinet in 1981, and then subsequently under a Rowling cabinet from 1981–84—there would have been some deregulatory momentum, and some scope and precedent for at least a mildly deregulatory policy line after 1984, even under a Muldoon-led regime. Were Muldoon to resist deregulation too strenuously, or to relapse into his old command-economy ways, the progressive market-liberalisation of the National caucus—and, after 1983, the spectacle of a deregulatory Labor government in Australia—might well have ignited new inclinations in National to replace him: having ousted him once, the 'colonels' would surely have been prepared to do so again. It bears remembering, too, that Muldoon's health was deteriorating in 1984 under the impact of alcohol and diabetes, and it is unlikely that he would have been able to exert the same iron control over his ministers and MPs as he managed while in power between 1981 and 1984. That constellation of factors would either have kept pushing Muldoon down the market-liberal route or encouraged an alternative prime minister to go there.

It is safe to conclude that there would have been economic liberalisation by a post-1984 National government, whether under Muldoon or under alternative management. Much the same goes for a post-1984 Labour cabinet, as the younger MPs gained more weight in the cabinet (with Rowling or, if he resisted, without him—he had, after all, only survived the December 1980 challenge by a single vote). Would that liberalisation also at some point have turned radical, as it did under Labour in 1984? Both Douglas and Ruth Richardson, who continued Douglas's radical reforms after 1990 in a National cabinet, were present in the two caucuses. The New Zealand Treasury was arguing for radical reform and there would still have been considerable and intense balance of payments and fiscal pressures. That might conceivably have led to a convulsion, resulting in Douglas or Richardson generating a burst of radical initiatives. But the odds are that reform would have fallen short of that. The particular circumstances of July 1984 are unlikely to have arisen under any of the alternative scenarios.

This gentler pace of liberalisation would also have yielded a gentler pace of improvement in economic performance. Productivity growth doubled in the 1990s compared with the preceding two decades. For all the disruption of the late 1980s and early 1990s, there was a payoff a decade later in a much more flexible, resilient and responsive economy which in the 2000s has delivered more to households than the unreconstructed economy would have. That payoff would have been delayed or attenuated by a gentler pace of economic reform.

And had it been the National Party carrying out the reforms post-1984, major-party politics would have been different. The Labour Party would have criticised the market-liberal reforms and would only gradually have come around to accept them. That is, it would have reached its present free-trade, moderately market-liberal position by a very different route, which might have influenced the composition of the leadership and the party caucus in the interim. Speculation on that, however, is for a different 'what if'.

Equally, it is beyond the scope of this 'what if' to inquire whether the country would have adopted the MMP proportional representation voting system. The predominant force behind that change was a strong sense of betrayal among previously loyal supporters of both major parties. Even so, however, the change was by a slender majority: 54 per cent to 46 per cent. It is possible to argue that the fraying of the combined major-party vote from an average of 92 per cent between 1949 and 1969 to 82 per cent from 1972–93 was symptomatic of deep changes in New Zealand society, developments which could not be reflected adequately in a two-party system and which would have led eventually to a change in the voting system. But it may well have taken much longer for that to occur.

Counterfactual contexts

There is a critical contextual factor for this 'what if' scenario.

The economic liberalisation was not an aberration by a few individuals, as many felt at the time. It occurred in the context of the globalisation of information and finance, which made it difficult to run 1970's orthodox economic policies, and in the context of the rise of an economic ideology predicated on open markets. There was also a severe terms of trade decline which required a deep adjustment response. Muldoon stood against all this like a latter-day and unwise Canute bidding the waves to recede. He was obstinate and mistaken, and that created the conditions for the particular configuration of the post-1984 economic reforms. But those reforms, or something like them, were bound to occur eventually.

Three other contexts need to be noted as well.

The first is the profound change within Maoridom. By the mid-1980s the Maori claim for indigenous status, redress of past injustices and a recognised place in the power structure was not the minority radicalism Muldoon dismissed it as but rather a powerful new social force. The post-1984 Labour government gave unwitting impetus to that force with the Treaty of Waitangi Amendment Act, the State-owned Enterprises Act and a number of other initiatives. But a National government would have had to make substantial changes, too, if it was not to intensify the civil unrest that had emerged in the late 1970s. One way or another, the Maori 'reindigenisation' could not have been denied. By the 1980s the demographics were making that clear.

The second is generational change. The generation that came to adulthood in the 1960s, began to influence the arts in the 1970s and took power in business and politics in the 1980s was the antithesis of the social and cultural conservatism of its parents' generation. It was more educated, economically secure and self-obsessed. This was a liberalising generation, and it was profoundly changing the mores and ethos of society even while Muldoon was hell-bent on freezing his own generation's mores in place. Homosexual law reform (to take one indicative legislative change) was bound to happen sometime. New Zealand society was changing profoundly and it was inevitable that profound changes would take place in the country's politics. If National wanted to run governments in the 1990s, it was going to have to liberalise on those issues.

The third grows out of the second: the new generation was in a sense an 'indigenous' generation. It did not need to distinguish itself from Britain; it was unselfconsciously New Zealand. That came through in an unprecedented outpouring of novels, plays, films, music and art—in popular culture as well as high culture. New Zealand had found a voice. It had decolonialised in mentality as well as in constitutional fact. This amounted to an 'independence revolution'.

Conclusion

In revolutionary times, events conspire to bring about a revolution. Talboys might have said 'yes' when offered the chance to lead New Zealand. He might have been prime minister. There might have been a failed Labour government between 1981 and 1984. There might have been a moderately reforming National government after 1984 instead of a radical Labour one. But would we, today, be in a greatly different policy environment, twenty-five years on? I think not.

I think the Talboys 'what if' scenarios indicate that while underlying forces shape events in the longer term, forceful individuals—and Muldoon was certainly one of those—can and do shape the course of events in the shorter term, delaying, detouring or quickening the pace of events. Muldoon hovers over all the scenarios. In actual history his descent into a sort of *götterdämerung* in his last term in office set up special conditions to which an incoming government of new-generation ministers reacted with zeal and urgency. If Muldoon had not done that, then even with the same players at the core of the post-1984 Labour government the pace of change might have been less immodest.

Of course, that says nothing about the future. After a revolution there is usually a consolidation (if there is no counter-revolution). We may be coming to the end of the Maori reindigenisation, and the social and moral liberalisation, and in due course a new government may bring about a rebalancing of those policy settings, as there has been under the present government of economic policy settings. But when, and how, and by whom this will occur is an altogether different 'what if' sequence of events on which to speculate.

12

What if the All Blacks had not won the final rugby test against the Springboks in 1981?

Bob Gregory

There was a young man named Hewson
Who ensured the Springboks were losin'
Though his kick did the trick and flew through the sticks
It scored three more years of Muldoonism.

In 1976 the All Blacks had lost the series against the Springboks in South Africa, three tests to one. New Zealand rugby followers were eager for payback in 1981 against the country's traditional and most respected rugby foe.[1] The 1981 tour of New Zealand by the Springboks gave rise to some of the strongest political protest movements, and most violent street conflict, ever seen in New Zealand. Prime Minister Rob Muldoon and his government effectively allowed the tour to go ahead, arguing that it was a matter for the New Zealand Rugby Football Union to determine. The Labour Party opposition appeared to be equivocal on the issue.

The opening match of the tour, at Gisborne, was marked by vigorous protest action. The second game, in Hamilton, had to be abandoned before it even started, after a large group of protesters had gained access to the playing field. The first test, in Christchurch, was won by the All Blacks, fourteen–nine, but then in Wellington the Springboks turned the tables in the second test, twenty-four–twelve. In the closing minutes of the third and final test, in Auckland on 12 September, the score was level at twenty-two all, when the Welsh referee, Clive Norling, awarded the All Blacks a penalty about forty-five metres from the Springboks' goalposts.[2] Allan Hewson, the All Black fullback, kicked the goal, and shortly afterwards the All Blacks had won the match, twenty-five–twenty-two, and the series, two–one.[3]

The general election was held on 28 November. The result: National forty-seven seats, Labour forty-three, Social Credit two—total ninety-two.[4] From a landslide fifty-five–thirty-two seat win in 1975, and a fifty-one–forty-one seat win in 1978, the National Party—following the appointment of one of its members as speaker—now had a mere one-seat majority in parliament.

What if Allan Hewson's final penalty kick in 1981 had missed?

How the flight of a rugby ball changed the fate of a nation

Hewson's kick swings just outside the upright and referee Norling blows the final whistle. The match is a twenty-two all draw and the test series is also drawn. New Zealand rugby supporters are deflated. Many of them assuage their frustration in the belief that the difficult conditions created by the protest movement have been a principal reason for this failure. Although most of them, and especially those living in provincial New Zealand, have enthusiastically hailed Rob Muldoon's decision not to intervene to stop the tour, they have not received the prize they had most fervently hoped for—a series revenge over the old foe. Had the All Blacks won the series they would have enthusiastically endorsed National candidates at the forthcoming general election. Now frustrated, a significant number are insufficiently motivated to vote at all. In the minds of many of them there now lurk doubts about whether the tour had actually been worth it, in light of all the mayhem and violence on the streets, and the social division.

Consequently, the 1981 general election sees the end of Rob Muldoon's two-term government. The Labour Party wins forty-six seats, National forty-four seats, and Social Credit two. Labour wins the seats of Taupo, Eden, and Gisborne by narrow margins.[5] With one of its members—Jonathan Hunt—elected by the house as its speaker, the government is reliant upon the two Social Credit MPs, Bruce Beetham and Gary Knapp, to support it on votes of confidence and supply. Bill Rowling is now prime minister, with Bob Tizard the minister of finance. They keep on with 'think big', the Muldoon government's industrial development projects, because of the funds already sunk into them. But there is no price and wage freeze (as instigated by Muldoon in 1982). Rowling and Tizard pursue largely orthodox economic management based on Keynesian assumptions. However, inflation continues to rise, along with interest rates and unemployment. After two years in office the Labour government's poll ratings are dropping badly.

Party discipline in the house holds firm during the government's three-year term, while MPs Beetham and Knapp bask in relentless media attention, only once threatening to abstain on a confidence vote, but at the last minute not following through with their threat.

Midway through the third year there erupts into full public view a Lange/Douglas versus Rowling/Tizard split in the Labour Party. With an eye to his own political future, party president Jim Anderton backs Rowling/Tizard. However, the Lange/Douglas challenge succeeds and Lange replaces Rowling as prime minister with Douglas as his deputy. The open and unseemly leadership struggle proves to be the final nail in the government's electoral coffin. The 1984 election is held, as scheduled, in November, and Labour is ousted. Neither Rowling nor Tizard have stood for re-election.

Early in 1985 Jim Anderton becomes the new leader of the Labour Party in opposition, having entered parliament at the 1984 election. Lange resigns from parliament mid-term, with Labour retaining his Mangere seat in the subsequent by-election. He returns to Mangere to resume his law practice. Douglas does not stand at the 1987 election. Instead, he becomes an unsuccessful pig farmer, subsequently writing his second book, this time entitled *There's got to be a better Whey.*

Meanwhile, early in 1982, following National's defeat at the polls, Muldoon has been replaced as opposition leader by Jim McLay. McLay thus becomes prime minister in 1984, with Bill Birch as minister of finance. (There is no economic or constitutional crisis.) The ANZUS treaty remains intact. Birch is wary of the radical economic advice being offered by Treasury and the Reserve Bank. He prefers more orthodox economic policies, along with a pragmatic 'modernising' of the public service and cuts in government spending. Industrial troubles develop, led by 'Red Ken' Douglas, president of the Federation of Labour. McLay is consistently portrayed by Labour as weak and indecisive, while Muldoon undermines his leadership from within the National Party caucus.

Although its impact on New Zealand investors is only

moderate, the international stock market crash in October 1987—just one month before the election—plays into the opposition's hands. Labour wins with a three-seat majority. Jim Anderton is now prime minister, with Helen Clark as minister of finance and Richard Prebble as minister of labour. Winston Peters succeeds McLay as opposition leader.

Just as Richard Nixon could open relations with China because he was known to be anticommunist, so too are Anderton and Clark able to introduce decidedly neoliberal economic policies, including deregulation of the economy and the phasing out of farming subsidies. Standing together, 'a job lot', they preach the same message: 'there is no alternative'. Graham Scott is now secretary to the Treasury. However, his advocacy of privatisation of state-owned utilities is not accepted by the government. A policy and personal schism develops between Clark and Scott, who resigns to stand at the 1990 election as a member of the New Zealand Party, a right-wing grouping formed and led by New Zealand businessman Robert Jones.

In 1990 the Anderton Labour government narrowly wins a second term, and Peters is replaced as leader of the National Party by Jim Bolger. On the back benches Peters attacks both opposition and government colleagues alike, earning for himself the sobriquet, 'the whine box'. He later resigns from parliament, so as to force a by-election and embarrass the government. Subsequently he takes up a position with a large Wellington law firm. Late at nights, often in a restaurant known as the Green Parrot, he muses over the prospect, unlikely though it seems, of one day returning to the political scene and becoming the country's minister of foreign affairs.

Following the 1990 election Clark becomes deputy prime minister. The election sees the New Zealand Party win 20 per cent of the vote, but no seats in the house. There are growing calls for the introduction of proportional representation, which are vigorously resisted by the Anderton-led Labour government.

National wins the 1993 election, and this time the New Zealand Party wins 25 per cent of the vote, but only one parliamentary seat (Robert Jones, who gave his opponent a thumping in the Turangi seat). The move for proportional representation now becomes unstoppable. At the first MMP election, in 1996, a minority coalition of National/New Zealand comes to office, led by Bolger, with Robert Jones as deputy prime minister.

At this juncture the elastic band of credulity is stretched to snapping point.

But seriously though . . .

Careful 'what if' thinking can help us develop a better sense of the relationships among (sometimes seemingly unconnected) significant variables. In doing so it is possible to distinguish between what we might call 'micro' and 'macro' events, on the one hand, and 'ripple' or 'tsunami' consequences, on the other (see figure 12.1).

Obviously, one person's 'micro' event may be another's 'macro', just as one's 'ripple' is another's 'tsunami', and there will be a vast grey area in between the polarities. Notwithstanding this, such a rudimentary matrix alerts us to the fact that contingency in human affairs is all pervasive, usually unpredictable, and often unknowable. On top of this, it may be a function of agency or structure, or both, meaning that the relatively small acts of individuals may be as decisive, or more so, than the effects of collectively defined social and other structures. And the consequences may be apparent immediately or become manifest over time, a crucial third dimension that could be built into figure 12.1.

Figure 12.1: Events and consequences

| | | Consequences | |
		Ripple	Tsunami
Events	Micro	x	Hewson's kick
	Macro	x	x

This is not the place to get bogged down in heady arguments about voluntaristic and deterministic interpretations of social change, so we may simply say that when Allan Hewson stepped up to kick that goal he did not and could not have realised what he was about to do. His act of individual agency, itself occurring within an immediate social structure of a sporting contest, had a major—if not tsunami-like—impact on wider political, economic and social structures.

The argument presented here is based on beliefs rather than hard evidence. (So, too, is most public policy, but that's another story.) The belief is that there is a relationship—if only we knew what it was—between some occasions of national sporting success and political behaviour, including voting. We might know just a little more if some serious research were to be devoted to seeing if there are any credible correlations to be found.

There is a certain symmetry about the 1981 rugby test series and that year's election, to the extent that both were knife-edged contests. The operating thesis here is that a drawn series would have been just enough to see the advent of a fourth Labour government. Had the All Blacks lost the series then perhaps Labour would have won convincingly.

We will never know. But what, if any, prima facie evidence exists of a relationship between elite sporting success and electoral outcomes? Because we are talking here of the 1981 Springbok tour of New Zealand, we could start by looking at what happened electorally in those years in which South Africa and New Zealand clashed on the rugby field. In 1937 the Boks toured New Zealand, winning the series two–one. The following year the first Labour government was returned to office by a resounding majority. In 1949 the All Blacks lost their series four–nil in South Africa. The first Labour government was soundly defeated by National in the subsequent election. Seven years later the All Blacks beat the South Africans in New Zealand three–one, in an epic test series which transfixed virtually the whole of the nation.[6] Yet the following year the National government was defeated by the Labour Party, led by Walter Nash. In 1960 the All Blacks toured South Africa, losing the test series two–one, with one test drawn. Later that year the Nash government was defeated at the election, and Keith Holyoake began his twelve-year incumbency as prime minister. During this period, in 1965, New Zealand hosted the Springboks, who were beaten one–three by the All Blacks, while five years later the tables were reversed, by the same margin, in South Africa. Two years passed until National lost office in 1972 to Norman Kirk's Labour Party. Then, in 1976, a year after Robert Muldoon had become prime minister, and two years before the next election, the All Blacks toured the republic, losing one–three. Muldoon won again in 1978, albeit with a much reduced majority.

There is little if any pattern in all of this, and even if there were it could easily be dismissed as specious and simplistic. Finding a way to assess the impact of any vague nationalistic 'feel good' element in determining the outcome of elections, as against more obvious and immediate political and economic factors, would tax the ingenuity of the most determined social scientist.

When one looks beyond All Black–Springbok encounters on the rugby field to links between other major instances of national sporting glory, including rugby, and political and electoral behaviour, the picture is no less ambiguous. In 1995 the All Blacks just failed to win the Rugby World Cup (losing the final in extra time to the South Africans) but the country celebrated Team New Zealand's historic winning of the America's Cup. Yet the following year's general election could well have resulted in the demise of Jim Bolger's prime ministership had it not been for the advent of MMP. In 2005, the All Blacks swept to a three–nil test series victory over the British and Irish Lions, won the Tri-Nations series (against South Africa and Australia), and retained the Bledisloe Cup against Australia. Yet in the weeks leading up to the election on 17 September the polls showed declining support for the Labour Party in the face of a strong challenge from National to replace it as the leading party in the next coalition government. So much for the elusive 'feel good' factor that could have been expected to boost the Labour Party's chances of remaining leader of the new government.

In the event, however, Labour has ended up doing just that, so perhaps the flush of rugby success was sufficient to carry it through? And if the National Party had ended up having the most seats in parliament we might then have concluded that a mood of national euphoria can mean that large—decisive—numbers of voters are emboldened to risk governmental change for the sake of change. Perhaps.

What we do know for sure is that many politicians believe there is a connection between elite sporting success and the electorate's political perceptions, and they act on those beliefs. A prime minister in New Zealand might even allow his or her drivers to shatter the speed limits on the road in order to get to an important rugby test match on time, even if that prime minister is not especially fond of the game.

Of course, public perceptions and assumptions can be fickle, and for a politician to be seen to be closely associated with a losing team may carry a political cost. For example, Prime Minister Helen Clark took considerable pains to front up personally in Dublin when the New Zealand Rugby Union (NZRU) made its final plea to delegates of the International Rugby Board (IRB) for the right to host the 2011 Rugby World Cup. In saying that it paid off handsomely for her we mean, of course, that she has derived significant political benefit, since the government fully backed the NZRU's successful bid. While she took a political risk in going to Dublin she also had little choice but to go. Had the bid been unsuccessful then by going she could not have been accused of not doing all she and the government could do to present the NZRU's case. The political impact would have been largely neutral. If she had not gone to Dublin and the bid had nevertheless been successful then she and her government could have expected some political kudos for fully backing it, but probably not as much as that derived from her presence in Dublin. The worst scenario for the prime minister would have been for her not to have gone to Dublin and for the IRB to have decided in favour of either South Africa or Japan (the other two contenders). This was just too great a political risk to take.

If the 2005 election had been held—as has often been the case—in late November, rather than in September—that is, just after the IRB had taken its vote, then the prime minister's political gamble would have been much more risky. The political impact of her decision would have been virtually immediate, and possibly decisive. As it is, the benefits are likely to be dissipated over time, as would have the costs, had other outcomes occurred.

It would seem that few analysts and commentators doubt that some sort of economic 'feel good' factor affects voting behaviour. Conventional wisdom has it that if the economy is doing well then voters feel more favourably towards incumbent governments (though it remains unclear as to whether voters are impelled by assessments of their own personal situation or of general economic conditions). By comparison, there is much more scepticism about the serendipity that ostensibly is aroused in the national psyche by elite sporting success. But if we do not—and perhaps cannot—know for sure what this general relationship is, if there is one, this does not mean that we cannot speculate more precisely about what the effects of a particular sporting moment might have been on a particular electoral contest. This is why those who wanted Bill Rowling to win in 1981 will argue that, indeed, Allan Hewson really does have a lot to answer for.

13

What if the fourth Labour government had allowed a visit by the USS *Buchanan*?

John Henderson

In February 1985 the newly elected fourth Labour government decided to reject a request from the United States government for a port visit by the USS Buchanan.[1] This is arguably the most significant single decision taken in New Zealand's foreign policy since World War II. Labour's policy of denying entry to nuclear-powered or nuclear-armed warships put it on a collision course with the US and jeopardised New Zealand's continued membership of the ANZUS alliance. The well-established US position was that its ships should be able to visit allied ports on the basis of 'neither confirming nor denying' the presence of nuclear weapons. The issue of nuclear propulsion could be determined by observation.

Labour's prime minister David Lange faced the difficult—if not impossible—task of keeping New Zealand within the ANZUS alliance while maintaining the ban on nuclear ship visits. The antinuclear policy had the strong support of mainstream New Zealand public opinion, based on both environmental and strategic considerations. The antinuclear stance also became bound up with a growing sense of New Zealand nationalism.

On the nuclear issue Lange had little political room to manoeuvre, as he discovered just two weeks after taking over the leadership of the Labour Party in 1981. In a speech at that time he suggested that there might be room for compromise with the US over the issue of nuclear propulsion. He expressed his own confidence in the safety record of the US navy, while reiterating his view that nuclear weapons should be kept out of New Zealand. But any suggestion of compromise brought forward howls of outrage from the Labour Party. Lange needed little convincing, and he did not pursue the proposal to separate the nuclear propulsion and weapons issues. Indeed, it was a lesson he never forgot. The nuclear issue lay at the core of Labour values and was not to be trifled with. If he was to remain party leader he realised that he must not deviate from the full implementation of the antinuclear policy.

Lange's position contrasted markedly with that of his Australian counterpart, Bob Hawke, who inherited a similar antinuclear policy from his Labor Party. But in Australia opposition to nuclear ship visits was largely restricted to the left faction of Labor. The *situation was very different in New Zealand, where there was widespread public support for the antinuclear stance—a point never appreciated by the US or Australian governments. The best evidence for the broad public acceptance of the antinuclear position was the failure of pro-US National Party governments to change the antinuclear policy when they had the opportunity.*

But Lange has confirmed that he did agree that the US should follow established procedures and submit its December requests for ship visits. He later admitted that he was 'naïve' not to have realised that the US would regard this as an indication that the requested port visits would be approved.

This is the background to the ill-fated US request for a visit by the USS Buchanan. Lange was visiting the New Zealand island dependency of Tokelau at the time and returned to receive a recommendation from his deputy prime minister, Geoffrey Palmer, that the US request be declined. Lange accepted the Palmer recommendation, which was endorsed by cabinet.

Negotiations on the port visit issue continued with the US after the rejection of the Buchanan. The US was unwilling to follow Lange's suggestion that it send an unambiguously non-nuclear ship (an FFG7 Frigate was suggested). In September 1985 Geoffrey Palmer unsuccessfully sought a resolution of the port visits issue at talks in Washington, DC. In June 1986 Lange held further talks with US Secretary of State George Shultz at the ASEAN meeting in Manila. Lange raised the possibility of resolving differences by following the precedent established for British naval visits to China. Under the 'China formula' each government would state that the naval visit was taking place in accordance with established policies. Neither would comment on the policies of the other. This would allow the US to restate its 'neither confirm nor deny' policy (which the UK also follows) and New Zealand to reaffirm its nuclear-free policy. New Zealand would have to accept nuclear-capable ships, but could make its own assessment of whether the US ships in question were nuclear armed. This would not entail searches, declarations, or questioning of crew. Nor would there be any public rejection of a US requested visit. But Shultz was not listening. He had made up his mind and declared to the waiting media: 'We part friends. But we part.' With this New Zealand's status changed from 'ally' to 'friend'.

Neither side changed its position. Lange argued that ANZUS was not a nuclear alliance and that New Zealand should be able to continue to meet its obligations to the Western alliance through non-nuclear means. The US position was that as an ally New Zealand should accept port visits on a 'neither confirm nor deny' basis. Even making its own determination of the nuclear status of a US ship was a violation of that policy by New Zealand. Bob Hawke's advice—'If you don't ask them you will probably be alright'— turned out not to be the case.

In February 1985 the Labour Party divided over the cabinet decision, announced by the acting prime minister, Geoffrey Palmer, that the government had agreed to a US request for a port visit by the USS *Buchanan*. The decision was announced by Palmer because Prime Minister David Lange's return from a visit to the isolated New Zealand territory of Tokelau had been delayed by bad weather. Palmer said that the government would consider requests from the US (and other nuclear powers) for ship visits on a case-by-case basis. New Zealand experts had determined that the *Buchanan*, an Adams class destroyer, was not nuclear powered, and that it was extremely unlikely that it was carrying nuclear weapons. This was because of the age and condition of the ship, and that it would be sailing directly to New Zealand from Japan. The US ambassador welcomed the decision as being in accord with what might be expected in terms of arrangements between close allies.

Labour Party hardliners and peace groups from the left attacked the decision. They claimed that Labour was opposed to visits of all nuclear-capable ships. In their view the *Buchanan* was clearly in this category. It was claimed that it could be carrying nuclear depth charges.

On his return from Tokelau, Lange initially refused to comment until he had been fully briefed. However, 'sources close to the PM' were reported to have told Radio New Zealand that Lange was not happy with Palmer's announcement. But the day after his return Lange publicly supported the decision to allow the visit— and pointed out that even the Cook Straight ferry was 'nuclear capable'.

At an acrimonious caucus meeting Lange was severely criticised for not giving stronger leadership on the issue. The opposition from Labour backbenchers was led by an MP first elected to the house in 1981, Helen Clark.

When the USS *Buchanan* visited Wellington it was met by massive protests. A number of Labour MPs joined the protests on land and on board the protest fleet. A new coalition of groups seeking to keep New Zealand nuclear free protested under the banner NFNZ (Nuclear-Free New Zealand). Environment groups were well represented in this antinuclear coalition. Public opinion polls showed a clear majority against the *Buchanan* visit. Polls also recorded a sharp dip in support for the Labour government and Lange's leadership ratings. One of the prime minister's speech writers, a young woman named Margaret Pope, who had written many of Lange's antinuclear speeches, resigned in protest from Lange's staff.

In the face of this storm of opposition, Lange agreed to review the policy to ensure all future ship visits were consistent with the spirit and letter of Labour's antinuclear policy. This caused alarm bells to ring at the US embassy. The ambassador sought a meeting with Lange, where he stressed the need for further ship visits to maintain the momentum of improving US–NZ relations created by the *Buchanan* visit. A follow-up visit should take place sometime in the next few months. The ambassador made it clear that the *Buchanan* visit alone was not enough to fully restore the health of the US–NZ relationship.

In September 1985 Lange despatched a negotiating team led by Palmer to Washington to discuss how requests for future ship visits should be handled. The US interagency group, led by Paul Wolfowitz and including Richard Armitage, insisted on discussing a schedule of visits that would include a number of 'ambiguous' ships—that is, ones that might well be nuclear armed—which would visit on a 'neither confirm nor deny' basis. During a meeting with Palmer, US Secretary of State George Shultz stressed that such visits were an essential part of being a US ally. He made it clear that over a period of time, New Zealand would have to assume that some of the US ships visiting New Zealand ports would be nuclear armed.

Palmer reported to Lange that there was no change in the US position, although they were prepared to allow a six to nine month 'cooling off' period before requesting a further visit. Lange told a press conference that the New Zealand policy remained unchanged, but that the US was welcome to request a further port visit. In November 1985 Lange faced a caucus revolt following his refusal to rule out media reports that a visit by a possibly nuclear-armed ship was imminent. The Labour caucus issued a strongly worded statement reaffirming its opposition to any visits by nuclear ships.

A further attempt to resolve the stand-off was made in June 1986 when Lange met with US Secretary of State George Shultz at an ASEAN meeting in Manila. Shultz repeated the lecture he had earlier delivered to Palmer on the obligations that went with being a US ally. Lange suggested that a resolution to the dispute could be to adopt the process followed by British naval visits to China—the so-called 'China formula'. This essentially involved visits on a 'no comment' basis, with each side simply confirming that the visit was in accord with established policies. Much to the surprise (and later consternation) of the Lange delegation, Shultz paused and responded: 'OK, it may be worth a try.' It was agreed that officials would work to provide a bit more substance to the proposal. Shultz ended the meeting, telling the waiting media that progress was being made on resolving differences and that he looked forward to the outcome of further talks.

What puzzled the Lange delegation was that Shultz and his advisers were clearly not surprised by the 'China formula' proposal. Although the New Zealand delegation rooms had been swept for 'bugs' (listening devices), somehow the US appeared to have gained advance notice of the proposal.

Lange had provided a diplomatic way forward for resolving differences with the US, but at the cost of creating severe domestic political problems for his leadership at home. The 'China formula' was a major concession for which Lange did not have prior agreement from either his cabinet or Labour's parliamentary caucus.

The New Zealand media contingent travelling with Lange had apparently been extensively briefed by US officials. Lange faced a barrage of hostile questioning. Headlines in New Zealand proclaimed: 'Lange backs down over nuclear ships'. He returned home to a groundswell of opposition demanding no compromises on the antinuclear policy. The 'China formula' was widely condemned as a convenient device to look the other way—to 'hear no evil, see no evil'.

The uproar led to Lange's continued leadership of the Labour Party being called into question. The Labour left—led by Helen Clark—had long been suspicious of the strength of Lange's commitment to the antinuclear policy. Most of the left had been strong supporters of Bill Rowling, the leader Lange had replaced. The hostility of the Labour left to Lange had greatly increased as a result of the 'Rogernomics' economic reforms. Disillusioned by both the 'China formula' compromise on nuclear ships and the government's economic policy, Jim Anderton split from the Labour caucus in July 1986 and formed a party that he chose to call 'New Labour'.

Those who had promoted Lange into the party leadership (the economic right faction—Roger Douglas, Richard Prebble, Michael Bassett and Mike Moore) were also increasingly unhappy with him. While the right were much more concerned with economic reform than foreign policy issues, they had welcomed the nuclear issue as a useful diversion for the party while the government pursued its 'Rogernomics' economic agenda. But with the Labour Party turning against its government over the nuclear issue, the economic reform programme also stalled. There seemed to be no common goals to hold Labour together. The process of government became paralysed in the face of divisions within both caucus and cabinet.

In February 1987 Lange lost office following a caucus leadership vote, coming in the wake of a further slump in Labour's poll ratings. Lange had put up only a half-hearted fight to hold on to the leadership. He seemed to have lost interest in the job. In the aftermath he was replaced by Palmer, who narrowly defeated Moore in the ensuing leadership contest. Lange announced that he would not be seeking re-election to parliament and hinted that he would like to be appointed high commissioner to India.

In the lead-up to the 1987 general election a realignment of New Zealand party politics took place. On the right, a number of Labour MP defectors (Douglas, Prebble, Bassett, Peter Neilson and Bill Jeffries) joined a new political grouping, the Liberal Party. It was made up mainly of ex-National MPs and was led by Derek Quigley. Roger Douglas was elected its deputy leader. The party was strongly pro-Rogernomics and mildly pro-ANZUS.

The left coalesced around Jim Anderton's New Labour Party. A rump of the Labour Party caucus continued on with Palmer as leader. Jim Bolger led what remained of the National Party caucus.

The new Liberal Party joined with the National Party to win a majority of seats in the 1987 election. Quigley became prime minister, with Roger Douglas his deputy and minister of finance. Other key appointments were Ruth Richardson (minister of economic development), Jim Bolger (foreign minister), Peter Dunne (minister of revenue) and Richard Prebble (minister of social welfare).

During the 1987–90 period the implementation of the 'Rogernomics/Ruthenasia' economic reforms proceeded at breakneck speed and with ever increased severity. The proposed antinuclear legislation was dropped and occasional US ship visits resumed on a 'neither confirm nor deny' basis. While they faced protests, most public anger and attention was directed to the radical 'new right' economic reforms.

In the 1990 election the Liberal government was soundly defeated by an electorate seeking relief from the severity of the economic restructuring. The new government was a centre-left Labour grouping led by Mike Moore, who had replaced Palmer as

Labour leader six months prior to the election. Moore's populist approach succeeded in rebuilding support for Labour and narrowly winning the 1990 election. Bolger also increased National's support by regrouping its traditional supporters. Neither leader favoured a proposal for a new electoral system (known as MMP) and the idea of electoral reform slipped quietly off the political agenda. The Liberals, increasingly seen as extremist, lost support, disappearing into political oblivion at the 1993 election. A Labour government was re-elected with Moore as leader.

Moore had long favoured the settling of the ANZUS dispute with the US. In 1991, following a visit to the White House, he announced a review of safety issues related to nuclear ship visits. While the review was underway the US did not request any further ship visits. On the basis of this review, and following victory in the 1993 election, Moore announced that US ship visits could resume, as the US government had announced publicly that its surface ships were no longer nuclear armed. This sparked a rift in the party, triggering the dramatic resignation of the foreign minister, Helen Clark. But a majority of the Labour caucus backed Moore, and the government went on to survive a no-confidence vote.

With Moore as prime minister, New Zealand made a substantial military commitment to the 1991 Gulf War and the 2001 Afghanistan conflict. In 2002 New Zealand joined the US, Britain and Australia in the invasion of Iraq. In a televised speech, Moore stressed the importance of the American alliance for ensuring New Zealand security. He also announced that New Zealand would remain on what he described as a 'high' terrorist alert for the foreseeable future.

14

What if Ruth Richardson had never delivered the 'mother of all budgets'?

Jon Johansson

I shall be telling this with a sigh
Somewhere ages and ages hence:
Two roads diverged in a wood, and I—
I took the one less traveled by,
And that has made all the difference.
                    Robert Frost, 'The Road Not Taken'

In July 1991 National's finance minister, Ruth Richardson, delivered what became known as the 'mother of all budgets'. Described by Colin James as 'Rogernomics-plus', Richardson took neoliberalism into social policy areas where even Douglas had feared to tread.[1] Major cuts to welfare benefits, changes to employment law, and new user-pays requirements in hospitals and schools were all announced. Shifting decision making dramatically back towards the individual, Richardson's budget proved a disastrous political document for the new Jim Bolger-led government. By August, only a month after Richardson delivered her budget, polls projected that National would be fortunate to hold twenty seats if an election were held (a projected loss of forty-five seats). Protests against the welfare cuts revealed widespread anger over the direction taken by the Bolger government and effigies of Richardson and welfare minister Jenny Shipley were burnt, for Bolger's government had been elected under a pledge to 'restore the decent society'.

Hampered by a still struggling, severely contracted economy, National limped back to power in 1993 with a mere one-seat majority (after enjoying its largest ever margin of victory in 1990). Importantly, 1993 also signalled the public's retribution for the concerted period of arrogant rule they had endured between 1984 and 1992. Given the opportunity to sanction political elites, the public, by a vote of 54 per cent for, and 46 per cent against, chose a new proportional election system (MMP) for the next election. With its vote only fractionally slipping in 1996, National managed to construct a coalition government with the newly formed NZ First Party, led by former National cabinet minister Winston Peters. Shipley deposed Bolger in late 1997, and New Zealand's first female prime minister then promptly lost the 1999 election, as

National continued to slide in voter support. Finally, in the 2002 election, National, now led by Bill English, suffered its electoral nadir as a political party, receiving a shocking and paltry 20.93 per cent of the vote. The National Party was in crisis.

Introduction

The question of what might have happened had Richardson not delivered her 'mother of all budgets' is one that I have dwelt on for a number of years, and one I alluded to during the 2002 election campaign when National's dramatic fall from grace gathered its tsunami force.[2] It is predicated on a number of premises, the major one being that Bolger made a dreadful failure of judgment upon taking office in 1990. After six years of large-scale policy volatility, further neoliberal reform carried out by Richardson (following Roger Douglas's template)—during a period when the country was yearning for consolidation, security and a pause from change—brought with it significant political costs, including a substantial decline in support for the National Party.

This chapter focuses exclusively on the political consequences of my counterfactual. My hypothesis is that the political costs of Richardson's 'mother of all budgets' were so great that popular support for National steadily eroded throughout the 1990s, culminating in the collapse of its vote in 2002.[3] The former 'natural party of government' had by 2002 become known for its continuing leadership instability, and by sharp divisions between its neoliberal/social conservative and more centrist and socially liberal rumps, resulting in disunity, confusing and often contradictory messages on policy, and equally confused political positioning as it struggled to resolve the residue of the Richardson era.

Colin James put National's conduct into context in 1993:

> For policy to be driven radically, in defiance to public opinion, by a tiny elite in *one* government was unusual. For the same thing to happen in *two* governments in a row is so rare as to defy the conventional wisdoms of democratic analysis.[4]

Figure 14.1: The decline in support for the National Party

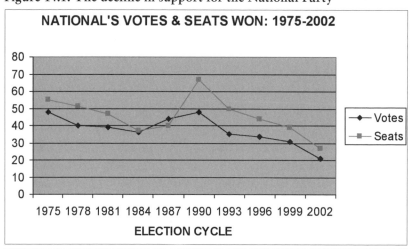

The 'mother of all budgets' was the tipping point for creating an enduring perception of National as a mean-spirited party, one that persisted throughout the 1990s, rightly or wrongly. Beneficiaries and workers, many of whom had already paid a significant price for being least able to adapt to the revolution's newly imposed burdens, then paid again as Richardson's benefit cuts and the Employment Contracts Act further eroded their sense of security. Voter support began a decline that culminated in National's disastrous 2002 election result, as depicted in figure 14.1.

By reneging on its promise to repeal Labour's superannuation surtax, and then taking the neoliberal revolution into social policy and labour markets, Bolger brought home to New Zealanders that successive governments could not be trusted to keep their promises. The result was to ensure majority public support for a change to a new electoral system, an outcome which became, in itself, the most significant unintended consequence of the entire Labour/National reform era.

Another consequence of the 'mother of all budgets' was to corrupt the language used during the neoliberal ascendency. This served to hamper successive National Party leaders' capacity to contest the battle of ideas, using language of their own choosing, because for the public terms like 'bulk funding', 'trickle down', and 'efficiency' were associated with negative feelings about the entire reform era.

Before developing my 'what if' scenario I have one or two general thoughts about counterfactual analysis as it pertains to this chapter.

Counterfactual analysis

'What if' questions are a fundamental part of our mental apparatus. They are like gatekeepers to the cognitive maps we all possess. As we walk down the street we are continually posing for ourselves 'what if' questions. Our next choice is frequently predicated on a 'what if' question as we subjectively calculate the costs and benefits of the next decision or non-decision that we take. Those choices, whether taken or not, form part of our shadow mental universe, but they also help to illuminate the choices we do make and form a backdrop to decisions reached, deferred and jettisoned. From an awareness about our internal thought processes we can, potentially, learn from our past actions and non-actions.

Counterfactuals thus help us to see, often in startlingly new detail, the essential forking points in our history, be it our personal history or indeed our perspectives on the far more impersonal and wider historical process. Although the standard objection to counterfactual analysis is that history should record what the evidence compels us to conclude actually happened,[5] by engaging in a thought experiment about how the future could have been different we gain new insights into decisions reached or consequences unfurled, for both good and ill. Another potential pitfall in counterfactual reasoning is to slip from asking 'what if' to pose the more problematic 'if only',[6] but there is more to counterfactual analysis than mere wishful thinking.

This last objection, however, is one that needs to be addressed in terms of this chapter, for in the counterfactual analysis provided below—where Prime Minister Bolger takes a dramatic decision to engineer Ruth Richardson's resignation, the consequence of which is to forever (and favourably) alter his political dynamic—it might be argued that Bolger's political situation and personality traits make such a decision highly unlikely. It is certainly true that in my counterfactual I allow Bolger to access the 'better angel of his nature'—perhaps even his 'best angel'—but I would argue that Bolger's innate pragmatism, canny political instincts and natural electoral insecurities would not rule out either of the two scenarios proposed, leaving readers to judge for themselves which scenario is the more likely, in keeping with Bolger's personality and its interaction with his political circumstances.

During the process of working out the political consequences of my counterfactual, it quickly became evident what other contributors to this book may have also experienced: namely, that multiple alternative futures can easily confound one's core analysis—and one's sense of equilibrium—because history's crucial forking points force us into several forced choices at different historical junctures. The longer the period of history encompassed by a counterfactual, the more such choices one must confront. In the end, a complex web of alternative futures complicates or confounds one's analysis. Rather than explore every branch of my counterfactual, I wanted, with this chapter, to quickly scale the treetop to reveal and enjoy the vista.

In my analysis the first and most significant point of departure concerns the question of whether a majority would have supported a change to the new MMP electoral system if Richardson's budget had not been delivered. On the face of it, one might conclude that, yes, MMP would still have been favoured by a majority of New Zealanders because deeper historical forces were at work, but the margin may have been much closer (51–49 per cent, perhaps), leading to a fresh set of complications for Bolger. Upon further reflection, however, I thought that attitudes towards electoral system change would depend upon the quality, nature and intensity of Bolger's repudiation of Richardson's intended budget—a *strong* or *weak* response. So, in order to simplify my counterfactual analysis rather than complicate it, what follows are two scenarios, one in which Bolger makes a strong stand against his own finance minister, and the other in which there is a weaker response from the prime minister.

Finally, my counterfactual analysis includes a significant narrative component that takes place between the chief protagonists. By providing a dialogue between Bolger, his chief lieutenant Bill Birch, and Richardson the aim is to help illuminate the behaviour and personalities of the major political actors in this drama, as well as the reasoning behind the decisions reached. While developing such a sustained narrative may not be the norm in counterfactual analysis, the temptation to do so was too alluring to resist.

Scenario One

Setting the scene: The genesis of a new history

It's late on the evening of 6 April 1991 and Prime Minister Jim Bolger is dining with his long time ally and friend, Bill Birch. The TV1/Heylen poll had, several hours earlier, delivered Bolger a sickening blow. National had dropped fourten points since December on the back of the public's negative response to its handling of the Bank of New Zealand crisis and the government's subsequent economic statement. The Labour Party led by Mike Moore, so recently discredited as the shambolic remnants of New Zealand's revolutionary government, was actually six points ahead of National.

Bolger, having just finished his entrée, downs his second large malt. 'That *expletive deleted* women is going to destroy me, Bill, if not before the budget then bloody well after it. You've seen what that woman wants to do!

'Honeymoon period, *expletive deleted*, this feels more like a bloody funeral—*mine!*

'I campaigned under the slogan of restoring a "decent society". Well it's not going to look very bloody decent when we take money from the poorest bloody people in the land, is it?

'It's not very bloody decent when we are breaking promises left right and centre, Bill.

'We have all these seats because we said we were going to restore legitimacy after Labour, not bloody piggyback their deceits. The surtax is killing us, Bill. The oldies will never forgive us. What Muldoon so generously gave we will be seen to be taking away.

'Bloody Ruth . . . bloody Treasury.'

Birch slowly contemplates his own whisky, then looks up at his old friend. 'Jim, Ruth is single-minded and focused. She's absolutely determined to get her and Treasury's way. She's an economic purist, an ideologue and she will never compromise, right?'

'Yeessss,' explodes Bolger, 'that's the *expletive deleted* problem, Bill. She thinks she's so bloody right—only *Ruth* knows the true path—yet we all know she's only a pale imitation of Douglas. The language is the same. The methods are exactly the same. Not an original thought there, mate.'

Bolger fumes on . . .

'All I hear from Ruth is that "There is No Alternative".

'"There is No Alternative". Of course there are bloody alternatives. There are *always* alternatives. She just refuses to discuss them, especially with me, Bill: thinks I'm a bloody plodder! *Expletive deleted*. Now I know how Lange felt about Douglas over the bloody flat tax.'

Jim pours another hefty tumbler. 'Anyway, Bill, what's your bloody point about Ruth?'

'Jim,' Birch says, 'don't you think it's about time we had a chat to Philip about the timing of his tariff reforms. He's been doing a really good job of getting caucus behind his far more *moderate* and *gradualist* approach. He has a lot of support in cabinet too. Perhaps, Jim, when you think about it, it wouldn't be very responsible of us, as a government, to sign off on the budget until cabinet has properly debated his *very* important proposals, which—upon greater reflection—I think are absolutely central to the way *you* want to present *your* government's budget.'

'She'll never go for it, Bill. She'd threaten to resign.'

'Mmmmm . . . well, she might,' replies Birch, raising an eyebrow.

Bolger looks up. 'Pour yourself another drink, Bill, then ring Philip.'

The Set-up

We are still on the ninth floor. It is the afternoon after cabinet approves Philip Burdon's gradual tariff reduction plan. All final budget decisions had been deferred until Burdon's (very late) plan had been debated and approved. To add insult to injury, Bolger told cabinet that he still wasn't happy on the tax front. He wanted Ruth and Wyatt Creech to work their way together through the details . . . however long it took.

Birch slaps his ashen-looking friend on the back. 'Well, Prime Minister, I did predict that Ruth would be enraged when Philip's plan was tabled so late. Didn't it work a treat!'

A furious Ruth Richardson had stormed out of cabinet, apoplectic in her rage: 'You just can't see it, Jim, can you! We really have *no alternative* but to tackle the deficit crisis! Our fiscal position demands it, the markets demand it, and Standard and Poor's were promised it.

'Health spending can't continue down this track, Jim! Welfare dependency must be tackled! You're *completely* undermining my ability to reduce the deficit! It's like a craw in the nation's throat, godammit!

'How can I deliver this government's budget when you have just signalled your lack of resolve to take the hard decisions? You have failed the leadership test, Prime Minister. You have also, in the process, completely undermined my credibility with the financial markets. My integrity is destroyed! This will not stand!'

With those words Richardson had slammed the door and left the cabinet room.

'Pour me a large malt, Bill,' pleads Bolger, who is wondering whether he has just given his ambitious colleagues—especially that infuriating Winston, or maybe even Burdon himself—the opening they've been looking for to shaft him.

Just then his chief of staff, Rob Eadie, enters the prime minister's office, grinning from ear to ear, holding a letter.

'Is that what I think it is?' inquires Bolger.

'Yes, Prime Minister', responds Eadie.

'Phone the Governor General, will you, Rob.'

The 'Avalon Address'

After publicly announcing his acceptance of his finance minister's resignation, Bolger avoids any further comment. He sits back and waits. Richardson's reaction, on the other hand, is very furious and very public. Still Bolger waits. Warren Berryman, of the *National Business Review*, castigates Bolger's failure of leadership:

> Institutional and overseas investors, business men and women up and down the country, and hard-working Kiwis everywhere are shocked at the prime minister's lack of staying power in the face of some difficult choices. There is no alternative to Ruth Richardson's courageous vision to end the good life for that lot of welfare bludgers and to transform our inefficient and decaying health system, through user pays, into the world-class system that is possible if greater market mechanisms are employed.

Still Bolger waits.

Fuming in public, Richardson signals her intention to undermine Bolger's leadership at every turn. Every news cycle has vivid images of yet another New Zealand government tearing itself apart. 'Why won't Bolger talk?' is the common refrain. Finally, the crescendo of vitriol against Bolger from Richardson's supporters meets with a response. It is three days since Richardson's resignation as minister of finance. Bolger chooses to address the nation directly in what our history now knows as the 'Avalon Address'. Public interest is intense as Bolger begins his speech. Is he going to resign? Will he reinstate Richardson? What *will* he say?

The time arrives and the prime minister appears on the nation's television screens. His address is brief and memorable.

> My fellow New Zealanders, tonight I want to address a real crisis in our country.
>
> This crisis is more serious than either the currency crisis that confronted my predecessors or the crisis that my government faced over the BNZ's imminent collapse.
>
> The crisis I want to address tonight is the crisis of confidence our people are feeling towards their government. New Zealanders

have quite rightly grown up with the belief that we will do what we say we're going to do, and if not, then we will explain ourselves. For six long years now we have failed you and tonight I pledge to all New Zealanders that the era of broken promises, of hidden agendas, of arrogant rule, is over. It ends tonight.

I utterly reject having my government driven by ideologues who know the value of nothing other than the purity of their imported theories. I completely reject these obsessed purists who put the balancing of the country's books ahead of balancing the nation's needs.

Fostering greater understanding between government and its people and restoring a social cohesion that has stretched beyond breaking point is my responsibility and tonight I exercise it. No ifs, no buts, no maybes. I resolve to do better in explaining the nature of the choices we face as a people. I will either bring you into my confidence or I will step down. That is my commitment to you here tonight.

The road ahead will prove a difficult one. We are in recession and our economy is not yet strong enough to provide jobs and security for all our people. But we *will* get there . . . together.

The reaction

Bolger's dramatic speech initially meets with shock, profound amazement, and, in some quarters, outright disbelief, but as its import slowly begins to penetrate the wider electorate, a huge wave of public support surges behind Bolger's call for greater integrity in government and a period of consolidation. Harsh criticisms coming from the business sector are drowned out by the surge of goodwill extended towards Bolger. Letters to the editor support Bolger's reading of the public mood by fifty to one. Astute *Listener* columnist Jane Clifton notes that by some form of cosmic coincidence the 'Avalon Address' was only 272 words long, exactly the same length as Lincoln's Gettysburg Address, concluding, 'Bolger's task was conceivably even more difficult than Lincoln's, for "Honest Abe's" opponent was General Lee, not a bucolic Sherman tank that goes by the name of Ruth.'

Such is the impact of the prime minister's inspirational address that despite a still sluggish economy, the National Party quickly recovers, and then flourishes in the polls. For the first time ever Bolger out-polls Winston Peters as preferred prime minister. The Richardson faction, in the wake of so much public support for Bolger, loses its power. Bolger is secure. Richardson resigns from parliament, forcing a by-election. The good people of Selwyn elect high-flyer David Carter as her replacement. Richardson enters the world of business, winning lucrative consulting contracts overseas. She later writes a book, chronicling her career. Originally planning to call it *Making a Difference*, she never falls free of her bitter resentment over her brief stint as finance minister. In the end it goes to the shelves as *It Makes No Difference*.

Through one dramatic moment of towering rhetorical splendour, Jim Bolger secures his leadership for as long as he wants to keep it. Even Winston Peters, Bolger's archrival, is forced to admit that the wily MP for King Country has outfoxed him. Peters abandons thoughts of setting up his own political party, at least for the moment.

In the 1993 election, National soundly defeats a Labour Party still struggling to resolve its own ambivalence about its role in the new right revolution. It is forced to fight on two fronts. On election night National wins 45 per cent of the vote, returning it to power with sixty-two seats in parliament. With only 28 per cent of the vote, Labour is reduced to thirty-three seats. Jim Anderton's breakaway Alliance Party wins two seats on the back of 20 per cent nationwide support. Labour is engaged in a real battle for survival from the younger and fresher brand, encompassing, as it does, the Green Party as well as Anderton's own New Labour Party.

Bolger's re-election had been widely predicted. The real drama on election night centres on the referendum to change New Zealand's electoral system. Despite a bitter public campaign—or maybe because of it—the well-funded Peter Shirtcliffe's 'Campaign for Better Government' fails in its bid to persuade the country to switch to MMP. Fifty-four per cent of voters preferred to stay with the status quo. First-past-the-post was here to stay. Bolger's leadership—and that key moment when he publicly rejected Richardson's 'There is No Alternative' approach to policy making—is widely acknowledged as the decisive factor in preserving things as they are. Douglas, Richardson and other significant figures on the right (Fay, Richwhite, Douglas allies like Michael Bassett, and business people like Alan Gibbs prominent among them) lament the fact that there was insufficient support to change to MMP, vowing to continue their fight for greater accountability in government.

Up in Te Kuiti that night, Prime Minister Bolger gives a short election night victory speech. He warns the country that while progress wasn't as fast as they had all hoped, and while there was still much work to do, he felt that with the confidence of the people his government could continue to try to steadily improve the lives of all. Later, Bolger receives a call from his old friend, Bill Birch.

'Congratulations Prime Minister. It turned out all right in the end, my friend. You are well on the way to becoming our great helmsman, Jim.'

'Yes, I am', replies a suitably humble prime minister.

By 1996, three years later, Jim Bolger understands the country and its people very well. They understand him, too, but familiarity has not yet bred contempt. During the past three years the major political upheavals have taken place almost exclusively on the left, although Winston Peters has finally made his break from National, complaining about the deluge of immigrants under Bolger's government and the burgeoning Treaty grievance industry that has been spurred along by National's settling of Treaty claims—Peters calls it 'the bro'ocracy'—none of which policies he has signed up for.

Helen Clark, survivor of the fourth Labour government, had replaced Mike Moore immediately after his defeat in 1993. However, she is unable to gain traction, fighting, as she is, on both left and right flanks. She and Labour poll miserably; Clark just doesn't seem to be able to resonate with the wider electorate. The Alliance is snapping at Labour's heels in the polls, even overtaking the party once or twice. When five senior members confront

Helen Clark just five months out from the election, she falls on her sword.

Mike Moore returns to the leadership and wastes no time in casting aside Labour's recent past:

> It was the best of times, it was the worst of times. But it's *now* time to force the spring, market our products anywhere, *everywhere*, ease superpower tensions, and reduce our debt burden while caring for our elderly as we forge new markets.

Despite Moore's flaky lack of focus, his ability to communicate with Labour's traditional supporters and middle New Zealand lead to an improvement in Labour's position vis-à-vis the government and the Alliance (which is having internal tensions of its own).

The right wing of National's caucus speculates (off the record, of course) that Bolger can conceivably win a third term, while complaining bitterly about the nation drifting along. Bolger, however, has mastered the art of staying close to public opinion. There are some burgeoning signs of recovery in the economy and the rebirth of optimism is enough to carry National through the campaign. On election night 1996 National and Jim Bolger win a coveted third term. National's vote has been slowly degrading, but the continued fracturing of the left has facilitated yet another comfortable election night victory for the still popular prime minister.

National receives 40 per cent of the vote (and fifty-three seats), as against Labour's forty-one seats and 34 per cent support. The Alliance sheds ten points—following a series of internal rifts spilling into the public arena—to end up with 10 per cent of the vote (while retaining its two seats). Winston Peters and his NZ First Party win the Tauranga seat. Labour, however, is finally on the road back to redemption.

By 1999 the grand old man of New Zealand politics, Jim Bolger is seeking a fourth successive term as prime minister. If successful, he will be up there with Keith Holyoake as National's most electorally successful prime minister. National has had to endure another cyclical downturn and it has also faced a much more focused opposition for the first time since Bolger became prime minister. Labour and the Alliance reach a pre-election agreement, following the Greens' split from its parent party, to reform under the banner of 'New Labour'. Tony Blair's win in the British elections has regenerated the left, and under Helen Clark, who has once again replaced Mike Moore, a more focused and more marketing savvy Labour Party has emerged.

The public remain supportive of Bolger, a leader with whom they have grown comfortable, but the concerted period of consolidation is starting to feel like drift to many voters. The decision to borrow Blair's credit card of promises proves a brilliant marketing ploy for Labour but, in a knife-edge election, Bolger gains a fourth term as prime minister by the narrowest of margins. After the votes are counted, National limps in with 37 per cent of the vote and forty-nine seats. Labour is not far behind, winning forty-seven seats with 36 per cent support. Winston Peters wins again in Tauranga, giving Bolger an effective majority of one. There is an exceptionally low turnout (only 73 per cent of all eligible voters) but this hurts Labour more than National on the day.

In 2000, Jim Bolger triumphantly relinquishes the National Party leadership. His career has proved an unlikely success. Genuine respect from other political actors in Wellington, and affection in the country at large, strengthen his place as one of the most enduringly successful prime ministers in our political history. Editorial writers and columnists pay tribute to Bolger for his steady and often inspiring leadership, particularly on Treaty and race issues. A run for president in a future New Zealand republic cannot be ruled out, write the pundits. Bolger may have returned from every overseas trip with a slightly different accent, but he was one of us. And Jim Bolger would always be remembered for that one moment in time, that dramatic day when he stopped the rot, that day way back in 1991 when he prevented a determined ideologue from finishing off the job. For that he had earned a nation's enduring gratitude.

Jenny Shipley wins the ballot to replace Jim Bolger. She had waited a long time for the opportunity. Shipley had done her homework, manoeuvring skilfully to gain just enough caucus support for the job. Now the race is on to see who will become the nation's first woman prime minister. It proves to be Helen Clark who succeeds, as in 2002 luck finally runs out for National. The country wanted change. The headlines scream the next day, *'Clark Breaks the Glass Ceiling'*. Soon afterwards, Bill English replaces Shipley. Her timing had been badly misjudged. There is a new generation of National MPs, impatient to make their mark in their own time.

Scenario Two

Another fork in the road: Bolger's weaker response

My second scenario is a much briefer one. This sees MMP voted in, predicated on a generally weak response from Bolger. Here, he still engineers Richardson's removal, but—and probably more closely in keeping with Bolger's motivations, personality and skills (for both good or ill)—he does not strongly repudiate Richardson's planned blitzkrieg of social policy reforms. Instead, he obfuscates much more and while an extended 'cuppa' satisfies many in the country, Bolger's levels of support are not nearly so high as in the preceding analysis.

Thus, MMP comes in with a bare mandate (around 52–48 per cent or 51–49 per cent) and the counterfactual is immediately complicated by the addition of multiparty politics, defections left, right *and* centre, and the idiosyncratic role of Winston Peters and other maverick politicians. Under the leadership of Maurice Williamson, with Richard Prebble as his deputy, and with Roger Douglas and Ruth Richardson acting as co-patrons, ACT carves out a niche for itself. Despite heavy funding, however, the party rarely polls more than 1 or 2 per cent. A young tyro, Rodney Hide, is encouraged to join the party.

Under this scenario Bolger still wins comfortably in 1993. Likewise, National outpolls Labour in 1996, forming a post-election coalition government with Peters, as actually happened, but Labour's leadership instability and its competition from the Alliance result in a weaker party vote and the loss of all the Maori seats to Peters, signalling Labour's continuing post-Rogernomics malaise. Bolger secures one last victory in 1999, but only because Labour has spent the last three years fighting with other parties on the left and the electorate considers the statesmanlike Bolger to be the safer bet. It's a tired government; there is a lot of tension between Bolger and Peters, with the later frequently threatening to pull the rug out from under the coalition. But it holds on, just.

Labour then finally wins in 2002, under Helen Clark. After the election Bolger steps down. His last act is to facilitate Bill English's elevation to the leadership. English by this stage is not just a widely respected ex-minister of finance, but one of a newer generation of National MPs who have gained vital experience in government. He immediately begins the process of revitalising National. John Key, Simon Power and Katherine Rich epitomise the new generation of National MPs. There is a real air of expectation as the 2005 election draws closer. English against Clark—who will win? The Labour-led government gets off to a promising start, but its popularity is tarnished after public unease over its 'closing the gaps' policy and a controversial Court of Appeal decision on the country's 'foreshore and seabed' that seems to many to favour Maori.

The Labour government also gets on the wrong side of the electorate by supporting prostitution law reform and legislating for civil unions. A feeling quickly develops that Labour is pandering to minorities. The result is a closely fought election, but ultimately favourable economic conditions carry Labour to a second straight term.

The story concludes: Alternative history

Jim Bolger came into office in extremely trying circumstances. Treasury Secretary Graeme Scott informed Bolger the day after victory celebrations that the collapse of the state-owned Bank of New Zealand was imminent. Bolger was persuaded that the future viability of the entire banking industry relied upon a government bail out of the bank. The country's fiscal deficit was also far worse than Bolger and Richardson had been led to expect. Bolger was persuaded that strong action was required. At the same time, however, Bolger had choices—even if during those first days in office he felt he had none—not least because of the strong public mandate he had received on the back of voters' repudiation of the fourth Labour government. This, in all likelihood, allowed Bolger more freedom of action than he may have felt at the time. This chapter identifies and discusses only two alternative choices, either of which would have seen a different outcome from what actually transpired.

Undertaking a counterfactual analysis has thrown light on several interesting features of the last fifteen years of our domestic politics. The first was that Bolger's failure of discernment, manifested through Richardson's ill-judged (and poorly named) 'mother of all budgets', was central to the new direction forged by the 1993 vote for MMP. In one political act Richardson's budget crystallised how successive governments had been driven by a narrow ideology entirely disconnected from its negative impacts on large numbers of New Zealanders unable to easily adapt to the requirements of the new economy. That budget created a perception, as well, that governments were intent on change for change's sake irrespective of the mounting human costs. In short, the public sensed—perhaps even unconsciously so—that an underlying cynicism drove the reformers' efforts. The public took its revenge when given the opportunity to do so.

Although somewhat contrived, the example of Peter Shirtcliffe leading a pro-MMP campaign underscores the underlying cynicism that drove the neoliberal project. The purpose of those who supported it—the names include Douglas, Richardson, Fay, Richwhite, Kerr and Gibbs, but there were others—was twofold. It was, in part, ideological, but it was also entirely power driven. The fact that many of these same individuals benefited financially from their roles in the revolution created a public relations disaster for all of those doctrinaire neoliberals who would follow. It also hamstrung their successors in terms of the political language that was available to them. This was evident in the 2002 election campaign, for instance, when Bill English tried to describe greater choice in education as 'self-management', only to be met with the retort that what he meant, of course, but was unable to say, was 'bulk funding'. There was no escaping the negative perceptions that were still attached to many of the centre-right's most cherished policy prescriptions.

My analysis also accentuates the centrality of Helen Clark's leadership in Labour's post-Rogernomics era. The switching of Labour's leadership between Clark and Moore in the preceding analysis was really predicated on the absence of any other viable alternative leader-in-waiting. Leadership talent was thin on the ground after Labour was decimated in 1990 and in many respects Clark's leadership is the single most influential factor in explaining the party's rehabilitation and success since 1996. She was able to talk freely about correcting the 'wrongs of Rogernomics' in a fashion that eluded her several National counterparts, each of whom has struggled to make sense of the politics of the post-Richardson reform era.[7]

This counterfactual analysis reveals and reminds us that politics is all about choices. 'What if' questions are continually posed in the domain of politics. Calculations are constantly made about costs and benefits and, thus, the likely outcomes of one's preferred set of policies. The law of unintended consequences also influences even the most carefully thought out policies. When combined, this reveals some of the complexity inherent in all decision making that confronts governments, irrespective of their political colours. Discernment is key and in my counterfactual I have attempted to analyse and comprehend the chain of circumstances that led to National's calamitous result in 2002. The catastrophe of that election, of course, then led National to depose Bill English and take a high-risk gamble on former Reserve Bank governor, Dr Don Brash, leading the party back into government. This desperation led, in turn, to Brash exploiting the race dimension to rehabilitate his party in the eyes of the voting public, which, if nothing else, provides a future opportunity to explore another counterfactual: what if Brash had not delivered his Orewa speech on race?

History provides a seamless web of continuity and the costs of poor cumulative decision making almost invariably return to haunt political parties. So, too, in the events associated with the topic of my counterfactual analysis: from one failure of judgment a chain began that resulted in an increasingly desperate political context for National, shielded for a time only by the unlikely success of Bolger in securing a third term in 1996, before finally coming home to roost in the 1999 election. Finally, counterfactuals remind us that history is not predetermined. Our very next choice might lead to wildly disparate outcomes from those envisaged. The vibrant potential of human agency makes individuals and the choices they reach central to our understanding of historical outcomes in a political world. And that is a reassuring thought, for one's next choice can always be different—and better.

15

What if Winston Peters had chosen to go with Labour in 1996?

Nigel S. Roberts

In New Zealand's first Mixed Member Proportional (MMP) general election, held on Saturday, 12 October 1996, the National Party won forty-four seats, the Labour Party thirty-seven, NZ First won seventeen (including the five Maori seats), the Alliance thirteen, ACT eight, and the United Party won one seat. Following the election, NZ First held protracted simultaneous negotiations with both Labour and National in order to determine with which of the country's two major parties it would form a government. Despite widespread initial expectations that NZ First and Labour would comprise the country's first MMP government, on 10 December 1996 Winston Peters (NZ First's leader) announced in a live television broadcast from the former legislative council chambers in parliament buildings that he and his party had decided to form a majority coalition government with the National Party. The two parties together commanded sixty-one seats in the 120-member House of Representatives, and National's leader, Jim Bolger, thus continued to be New Zealand's prime minister (the post he had held since late 1990), with Winston Peters appointed deputy prime minister. The cabinet included fifteen National ministers and five NZ First ministers, while there were two National and four NZ First ministers outside the cabinet.

In early 1997 NZ First back-bench MP Tukuroirangi Morgan encountered heavy criticism for his lavish spending habits prior to entering parliament, and the five Maori MPs rapidly acquired a reputation for arrogance. They became known as 'the tight five' and the coalition government's image was indelibly tarnished. In September 1997 proposals for a compulsory superannuation savings scheme promoted by Winston Peters and supported by Jim Bolger but publicly opposed by the coalition government's fifth-ranked minister, Jenny Shipley, were overwhelmingly defeated in a referendum; and a few months later, National Party MPs replaced Jim Bolger with Jenny Shipley as their leader, much to Winston Peters's annoyance. In mid-1998 open disagreements surfaced between National's health minister, Bill English, and the NZ First associate minister of health, Neil Kirton. Kirton was dismissed from the government and left NZ First. Soon afterwards, Peters sacked Tau Henare from his position as deputy leader of NZ

First, and in August 1998 Prime Minister Jenny Shipley dismissed Winston Peters from her cabinet because of his open opposition to the government's proposals for privatising Wellington airport. Peters pulled NZ First out of the government, but Shipley and the National Party constructed a minority coalition government with the help of Tau Henare and the Mauri Pacific Party (formed by Henare after his contretemps with Peters) as well as other former NZ First MPs, such as Tuariki John Delamere and Peter McCardle, who had declared themselves to be independents after the Shipley–Peters imbroglio. Supported in parliament by parties such as ACT and United, the Shipley-led minority government survived until the end of the 1996–99 parliamentary term. It was defeated in New Zealand's second MMP election, held on 27 November 1999, when the Labour Party won the most seats and formed a minority coalition government in conjunction with the Alliance.

Many of the events described in this chapter did take place and most of the quotations in it are real. Sometimes, however, quotations and events have been taken out of context, or—in light of the composition of the third Labour-led minority coalition government formed by Helen Clark in October 2005—were they?

Creation and destruction: A brief history of the 1996–97 Labour–NZ First government

On Sunday evening, 13 October 1996—the day after the 1996 general election—Television New Zealand finally got its graphics pièce de résistance to work. Accompanied by audible gasps of admiration from the TV studio's floor managers and technicians, party groupings in the House of Representatives dramatically changed places while TVNZ's election-night commentator made his public prediction as to which political parties would form New Zealand's first MMP government:

If I were a betting person I would say it's going to be a minority coalition government led by Labour; Helen Clark as prime minister; NZ First there in the coalition; and probably Winston Peters at least as deputy prime minister and maybe some other portfolio.[1]

This was a bold prediction that flew in the face of many political science theories. For a start, one might have expected a minimum winning coalition to have been formed—that is, a coalition 'with the minimum number of parties necessary to secure a parliamentary majority'.[2] National (with forty-four seats) and NZ First (with seventeen seats in the House of Representatives) could have done just that, with the added advantage that it would also have been a 'connected coalition [of] parties relatively close to each other on the relevant issue dimensions'.[3] Indeed, a National–NZ First coalition is exactly what Rein Taagepera, University of California political science professor and co-author of the seminal work, *Seats and Votes*, predicted in Denmark at a November 1996 conference of electoral systems experts from around the world.[4]

Creation

It took a long time to find out which of us—Rein Taagepera or myself—was going to be proved correct, because the 12 October 1996 election was followed by what Jonathan Boston has called a 'very protracted' process. Boston has also noted that 'by international standards, the events surrounding the formation of the first MMP government were unusual', not least because 'NZ First decided to conduct simultaneous, parallel negotiations with Labour and National'.[5] Nevertheless, by early December—seven weeks after the election—the signs were clear that NZ First was going to form a minority coalition government together with the Labour Party. Few students of New Zealand politics can have forgotten the scene—or, surely at the time, could have failed to have interpreted correctly the message conveyed by the sight—of Mike Moore and Winston Peters having a congenial cup of coffee together at the 'Paris' café's roadside tables in downtown Wellington.[6]

There were good reasons why—despite coalition theory—NZ First and Labour formed their 1996 coalition. Michael Laver and Kenneth Shepsle have pointed out that 'it is simply not enough for a proposed government to command the majority of legislators— it must also command the support of its own participants',[7] and from opinion poll evidence we know that NZ First supporters and voters favoured a coalition with Labour rather than National by a ratio of five to one.[8] As Raymond Miller has noted, 'NZ First's voters were as dismissive of National as National's were of NZ First. The clear preference was for a coalition involving Labour.'[9]

Jonathan Boston and Elizabeth McLeay have also pointed to the reasons why National was more reluctant than Labour to form a coalition government in concert with NZ First. National knew that 'it risked being seen by the electorate as having "sold its soul" in order to retain power'. And, what is more, 'Peters had anything but a good working relationship with the prime minister, Jim Bolger. Bolger had removed Peters from the National cabinet in 1991 because of his failure to abide by the conventions of collective responsibility.' Possibly most important of all, key figures in the National Party's hierarchy realised that 'by going into opposition, National would be in a better position to change its leader and rejuvenate its front bench'.[10]

As a result, as Boston and McLeay remind us, it was widely felt that 'the net risks for Labour were probably fewer than those for National. Further, Labour and NZ First enjoyed a greater overall commonality of purpose, policy stance and electoral base than National and NZ First'.[11] On Tuesday, 10 December 1996, just three days before parliament was required (under the terms of the 1986 Constitution Act) to assemble, Winston Peters announced his coalition decision to a packed press conference in the former legislative council chamber of the New Zealand parliament. The detailed coalition agreement hammered out between the Labour and NZ First negotiating teams was signed by Helen Clark and Winston Peters on 11 December; parliament met on 12 December; and (as Boston and McLeay have recorded) 'the new government was sworn in on Monday, 16 December'.[12]

Portfolio politics

One of NZ First's 1996 election promises was to reduce the size of cabinet. Although this did not occur—the Labour–NZ First cabinet consisted of twenty ministers (the standard size for New Zealand cabinets in recent years)—one unusual feature of the government sworn in on 16 December 1996 was that it consisted solely of full cabinet ministers. The coalition government's genuflection in the direction of the NZ First policy was to axe all sub-cabinet posts. A feature of New Zealand politics brought in by the fourth Labour government[13] was thus discarded by what some in the Labour Party, at least initially, tried to portray as the fifth Labour government. Details gleaned from interviews during the past nine years with senior National Party politicians have revealed another reason why NZ First eventually favoured the Labour Party as its coalition partner: National's negotiating team baulked at the idea of reducing the size of cabinet. As Boston and McLeay have also noted, they believed that it would 'be necessary [for National] to demote up to six cabinet ministers'.[14] During the eight-week period in which NZ First's simultaneous negotiations with Labour and National took place, National, almost unbelievably, even went so far as to propose a ministry of twenty-six people. Although six of the ministers in their proposal would apparently have been outside cabinet, all of them—even the most inexperienced NZ First newcomer—would have held at least one full ministerial (as distinct from associate ministerial) portfolio.[15]

Overseas experience with coalition governments pointed to the likelihood that the smaller party in a New Zealand coalition was likely to be somewhat overrepresented in the cabinet. Jonathan Boston and Elizabeth McLeay have observed that 'normally parties receive Cabinet posts in relation to their relative proportions of parliamentary seats, though junior coalition partners are frequently over-rewarded'.[16] This is exactly what happened in the case of the Labour–NZ First cabinet. Labour had thirty-seven seats in the House of Representatives; NZ First had seventeen—in other words, Labour held 68.5 per cent of the government's seats compared with NZ First's 31.5 per cent. Their cabinet, however, contained thirteen Labour and seven NZ First posts (which is a 65:35 per cent split).

Helen Clark was, of course, prime minister (as well as being minister in charge of the Security Intelligence Service). As expected, Winston Peters became deputy prime minister; and—in what was a surprise move that caught commentators, journalists and academics unawares—Peters was also appointed minister of finance. However, in a superb example of the mixing-and-matching that Helen Clark and Winston Peters employed to create their cabinet, Labour's number two—deputy party leader Dr Michael Cullen—was appointed treasurer (unlike Australia, it was a previously unused post in New Zealand), and the fine print of the Labour–NZ First fifty-seven-page coalition agreement revealed that the post of treasurer was (and I quote) 'the senior position of the finance portfolios'.[17] Interviews with senior negotiators on both sides, Labour and NZ First, have since revealed that Labour insisted that if Peters rather than Cullen had been appointed treasurer, there would have been a drastic decline in confidence in the government by international and domestic financial markets, and that it was only at almost the last minute of the negotiation process that Peters accepted Labour's view.

The cabinet contained other surprises. Labour's caucus elected Mike Moore to a higher position in Labour's cabinet ranking than most commentators had predicted. In what was clearly a display of gratitude to the former Labour leader for his willingness to support Helen Clark during the election campaign, as well as a realistic recognition of the close links Moore had with Peters, Moore was the first person Labour elected to cabinet. He was thus fourth in the overall cabinet hierarchy and was made foreign minister. Not surprising was that fact that Steve Maharey was fifth in the cabinet rankings and minister of social welfare.

A major tussle took place during the coalition negotiations as to who would be minister of Maori affairs. NZ First insisted that its deputy leader, Tau Henare, get the post. The party pointed to the fact that he already had parliamentary experience (he was first elected to the former Northern Maori seat in 1993) and that NZ First had, after all, made a clean sweep of all five Maori seats in the 1996 election. Labour was eventually forced to concede that after fifty years of unrivalled domination in the Maori seats, its mana among Maoridom had been considerably (if not necessarily irreparably) reduced, and thus conceded both the post and the number six cabinet slot to Tau Henare. Labour's one supposed crumb of comfort in this regard was the appointment of Dover Samuels as minister of racing (a portfolio in which he clearly had next-to-nothing to do) and associate minister of Maori affairs. Samuels was, though, number eighteen in the cabinet line-up.

Seventh in the cabinet rankings was Phil Goff, who, as well as being made minister of state services, was also given the portfolios of minister of justice and of the courts. He was thus, in effect, paired with his former Auckland Labour Party colleague but now new NZ First member, Jack Elder, who was made minister of police, internal affairs and civil defence (and was eleventh in the cabinet hierarchy). Eighth was Annette King, minister of health, but in one of the cabinet's typical 'mix-and-match' appointments, NZ First's Neil Kirton (a former health administrator) was made minister of ACC and associate minister of health. He was also last—twentieth—in the cabinet rankings. Peter McArdle (a former National MP) was ninth in the cabinet and given his pet area: he was made minister for employment.

NZ First's highest ranked newcomer to parliament in the cabinet list was Brian Donnelly. He was number twelve in the cabinet and was made minister of education. This was another major concession on the part of the Labour Party. As a result of 'NZ First's desire to achieve policy change in [the] areas' of health, education, and social welfare, NZ First had insisted during the long and drawn out coalition negotiations that part of its price for going into government with the Labour Party was that it be given at least one of these three 'high spending portfolios'.[18] As already noted, Labour refused to concede the health portfolio, regarding it as far too sensitive; and NZ First probably realised that it had no one to match Maharey's expertise in the field of social welfare. That left only education, and Labour eventually and reluctantly relinquished the portfolio to NZ First. This meant that the biggest loser among Labour's high profile performers was Trevor Mallard, who was (symbolically?) ranked thirteenth in the cabinet and given the post of associate minister of education in addition to being the minister for sport and the minister responsible for the Education Review Office.

By contrast, Jim Sutton, three places above Trevor Mallard in the cabinet line-up, was an obvious and utterly uncontested candidate for the position of minister of agriculture, forestry and fisheries. Likewise, Lianne Dalziel's legal background gave her a smooth ride to the post of attorney general. She was also made minister of women's affairs. Dalziel was fourteenth in the cabinet hierarchy. Pete Hodgson was number fifteen, but with a plethora of ministerial responsibilities including environment, science, and the crown research institutes. NZ First newcomer John Delamere (later to become Tuariki Delamere) was the sixteenth-ranked cabinet member and minister of immigration and of revenue. Mark Burton at number seventeen was a fairly obvious appointee as minister of defence. As we have already seen, Dover Samuels and Neil Kirton filled the eighteenth and twentieth cabinet slots.

Four women stood for election to Labour's last cabinet slot: Ruth Dyson (who was first elected to parliament in 1993) and three 1996 newcomers—Tariana Turia, Judith Tizard and Marian Hobbs.[19] Possibly because of her administrative experience as the principal of a large and highly successful girls' high school, Marian Hobbs eventually defeated Dyson for the post and became the nineteenth ranked minister. She was given the conservation portfolio and also made an associate minister of education.

Helen Clark thus became New Zealand's first (and thus far only) female prime minister. Her cabinet, however, contained only four female ministers—Clark, King, Dalziel and Hobbs. This meant that while 29.1 per cent of the members of New Zealand's first MMP parliament were women,[20] only 20 per cent of the first MMP cabinet were women. The first MMP cabinet also contained four Maori—namely Peters, Henare, Delamere and Samuels. This was historic: no ministry had ever before contained four Maori. The new cabinet was also distinguished by the fact that for the first time in the twentieth century it contained a significant portion of members who had never before even sat in the House of Representatives: fully a quarter of the cabinet consisted of parliamentary neophytes (Donnelly, Delamere, Samuels, Hobbs and Kirton).

First steps

Although the Labour Party and NZ First had a combined total of only fifty-four MPs compared with fifty-three for National, ACT, and United, both Labour and NZ First recognised that as long as the Alliance agreed either to vote with the government or to abstain, a one-seat plurality over the combined forces of the opposition parties on the centre-right was perfectly sufficient for governing New Zealand. This was quickly proven to be the case.

As Boston and McLeay have noted, 'Parliament's formal opening was on Thursday, 12 December, and it met again the next day to elect the Speaker and Deputy.'[21] Choosing Labour's longest-serving MP, Jonathan Hunt,[22] as speaker was not a problem for the government despite its wafer-thin margin over the opposition parties in parliament. Parliament's standing orders were specially amended in 1995 to cater for the likelihood of multiparty parliaments and the possibility of minority governments. Parties were given the ability to cast party votes in parliament, which meant that Labour's chief whip could cast Labour's thirty-seven votes for or against any remit even though one of its members was in the speaker's chair.[23]

The first session of New Zealand's first MMP parliament was a short one. Despite the fact that Laila Harré severely criticised the idea in an Alliance Party caucus meeting, Jim Anderton declared that the Alliance would support the new government when National, ACT and United challenged Labour and NZ First's decision to adjourn parliament from 13 December 1996 until 20 February 1997, thus successfully thwarting the opposition parties' desire to deal with unfinished legislative business and set up select committees.

The 1996–97 Christmas–New Year break briefly turned the country's gaze away from the political debates and manoeuvrings that had dominated the media constantly for the previous four months. Helen Clark soared up the preferred prime minister stakes from 19 per cent support at the time of the general election (six per cent *below* Jim Bolger)[24] to 52 per cent in the first opinion poll results released in February 1997. The prime minister's debating skills—displayed so keenly during the 1996 election campaign[25]— were used to good effect in a barrage of statements and media appearances. The country also began to take quiet pride in, and even admire, a prime minister with interests as varied as cross-country skiing, military history, music and opera. The deputy prime minister came across in a good light too. Tanned and as good looking as ever, photographs of Winston Peters fishing in the Bay of Plenty or striding in an impeccable suit towards his Beehive office contributed to an initial image of a government of both style and substance.

The opposition also did its bit to help the government. As Radio New Zealand's political editor noted in a mid-January 1997 *Summer Report* programme, the clamour stemming from in-fighting and dissatisfaction within the National Party threatened at times to displace the sounds of beach barbecues and cricket. National caucus soundings rapidly revealed a widespread belief that the party had to find a new leader; the only problem was who would it be? When Bolger said he would stand down if a new leader were chosen at the parliamentary party's three-day retreat in Whitianga during the second week of February, six people publicly indicated that they would like to be the National leader— Bill Birch, Don McKinnon, Lockwood Smith, Jenny Shipley, Max Bradford and Bill English. 'The trouble with my old party,' a former National cabinet minister reputedly said from the sanctuary of his South Island farm, 'is that it is full indians wanting to be chiefs when most of them are really clowns.'[26] Lockwood Smith was the first to withdraw from the race, and a little later Bill Birch, the party's éminence grise, apparently concluded that he could continue to be both more effective and more efficient in nominally secondary roles. That still left four people with their hats in the ring. From the evidence gleaned from extensive discussions with National MPs by political scientist Jon Johansson, it appears that it took three ballots for the forty-four members of the National

Party caucus to elect their new leader. Bradford was eliminated in the first vote, Shipley in the second. Their supporters then switched predominantly to Bill English, the brightest and most successful of National's large crop of new MPs in 1990. Combined with feelings not only that it was time for a change—especially a generational change—but that it would also be wise for the party to move towards the centre of the political spectrum in the new MMP environment, National's caucus narrowly opted for English rather than McKinnon. (The most reliable estimate of the vote is twenty-three to twenty-one in English's favour.)

Labour and NZ First were cock-a-hoop at the news. English would be an easy beat, they concluded. What is more, the coalition partners were in substantial agreement about many aspects of policy, and they set about—with a high degree of determination—implementing their coalition agreement. Details of the Labour–NZ First coalition agreement are contained in former Victoria University of Wellington student Fiona Barker's excellent chapter, 'Negotiating With NZ First', in *From Campaign to Coalition*, the book that Jonathan Boston, Stephen Levine, Elizabeth McLeay and I edited.[27] (Barker's chapter outlines not only the Labour–NZ First coalition agreement, but also the draft National–NZ First agreement. I hope that someone some day uses the information Barker gathered to ask what I think is a neglected question in New Zealand politics: What would have happened if Winston Peters had chosen *National* rather than Labour in 1996? Of course, that's a counterfactual question and obviously not properly a subject of political history.)

The Labour–NZ First coalition agreement built on the common ground that the two parties shared. It 'emphasised the way the state could use . . . growth to invest in social spending', but—at the same time—pledged to 'adopt sound fiscal and monetary policy while addressing the urgent social and economic needs of the nation'.[28] The latter clause was regarded as an attempt by both Michael Cullen and Winston Peters to assure financial markets and foreign investors that the new minority government was going to be, above all, a responsible government. Both parties were urgently signalling that the Labour–NZ First regime was not going to model itself on either the third Labour government (1972–75) or, equally importantly, on the fourth Labour government (1984–90).

Coordinated by Cullen, cabinet committees immediately began the groundwork for the 1997 budget. Health was given a high priority, especially NZ First's pledge (incorporated into the coalition agreement with Labour) that visits by children to GPs would be 'free for children up to five years' (with a commitment eventually to increasing this to twelve years).[29] There were, nevertheless, early indications that the working relationship between Annette King and Neil Kirton was less than smooth. 'He's a prickly, interfering know-all' was one comment that emanated from a source close to the minister.

At Te Puni Kokiri, however, all was sweetness and light. Tau Henare and Dover Samuels enthusiastically planned the fulfilment of a range of policies in the Labour–NZ First coalition agreement, including abolition of the previous National government's 'fiscal envelope', extending time limits for Treaty settlements, funding the Waitangi Tribunal more adequately, and ensuring better Maori representation on government and statutory agency boards.[30] Cabinet quickly agreed on a range of measures to help Maori, and someone (not Henare; it is thought it may have been Trevor Mallard) came up with the suggestion to call it the 'closing the gaps' programme, an idea that was enthusiastically endorsed by both parties.

Twin troughs

The coalition government was utterly unprepared for the first storm to hit it. All had been plain sailing until mid-February 1997. Until then it was the opposition that was in the doldrums. But when the news media broke a series of stories about lavish expense account spending by Tukuroirangi Morgan, a back-bench NZ First Maori electorate MP and a former television broadcaster, the new government soon shuddered. Mr Morgan's purchase of $79 underpants rapidly came to symbolise what was ceaselessly portrayed as a story of greed and even possibly corruption. It is interesting to reflect how in a small society like New Zealand, the story—well known in entertaining and retailing circles even prior to the election—was bound to come out sooner or later (as it happened, it was sooner), no matter which parties were in government. Most MPs and commentators were agreed that the scandal would probably have hit a National–NZ First government equally severely, and for the first time National's MPs really heaved a collective sigh of relief that they were in opposition and *not* in government.

The response by Tuku Morgan and the other four Maori MPs exacerbated the affair and prevented it from losing traction in the media. Instead of keeping a low profile, they were the very opposite of meek. Mr Morgan's fellow Maori electorate MPs rallied round him. Using a rugby analogy, they were, they said, 'the tight five' in the new parliament, and tackling them would prove painful. At a NZ First caucus retreat in Akaroa, they swaggered round the picturesque holiday town wearing 'Dirty Dog' sunglasses and looking for all the world like thugs or the mafia. The public was not impressed. In early March, a *Sunday News* poll found that more than 72 per cent of people interviewed thought that Tuku Morgan was not 'a fit and proper person to be a member of parliament'. More worrying for the new government as a whole were the facts that 54 per cent did not think that the coalition was working, and that support for Helen Clark as prime minister had fallen back below 30 per cent. The paper noted that 'political scientist professor Nigel Roberts says our *Sunday News*/Redman Research opinion poll will sound deafening alarm bells for the coalition government's lead partner as well as NZ First.'[31]

The government might possibly have been able to allay the worst effects of this storm, but another followed hard on its heels. A leak to the media alleged that Dover Samuels had had a sexual relationship with a fifteen-year-old girl when she was living in his home under the care of his family. As a Labour member of the cabinet, Dover Samuels came under Helen Clark's purview. Although he had been elected to the cabinet by the Labour Party caucus, Helen Clark could—and did—dismiss him. She announced that she was setting new high standards of propriety for New

Zealand politics, pointedly comparing her actions with the former National government's refusal to dismiss Denis Marshall from the cabinet or even from his conservation post for a period of almost a year following the April 1995 Cave Creek disaster.[32]

Clark's relationship with her deputy prime minister, Winston Peters, had been somewhat stiff and formal but, nevertheless, reasonably congenial until this point. However, when she demanded that Peters also take a strong stance regarding his Maori electorate MPs, who included two cabinet ministers (Henare and Delamere), Peters was incensed. He angrily told Clark that the management of NZ First's MPs was his responsibility, not hers. He stressed that Morgan had not been accused of committing a crime (unlike Samuels, he added pointedly), and said that Henare and Delamere had simply been doing what any decent party colleagues would do in any caucus—helping a fellow MP under attack from a rumour-mongering salacious media. The NZ First leader also pointed out that the Labour Party had achieved (if 'achieved' is the right word, he added caustically) its lowest share of the vote (28 per cent) at any election since 1928, and that Labour would not have been in government and that Clark would not have been prime minister were it not for him.

Helen Clark's relationship with Winston Peters never improved after this dramatic contretemps on the ninth floor of the Beehive.[33] Clark began to see less and less of Peters and started to rely increasingly on Michael Cullen and Heather Simpson (her chief of staff) for advice. Peters, on the other hand, kept his links to the Labour Party open via Mike Moore. During late night whisky sessions in the minister of foreign affairs' office, Peters and Moore began to share their sense of frustration and bitterness over Clark's leadership style.

What took many journalists and political scientists by surprise was the public reaction to the 'undie-gate' and Samuels scandals. A strong streak of anti-Maori feeling had previously been discerned in the New Zealand electorate (see, for example, the findings in the New Zealand Study of Values surveys),[34] but few commentators, if anyone, realised quite how pervasive—or even pernicious—it was. There was a seeming tidal wave of anti-Maori feeling, which even Winston Peters recognised. In cabinet he supported Helen Clark's proposal to stop using the title, 'closing the gaps', to describe the coalition government's Maori affairs policies, and agreed ironically that Trevor Mallard should be put in charge of changing the government's focus away from race-based policies to ones based on need. However, as a perceptive article by Jon Johansson in a recent edition of *Political Science* has pointed out, since the twin scandals—one focused on NZ First MPs, the other on a senior Labour politician (Samuels, it should be stressed, was number three on the Labour Party list in 1996)[35]—'the scars are still evident from the political bombshell[s] . . . Noise at the extremes has received more coverage than before . . . Incendiary talk of civil war has further polluted our race discourse.'[36]

The government plummeted in public opinion polls. At the same time, as Johansson reminds us, 'National, under English, launched a billboard campaign under the slogan "One standard of citizenship for all".'[37] It resonated with voters. But worse, far worse, was to come for the government.

The Labour–NZ First budget was delivered by Michael Cullen on Thursday, 26 June 1997. It did the government no favours at all. The financial plans in the Labour–NZ First coalition agreement were, to quote Fiona Barker's astute analysis, 'contingent on achieving [a] targeted rate of growth and consequential budget surpluses'.[38] As growth in the New Zealand economy had been comparatively sluggish (reflecting investors' concerns both in the lead-up to the October 1996 general election and about the character and composition of the coalition government), the coalition agreement had, in effect, promised more than it could deliver. While the government introduced its plans for free health care for under-five-year-olds (it actually drew the line at six years) and announced that the superannuation surcharge would be abolished the following financial year, among the widely heralded features that the budget failed to deliver were lower tertiary education fees; a 'Schools Out' programme to fund childminding services at schools; an FM non-commercial radio network for young people; the legal costs for a class action for veterans suffering the effects of Agent Orange; and expanding the cervical screening programme.

On the one hand, the budget was criticised by the financial sector for being too profligate; on the other hand, it was also criticised by students, war veterans, and women for being too parsimonious. Memorable headlines generated by the 1997 Labour–NZ First budget included 'Cullen's clanger' and 'Reform Peters out'.

The Labour–NZ First coalition agreement had included proposals both for a dedicated New Zealand Superannuation tax and fund regime if approved by a referendum held in conjunction with the 1999 general election (something that Michael Cullen strongly favoured) and for a second-tier compulsory superannuation scheme based on individual accounts (which Winston Peters wanted).[39] Detailed, complex negotiations between the treasurer and the minister of finance made little or no progress towards these goals. Cullen—with a reputation for not suffering fools gladly—railed against Peters's laziness and lack of attention during their discussions. For his part, the NZ First leader found Cullen increasingly arrogant and stubborn, and began—none too secretly—to blame Cullen for the budget's bad reception. The coalition government plumbed new depths in political unpopularity.

Labour MPs, elected on the basis of a post-Depression low in support for their party, became increasingly nervous. As Jonathan Boston and Elizabeth McLeay so tellingly wrote in 1997, 'if a Labour–NZ First government were widely perceived to be ineffective and divided, [Labour] risked a significant loss of support . . . This could render the centre-left impotent for many years to come.'[40] From all the available evidence, it was Harry Duynhoven and Damien O'Connor—both Labour backbenchers on the right of the party—who began taking quiet soundings among their colleagues. Who could talk to the country's voters? (The prime minister was increasingly seen as out of touch—too academic, too esoteric, and too intellectual were just a few of the criticisms being levelled at her.) Who could talk to Winston Peters? (Relations between the prime minister and her deputy were, in the words of one South Island MP, believed to be Mark Peck, 'colder than winter on the Taieri Plains'.)[41]

The answer was, not surprisingly, Mike Moore. Colleagues

recalled his personal popularity: even in 1990, on the very edge of defeat, he was far more strongly supported as prime minister than Jim Bolger.[42] Colleagues recalled his affability and vitality. Crucially, colleagues also recalled his ability to communicate and work with Winston Peters. The consequences were almost inevitable. On Tuesday, 5 August 1997, Helen Clark's leadership of the Labour Party ended as it had begun—as a result of a well-planned and neatly executed coup. Mike Moore was elected leader of the Labour Party by a margin of twenty-two votes to only fifteen for Helen Clark. One member of Labour's anti-Clark faction in both 1993 and 1997 was overheard saying in an off-hand manner, 'Well, she who lives by the sword dies by the sword.' In this instance, of course, he was correct.

The treasurer, Michael Cullen, saw that having a party leader and deputy leader both representing South Island electorates was not electorally appealing (especially when more than three-quarters of New Zealand's voters live in the North Island), and he resigned without a fight. An intense battle for the deputy's post took place, with Annette King narrowly defeating Phil Goff for the post (some say the vote was as close as nineteen to eighteen). Moore consoled the immensely capable Goff by promising to appoint him minister of foreign affairs in his stead. Naturally, Winston Peters was pleased by the overall outcome[43] and quickly pledged publicly to work closely with Labour's new leadership team.

Headlines such as 'Return of the (Lamb) Burger King' greeted Moore's accession to the prime minister's office for the second time. Spirits rose in government quarters. MPs from both parties in the coalition government hoped that things would settle down and that the Labour–NZ First government would pursue a sensible, centrist course. They were soon to be bitterly disappointed.

Final days

When parliament assembled the following week (after a three-week recess), National leader Bill English moved a vote of no-confidence in the government. Jonathan Hunt reluctantly accepted the motion, as he had in all fairness to concede that it was not out of order. The leader of ACT and MP for Wellington Central, Richard Prebble, took particular delight in castigating his former Labour cabinet colleagues during the debate. His wit was withering. However, the government was fairly relaxed during the debate. 'We'll win this vote by fifty-four votes to fifty-three,' Labour and NZ First MPs reasoned. Even so, Phil Goff, Judy Keall and Trevor Mallard gave speeches so loud that technicians had to turn down the volume on the House of Representatives' microphones.

But unbeknownst to Labour or NZ First, the Alliance had reached a crucial decision. Most of the party's MPs had been outraged by the Labour–NZ First government's treatment of Maori. Ditching the 'closing the gaps' programme was seen as an affront, and the denigration of Dover Samuels and even of NZ First's Maori MPs rankled the members of the furthest left-wing party in parliament. Even more important, though, were the sins the government had committed in its budget. Alliance MPs Pam Corkery and Phillida Bunkle were not in a mood for compromise because of what they saw as the coalition government's 'cavalier treatment of women'. Bunkle is said to have argued in the Alliance caucus room that what the Labour–NZ First government had done to women was 'worse than the National Women's [Hospital] experiment'. Most damaging of all, though, was the conviction among Alliance MPs that the promotion of Moore, King and Goff indicated a sharp swing to the right in the Labour Party. 'The fourth Labour government rides again' was the irate comment of one Alliance MP. The leader of the Alliance, Jim Anderton, argued in vain for caution. He was apparently supported by Alliance whip Grant Gillon but by few if any others in his caucus.

As Boston and McLeay noted tellingly when the Labour–NZ First government was formed, it 'ran the risk that the Alliance could make life difficult'[44] for the coalition. It did indeed.

Thursday, 14 August 1997, thus became an historic day in New Zealand politics. At 4.53pm, the House of Representatives voted—by sixty-six votes to fifty-four—that it had no confidence in the Labour–NZ First coalition government. It was nearly seventy years since an event of this kind had occurred in New Zealand. The previous time a government had been defeated in a confidence vote in the New Zealand House of Representatives was on Friday, 7 December 1928, when Gordon Coates's Reform government lost by twenty-eight votes to fifty.[45]

New Zealand may have a largely unwritten constitution, but many of the country's constitutional conventions are nonetheless reasonably clear. It is widely understood that the 'reserve powers' of a Governor General includes their right 'to refuse to dissolve a parliament.'[46] The convention was outlined by law lecturer Caroline Morris in further detail after the adoption of MMP but prior to the first proportional representation election: 'Parliament should not be dissolved if an alternative government exists in the House.'[47] After Mike Moore formally told the Governor General, Sir Michael Hardie Boys, that he (Moore) no longer had the confidence of the House of Representatives,[48] the Governor General sought to determine whether a possible alternative government existed. It was quickly made quite clear to him that neither the Alliance nor NZ First would support a National-led government. Winston Peters was alleged to have said, almost apoplectically, that as those two parties had just betrayed him, he would 'have no truck with traitors'. Sir Michael then dissolved parliament and called a general election.

'Bye Bye Miss MMP Pie'

The 1997 general election was held on Saturday, 20 September. Five years and one day after a massive 84.7 per cent 'vote for a change to the voting system' in New Zealand,[49] the electorate voted in its second (and what proved to be its last) MMP election. Not surprisingly, National gained an overwhelming victory over Labour, capturing 48.6 per cent of the party vote. Even though this was less than half the valid votes cast in the election, it translated into sixty-two seats—an absolute majority in the House of Representatives.

Table 15.1 details the shares of the votes and seats won by New Zealand's political parties in the 1997 general election.[50] Both ACT and the Alliance improved their standings in the September 1997 general election. United's party vote fell marginally, but Peter

Table 15.1: The results of the 20 September 1997 MMP election

Party	Party votes %	Electorate seats	List seats	Total seats	Total seats %
National	48.6	35	27	62	51.3
Labour	19.1	21	3	24	19.8
Alliance	14.3	2	16	18	14.9
ACT	8.2	1	10	11	9.1
NZ First	3.1	5	0	5*	4.1
United	0.8	1	0	1	0.8
Chr. Herit.	2.1	0	0	0	0.0
ALCP	1.8	0	0	0	0.0
Chr. Dem.	1.4	0	0	0	0.0
Others	0.6	0	0	0	0.0
Total	100.0	65	56	121 *	100.0

* The total seats includes one 'overhang' seat.
Electoral Roll Turnout: 89.5 per cent; Population-Based Turnout: 84.7 per cent.
Source: The Chief Electoral Officer, 'The General Election 1997' (Wellington, *Appendices to the Journals of the House of Representatives*, E9, 1998), p.5.

Dunne retained his Ohariu-Belmont seat comfortably. The Labour Party's party vote fell below 20 per cent and the party won only twenty-four seats. As Labour managed to hold twenty-one of the electorates it contested, the party was awarded just three list MPs (Lianne Dalziel, Mark Gosche and Jonathan Hunt).

The biggest loser, not surprisingly, was NZ First. Its party vote slumped from 13.4 per cent in 1996 to just 3.1 per cent eleven months later. Winston Peters lost his Tauranga seat to National's Katherine O'Regan by a margin of 2630 votes. At the same time, however, intense anger in the Maori electorates about what was perceived to be the 'Pakeha brutalisation of our MPs' (to quote one respondent in VUW's 1997 election survey) and over negative political attitudes and actions towards policies and programmes for Maori saw all five NZ First Maori electorate MPs returned to parliament. As NZ First's party vote entitled the party to only four MPs, there was an 'overhang' seat (what Germans call an *überhangmandat*) in parliament. Instead of having a parliament of 120 MPs, New Zealanders found that the second MMP election had unexpectedly delivered an even larger parliament (namely, one with 121 seats in it).

The popularity of Bill English's MMP single-party majority government has been described and analysed in a host of other publications, so there is no need to canvas old ground in this paper, other than to note that the relief with which Kiwi voters accepted Bill English, his attractive and capable wife Mary, and their host of pleasant children has no parallels in New Zealand political history. English's longevity as prime minister has now overtaken Sir Robert Muldoon's, and some commentators have even referred to the youthful Southlander as the country's 'new Holyoake' as a result of his canny dominance of National's caucus and cabinet.

English has, of course, been helped by the decision his government made almost immediately it took office to hold a binding referendum on whether or not New Zealand should abolish MMP and return to a first-past-the-post electoral system. The fact that the proposed first-past-the-post system meant both a smaller House of Representatives (reduced to 101 members for the general election in October 2000) and a parliament without separate Maori electorates[51] was an irresistible combination for voters. Claims by minor party MPs and their supporters that what was, in effect, a constitutional referendum should not be held separately from a general election were easily countered by the new National government. It pointed out that the question of a four-year term had been put to voters in a stand-alone referendum in September 1967; and the government then proceeded—with almost indecent haste—to hold New Zealand's second binding electoral reform referendum, which took place on Saturday, 28 March 1998.[52]

The vote was 61.8 per cent in favour of returning to a first-past-the-post electoral system. A disgusted Rod Donald, then a second-term Alliance MP, commented dejectedly, 'This day will go down in infamy. As far as New Zealand politics is concerned, it really is the day the music died.'

Epilogue

Stephen Levine

This book provides fifteen scenarios exploring ways in which New Zealand might have developed differently. The process, creative and thoughtful, draws attention not only to paths nearly (but not) taken, but also to unfulfilled hopes and unrealised aspirations. In thinking about what might have happened 'if only' something slightly different were said or done, human beings tend more readily to dwell (with regret) on things that did not work out quite as hoped rather than on those that did. These 'what if' chapters, for instance, do not generally dwell on happy results and successful outcomes that might—had but one or more factors developed differently— have been disastrous. Yet there are innumerable experiences that work out well that might, very easily, have gone terribly wrong had people behaved differently at the crucial moment.

So these fifteen chapters, perhaps characteristically, look predominantly at events that, in the view of their authors, might well have had a better outcome. In some measure the choice of topic, and the interpretation given to it, reflects contemporary preoccupations. Looked at as a group, it is possible to say something about the sort of alternative New Zealand the 'what if' scenarios conjure up. It is, of course, one with a different capital, warmer both in temperature and in relationships. That preferred consequence, a more harmonious society, is a feature of other chapters as well. Indeed, each contribution to the first section of the book—the two dealing with the Treaty of Waitangi and the one speculating about New Zealand's presence in an Australian nation—dwells on 'race relations' in one form or another. So, too, does the chapter that imagines a more forthright and resolute Jim Bolger staring down Ruth Richardson and her budgetary programme.

These chapters thus say something about what their authors find lacking in New Zealand as it is or has become. Other chapters, too, reveal some disquiet about how New Zealand has evolved. Inevitably there is an emphasis on missed opportunities. These reflect concerns about contemporary developments as well as a consideration of historical possibilities. The book offers a New Zealand in which there was at least the possibility of a more steadfast trade union movement, its working class dedicated to causes greater than their own comfort. It seems more factual than fanciful to discover a New Zealand in which 'think big' succeeds, the term no longer a monument to government intervention or grandiose industrial schemes, but, remarkably, as a far-sighted forerunner to energy self-reliance and greater environmental sensitivity.

The New Zealand of these scenarios is also one in which leadership and language are closely interrelated. Several chapters build up to speeches in which visions of a different and more hopeful future are laid out. Janine Hayward's chapter on the Treaty and citizenship ends with a speech—'Yes, we are New Zealanders now, but we are also more than that. We are Maori.'—and Jon Johansson's search for a Jim Bolger guided by his 'best angel' very nearly begins with one, a televised address providing the decisive turning point in a nation's history. The chapter about Nelson likewise finds a prime minister, Helen Clark, at least imagining rhetoric as an instrument of leadership, a means of summoning up the values and purposes not only of her government but of the society she has chosen to serve.

Denis McLean's chapter has no New Zealand-style 'Gettysburg Address', but in an inspired moment of authorship he turns around Michael Joseph Savage's famous words explaining New Zealand's choice to enter World War II against Germany—'where Britain goes, we go', words inspired by scripture (*The Book of Ruth*)—

plausibly superimposing contemporary New Zealand perspectives on what was a self-evident reflex response several generations ago.

John Henderson's chapter on New Zealand–United States defence cooperation under a Lange-led government also pivots around the use of words, as US Secretary of State George Shultz emerges from a meeting with Lange to say what he probably should have said, rather than what he actually did. US President Harry Truman once said that a large part of his job involved persuading people to do what they ought to have the good sense to do (in their own interest) in any case, without his intervention, and Henderson's chapter deftly shows that there was scope for the US to get a better outcome for itself more than twenty years ago.

If some chapters reveal their authors to be closet speech writers, others find scholars selecting cabinets, allocating ministerial portfolios, appointing and deposing party leaders, exiling and bringing back prime ministers and their companions. This is a particular facet of the more contemporary chapters—those that relate to the Muldoon, Lange, Bolger and Clark years—though even Ian McGibbon, in reporting on the aftermath of a Japanese invasion, finds time to set up a new government (while imprisoning a significant proportion of the old one).

Concerns about the environment, and economic development, are a feature of two of the chapters, one dealing with 'think big', the other with Lake Manapouri. Energy and the environment are economic and security preoccupations that have grown more urgent in recent years. Other chapters are reminders of grim threats to New Zealand security—and the lives of those who fought for the country—in the two great armed struggles of the twentieth century.

If, as noted, the natural impulse is to discover how something that went wrong might perhaps have been made right—rather than the opposite, focusing on what a close call we actually had just this side of catastrophe—little wonder that World Wars I and II should be a feature of several chapters. Not everything can be readily altered, of course, even giving weight to alternative possibilities. Whatever might have been done differently at Gallipoli, the tragic answer seems to be that the New Zealand soldiers who departed the country in the First World War were doomed wherever they went. The Western Front was a graveyard waiting for the men to come to fill it. Here we see the wisdom of the Arab tale of the man glimpsing Death in one town and fleeing to another, Samarra, where Death has already determined that they have an appointment.

As for the Second World War, the two chapters envisage a New Zealand very different from the one that survived the conflict. Ian McGibbon's tour de force—so compelling that it is necessary to remind ourselves, at the end, that it didn't happen—is premised on what was in fact a very narrow escape—and not only (or even principally) for New Zealand—based upon a highly fortuitous victory by the United States over the Japanese navy in the battle of the Coral Sea. Had fortune favoured the Japanese, New Zealand's experience of the Second World War—as a country occupied by an unsympathetic invader—would have been very different from what it was. Nor is it likely that we would today welcome visiting Japanese, seeking to memorialise their soldiers' sacrifice, with the same warmth extended by the people and government of Turkey to New Zealanders and Australians making pilgrimage to the site of the failed Gallipoli invasion.

Denis McLean's musings on New Zealand's response to news of a German invasion of Poland—and the subsequent declaration of war by Great Britain and France—reflects the considerable changes in New Zealand culture, and outlook, on which he has commented elsewhere. What New Zealand undertook so naturally in 1939—that 'where Britain goes, we go'—this country would perhaps never do again: that sort of instinctive bond with another country no longer exists. New Zealand considers its own interests first and acts accordingly. Unspoken in that chapter, but underlying its thinking, is the sense that New Zealand as it exists today would not have responded to that event as it did then. Transposing New Zealand as it is now to those times, and analysing plausible and likely outcomes, that chapter manages to discover a future—an alternative present, really—in which New Zealand's relations with Australia come to rest on a firmer footing.

John Henderson's chapter on the nuclear-free dispute with the

United States, and the breakdown of ANZUS, is another in which New Zealand's security and sovereignty are fundamental issues. His analysis also demonstrates another feature of counterfactual thinking: namely, that especially in hindsight it is possible to envisage more rational thought processes and more intelligent ways of proceeding.

Indeed, as Henderson's and Johansson's chapters show, a further feature of these reinterpreted events—altered scenes from New Zealand's history—is that they identify ways that people could have behaved more sensibly in pursuit of their own interests, the goals of their party, and the needs of the country. Of course there will always be scope for more rational and harmonious outcomes. In this sense critical reflection on our history and our politics, both distant and recent, will probably always have elements of disappointment and unfulfilled possibility. These fifteen chapters, looked at as a whole, thus represent something of a search, as their authors try to find their way towards a New Zealand with less conflict, less social pain, fewer economic disparities. For the latter chapters, what this means is a New Zealand with less of Muldoon, and rather less of the fourth Labour government as well.

It has been suggested that the aim of a counterfactual is not 'to blame or to excuse the protagonists for what they did and did not do'. It is agreed, however, that this is a common impulse. Even with a judgemental approach, however, it is necessary 'to ask whether any of the protagonists could have acted differently'.[1] In *this* book only a few of the fifteen scenarios could be said to have decision makers squarely in their sights: Talboys, who 'could have acted differently' but chose not to; nineteenth-century parliamentarians, who had the opportunity to consider not only the site of a capital but who ought to be responsible for choosing it; Winston Peters, in 1996, opting for one party rather than for another. Other scenarios are entirely free of retrospective criticism: New Zealand politicians are untouched by reproaches for their 'failure' to join Australia; New Zealand's military and political elite is unscathed despite the limited resources available to deal with a possible Japanese occupation; and even the planners of 'think big' go largely untouched by second guessing.

If making history (that is, real life) were more like making a movie, many of the scenes and incidents that characterise our national life would have worked out differently. Few leaders, and even fewer voters, can ever be fully satisfied with their decisions—followed, as they so often are, by unexpected consequences and unforeseen developments.

The chapters in this book are thus in a sense scripts for a second or third take; no doubt if it were possible to intervene to stop the action, and start from the beginning again, we would all do many things differently. Alas, we do not have that capacity, but in looking at the past—and reflecting, inevitably, on the present and the future—perhaps these imaginings can provide a greater degree of caution, and humility, encouraging us to proceed more deliberately in life, with a greater awareness of all that can be achieved, and so much that is possible, and how little separates tragedy from triumph.

Acknowledgements

Organising the New Zealand 'counterfactuals' conference—a first for New Zealand—was a terrific experience. The two days were everything they could have been hoped for—stimulating, informative, thought provoking, creative, and—equally importantly—a great deal of fun. Much of what took place was light-hearted and hilarious; some of it, filled with the unexpected, was mesmerising.

There is, of course, a wistful and whimsical aspect to counterfactuals. C.P. Snow, describing Sir Arthur Conan Doyle, saw in Sherlock Holmes's creator 'a singularly powerful romantic imagination' whose 'essence . . . is that it simplifies and heightens'.[1] Obviously there is in the counterfactual approach something of a romantic impulse, with authors imaginatively re-creating an event in order to suggest other ways it might have unfolded. As with Holmes's own energetic leaps of logic, what is required is to remain reasonably faithful to the evidence. In the process, those involved inevitably need to simplify, emphasising certain factors while giving less weight to others.

All participants entered thoroughly into the spirit of the counterfactuals conference, lending it an atmosphere and character unlike any other academic meeting any of us had attended. My thanks go to all the participants: to all who took part, giving of their time and their intelligence, I am truly grateful. My further appreciation goes to the authors for having taken the time to revise their papers for publication.

The project could not have succeeded without support and encouragement. The conference itself was assisted by Jane Fogden in Victoria University's history programme, who prepared the programmes for the small group of participants invited to attend.

Nicola Kean, a student at Victoria University, gave generously of her time to make sure that everything over the two days, from PowerPoint presentations to the preparation of morning and afternoon teas, worked to perfection. Nicola also assisted subsequently by working through my editorial notes about some of the chapters, tidying up the manuscript with a much-appreciated efficiency.

The idea for a counterfactuals conference took some time to develop. My closest colleague, Nigel Roberts, was pivotal in propelling this project forward. His enthusiasm was terrific and sustained, as periodically I would go into his office to talk over possible topics and participants, and review progress towards the conference (and the book). I thank him for this as for so much else.[2]

Victoria University professor of political science Margaret Clark, my colleague, was also supportive of this conference right from the start, providing encouragement every time I broached the subject of a conference with her. She unhesitatingly predicted that it would be 'great fun'—as, indeed, it was—and I appreciated her enthusiastic support and suggestions.

A brilliant conversation with Denis McLean helped me to move this counterfactuals conference idea along. I broached the subject with him on a taxi ride to Christchurch airport and immediately, both in the taxi and then on the flight back to Wellington, Denis showed such enthusiasm for the project that by the time we had left the plane he had come up with three scenarios on his own (each represented in this book). When I said goodbye to him at Wellington airport, he stopped me from leaving for a moment, telling me, about his own scenario, 'Wait: I've got my opening line.'

A conversation with Giselle Byrnes likewise played an important role in shaping my thinking as to how to proceed. That talk that I had with Giselle—and I still have the notes of it—contributed greatly not only in terms of ideas, but also simply by providing a response from an historian to what I was setting out to do with this projected conference. And really Giselle's very positive and warm response helped to give me the feeling that we were going to be able to make this work.

Another member of Victoria University's history programme, Melanie Nolan, also gave me very useful advice, support and encouragement which proved critical to the eventual counter-factuals gathering. It was Melanie, for instance, who contacted me after seeing Donald Anderson's description of himself as someone interested in 'counterfactuals', bringing him to my attention.

Victoria University Press has been wonderfully supportive in respect of this project. Fergus Barrowman showed his interest and enthusiasm for the book as soon as I began to discuss it with him, after the conference had already taken place, and his genuine commitment to the publication has been much appreciated. Many thanks as well to Sue Brown for all her efforts in preparing the book for publication; and to Craig Gamble for his assistance in setting up and sourcing the photographs that are found at the beginning of each chapter. Thanks, as well, to my son Spencer Levine (of Base Two, Wellington) for the very effective and attractive cover design, complete with Japanese foliage

This 'what if' conference (and this book that has followed) finds its beginnings in efforts by a youthful and engaging political science student, Simon Sheppard, striving to interest me in the topic of 'counterfactuals'. It took him quite a while to do so, but Simon proved persistent. Simon Sheppard was a remarkable student at Victoria University and subsequently he enrolled as a Ph.D. student in political science at Johns Hopkins University in Maryland. It is a tribute to his perseverance and enthusiasm—and the range of his interests—that eventually I focused on what he was urging upon me, seeing the possibilities in the topic and, in due course, developing the idea for a conference on New Zealand counterfactuals. Over time Simon wore down my resistance, and in doing so he once again demonstrated the wisdom of the Talmudic precept inscribed at the top of one of Victoria University's political science and international relations programme's honours boards listing the names of its award-winning students: 'I have learned from all my teachers, and from my students most of all.'

I can go further and say, in the spirit of the conference and this book, 'what if Simon Sheppard had not been a student in political science at Victoria University?' The answer is clear: no Simon Sheppard, no conference. But these 'what if' statements have a way of running into each other, for I could go on to observe that if

I hadn't been at Victoria University while Simon was here similarly no such conference would ever have occurred. And my arrival in New Zealand, to Victoria University, ultimately is attributable to my having seen an advertisement in the *New York Times* one Sunday. So . . . 'what if' I hadn't bought the *Times* that day? But I did . . . and the rest, as they say, is history.

Stephen Levine
Wellington
October 2006

Notes

Introduction

1 Philip Roth makes much the same point in his 'alternative history' novel, *The Plot Against America*, Houghton Mifflin, New York, 2004, with his main character observing that 'history' took the unknowable chaos and changeability of everyday life and, after the fact, turned it into something far less terrifying: 'harmless history, where everything unexpected in its own time is chronicled on the page as inevitable' (pp.113–14).

2 The lines appear in Dag Hammarskjold, *Markings*, Faber and Faber, London, 1964, p.181.

3 Here we have an unusual case of a minister of finance inspired by Saddam Hussein's 1991 Gulf War rhetoric about a 'mother of all battles' to describe her first budget in similar terms. Notwithstanding their very different circumstances, there is a degree of similarity in the way the two 'battles' developed, with each characterised by destruction, retreat and defeat.

4 See Richard Ned Lebow, 'What's so different about a counterfactual?', *World Politics*, vol.52, July 2000, pp.550–85; quoted on p.551.

5 Lebow, 'What's so different about a counterfactual?', p.557.

6 See Geoffrey Hawthorn, *Plausible Worlds: Possibility and understanding in history and the social sciences*, Cambridge University Press, Cambridge, 1991. Professor Hawthorn's study—the opening chapter is entitled 'Counterfactuals, explanation and understanding'—draws attention to a number of 'what if' treatises—none of them focusing in any way on New Zealand's history, not surprisingly—including J.C. Squire's thought-provoking *If it had Happened Otherwise: Lapses into Imaginary History*, Longmans, London, 1932.

7 Hawthorn, *Plausible Worlds*, p.xi.

8 Otte's comments very closely resemble one of Victoria University of Wellington's slogans, advertising at times startling propositions from the university's courses and lecturers with the motto 'it makes you think'. Otte's observations about counterfactuals were made in his *Times Literary Supplement* review, 'Roads not taken', of Andrew Roberts, ed, *What Might Have Been: Imaginary history from twelve leading historians*, Weidenfeld and Nicolson, London, 2004.

1 What if the Treaty of Waitangi had not been signed on 6 February 1840?

1 Claudia Orange, *The Treaty of Waitangi*, Allen and Unwin/Port Nicholson Press, Wellington, 1987, p.60. Orange has pointed out that, '[f]or Hobson, the initial signing at Waitangi was the "de facto" treaty; the later signings

Notes

he represented as merely acts that "further ratified and confirmed" it.'
Orange, *Treaty of Waitangi*, p.60. Thanks also to colleagues in the history
department, Georgetown University, for their comments on this paper.

2 Orange, *Treaty of Waitangi*, pp.51, 52.

3 Orange, *Treaty of Waitangi*, p.51.

4 Orange, *Treaty of Waitangi*, pp.52–5.

5 Orange, *Treaty of Waitangi*, pp.52–5.

6 Johannes Bulhof, 'What If? Modality and History', *History and Theory*,
vol.38, no.2, 1999, pp.145–6.

7 See, for instance: Waitangi Tribunal, *The Muriwhenua Land Report*, WAI
45, Waitangi Tribunal, Wellington, 1997.

8 Paul McHugh, *The Maori Magna Carta: New Zealand Law and the Treaty
of Waitangi*, Oxford University Press, Auckland, 1991, p.30.

9 James Belich, *Making Peoples: A History of the New Zealanders from
Polynesian Settlement to the End of the Nineteenth Century*, Penguin,
Auckland, 1996, p.196.

10 Orange, *Treaty of Waitangi*, p.29.

11 Claudia Orange, *An Illustrated History of the Treaty of Waitangi*, Bridget
Williams Books, Wellington, 2004, p.16.

12 Paul Moon, *Te Ara ki te Tiriti: The Path to the Treaty of Waitangi*, David
Ling, Auckland, 2002, pp.10–11.

13 Moon, *Te Ara ki te Tiriti The Path to the Treaty of Waitangi*, pp.10–11.

14 Normanby to Hobson, 14–15 August 1839, *GBPP (Great Britain
Parliamentary Papers)*, vol.23, pp.37–45. Subsequent references to the
instructions are to this source. See also Moon, *Te Ara ki te Tiriti*, pp.108–
18.

15 Orange, *An Illustrated History of the Treaty of Waitangi*, p.19.

16 Cited in Orange, *Treaty of Waitangi*, p.28.

17 Andrew Sharp, 'The Treaty in the Real Life of the Constitution', in Michael
Belgrave, Merata Kawharu and David Williams, eds, *Waitangi Revisited:
Perspectives on the Treaty of Waitangi*, Oxford University Press, Auckland,
2005, p.311.

18 McHugh, *Maori Magna Carta*, pp.11–12.

19 James Belich, 'Hobson's Choice', review article, *New Zealand Journal of
History*, vol.24, no.2, 1990, p.205; Vincent O'Malley, 'Treaty-Making in
Early Colonial New Zealand', *New Zealand Journal of History*, vol.33,
no.2, 1999, pp.137–54.

20 O'Malley, 'Treaty-Making in Early Colonial New Zealand', p.140.

21 See Francis Paul Prucha, *American Indian Treaties: The History of a
Political Anomaly*, University of California Press, Berkeley and Los
Angeles, 1994; and Vine Deloria Jr. and David E. Wilkins, *Tribes, Treaties
and Constitutional Tribulations*, University of Texas Press, Austin, Texas,
1999.

22 For historical analyses which suggest the Treaty's 'exceptionality', see T.
Lindsay Buick, *The Treaty of Waitangi*, Wellington, 1914; and Keith Sinclair's
History of New Zealand, 1st edition, Penguin, Harmondsworth, 1959.
Those who emphasise the wider imperial and international context include
(but are not limited to): Peter Adams, *Fatal Necessity: British Intervention
in New Zealand 1830–1847*, Auckland University Press, Auckland, 1977;
Orange, *Treaty of Waitangi*, pp.2–3; and M.P.K. Sorrenson, 'Treaties in
British Colonial Policy: Precedents for Waitangi', in William Renwick, ed,

Sovereignty and Indigenous Rights: The Treaty of Waitangi in International Contexts, Victoria University Press, Wellington, 1991, pp.15–29.

23 See Ken S. Coates, 'International Perspectives on Relations with Indigenous Peoples', in Ken S. Coates and P.G. McHugh, eds, *Living Relationships Kokiri Ngatahi: The Treaty of Waitangi in the New Millennium*, Victoria University Press, Wellington, 1998, pp.19–103; Paul Havemann, ed, *Indigenous Peoples' Rights in Australia, Canada and New Zealand*, Oxford University Press, Auckland, 1999; Marcia Langton, Maureen Tehan, Lisa Palmer and Kathryn Shain, eds, *Honour Among Nations? Treaties and Agreements with Indigenous People*, Melbourne University Press, Melbourne, 2004; Janine Hayward and Richard T. Price, 'Indian Treaties and Land Claims in Canada', in Janine Hayward and Nicola R. Wheen, eds, *The Waitangi Tribunal: Te Roopu Whakamana it te Tiriti o Waitangi*, Bridget Williams Books, Wellington, 2004, pp.139–53.

24 Bulhof, 'What If? Modality and History', pp.145–68.

25 Gavriel Rosenfeld, 'Why do we ask "What if?" Reflections on the Function of Alternate History', *History and Theory*, Theme Issue 41, December 2002, pp.90–103 (p.90).

26 For popular expressions of alternate histories, see the bibliography available at http://www.uchronia.net. Scholarly investigations and critiques include: Niall Ferguson, ed, *Virtual History: Alternatives and Counter-Factuals*, Basic Books, New York, 1999; Robert Cowley, ed, *What If? The World's Foremost Military Historians Imagine What Might Have Been*, Pan MacMillan, New York, 2001; Robert Cowley, ed, *What If? 2: Eminent Historians Imagine What Might Have Been*, Putnam, New York, 2001. Other works include Alexander Demandt, *History That Never Happened: A Treatise on the Question, What Would Have Happened If . . .?*, McFarland, Jefferson, N.C., 1993; Karen Hellekson, *The Alternate History: Refiguring Historical Time*, Kent State University Press, Kent, Ohio, 2001; William J. Collins, 'Paths Not Taken: The Development, Structure and Aesthetics of Alternative History', PhD thesis, University of California, Davis, 1990; Edgar V. McKnight, Jnr., 'Alternative History: The Development of a Literary Genre', PhD thesis, University of North Carolina, Chapel Hill, 1994.

27 Demandt, *History That Never Happened*, pp.70, 122; McKnight, 'Alternative History: The Development of a Literary Genre', p.10.

28 Rosenfeld, 'Why do we ask "What if?"', p.92.

29 Rosenfeld, 'Why do we ask "What if?"', p.90.

30 Rosenfeld, 'Why do we ask "What if?"', p.93.

31 Rosenfeld, 'Why do we ask "What if?"', p.93.

32 The New Zealand Futures Trust is one such example. This organisation aims to: 'identify developments and changes affecting the lives and aspirations of New Zealanders, and to promote debate about possible futures'. http://www.futurestrust.org.nz, accessed 3 May 2005.

33 On the Waitangi Tribunal, see Giselle Byrnes, *The Waitangi Tribunal and New Zealand History*, Oxford University Press, Melbourne, 2004; W.H. Oliver, 'The Future Behind Us: The Waitangi Tribunal's Retrospective Utopia', in Andrew Sharp and Paul McHugh, eds, *Histories, Power and Loss—Uses of the Past: A New Zealand Commentary*, Bridget Williams Books, Wellington, 2001, pp.9–29.

2 What if Maori had not been made British subjects in 1840?

1   Claudia Orange, *The Treaty of Waitangi*, Port Nicholson Press, Wellington, 1987, pp.42–3. In writing this counterfactual, I am grateful to Claudia Orange's *Illustrated History of the Treaty of Waitangi*, Bridget Williams Books, Wellington, 2004 for reminding me of the facts of New Zealand's Treaty history. Thanks also to Mike Murphy (University of Northern British Columbia) for bringing a little reality to these imaginings.

2   Paul Moon, *Te Ara ki te Tiriti: The Path to the Treaty of Waitangi*, David Ling, Auckland, 2002, pp.84–9.

3   See, for example, Alan Cairns, *Citizens Plus: Aboriginal Peoples and the Canadian State*, University of British Columbia Press, Vancouver, 2000.

3 What if Nelson had been made the capital of New Zealand?

1   An overview of these events is provided by John E. Martin in *The House: New Zealand's House of Representatives 1854–2004*, Dunmore Press, Palmerston North, 2004, pp.38–41. The reference to FitzGerald's 15 September 1854 proposal, and his failure to organise his colleagues on its behalf, is from Edmund Bohan's *'Blest Madman': FitzGerald of Canterbury*, Canterbury University Press, Christchurch, 1998, p.130. Bohan has also produced *Edward Stafford: New Zealand's First Statesman*, Hazard Press, Christchurch, 1994. The record of parliamentary debates and votes is from New Zealand's *Hansard*: 15 September 1854, p.444; 26 May 1856, pp.99–100; 3 July 1856, pp.251–4; 4 July 1856, pp.255–61; 12 August 1856, pp.354–6; 16 August 1856, pp.365–6; and 25 November 1863, pp.926–9. The quotation about Lord Auckland is from Michael King, *The Penguin History of New Zealand*, Penguin Books, Auckland, 2003, p.165. King (p.165) also notes the progression of the seat of government from the Bay of Islands to Auckland. A brief entry on Russell as 'the country's oldest centre of permanent European settlement, originally known as Kororareka', is found in *Bateman New Zealand Encyclopedia*, 5th edition, David Bateman, Auckland, 2000, p.557.

2   Clark's thought processes take place in mid-2005—that is, prior to the September 2005 general election—and they range over a number of people. To identify them in terms of their roles at the time that this takes place: Koizumi Junichiro is Japan's prime minister; Michael Howard is a former leader of the British Conservative Party, defeated in the 2005 general election by Labour's Tony Blair; Lockwood Smith is a National MP; Simon Power is also a National MP and the parliamentary caucus's senior whip; Mike Ward is a Green MP; Jeanette Fitzsimons is one of the Green Party's co-leaders; Michael Cullen is minister of finance and deputy prime minister; Mike Williams is the Labour Party president; Mike Munro is the prime minister's chief press secretary; and Heather Simpson is the prime minister's chief of staff. Others points of identification are as follows: Jenny Shipley was National's leader at the time of the 1999 election; Bill English was National's leader at the time of the 2002 election; Don Brash was National's leader going into the 2005 election; and only five New Zealand prime ministers have died in office—John Ballance, Richard John Seddon, William F. Massey, Michael Joseph Savage and Norman Kirk. Matai Industries was an ultimately unsuccessful venture that had been set up under the third

Labour government's regional development programme. Tony Brunt was a Victoria University political science honours student who, with others, did set up the Values Party in 1972. There was indeed a Nelson 'notional railway'; there was and is, however, no tunnel at Takaka.

3   Martin, *The House*, p.32.

4 What if New Zealand had joined Australia in 1901?

1   Federation Commission, *AJHR*, 1901, vol.1, p.v.
2   John Hirst, 'Western Australia', in Graeme Davison, John Hirst and Stuart Macintyre, eds, *The Oxford Companion to Australian History*, revised edition, Oxford University Press, Melbourne, 2001, pp.683–4. For an overview of Australian federation and new Zealand's position, see Stuart Macintyre, 'The Nation-building Project in the Antipodes' in Arthur Grimes, Lydia Wevers and Ginny Sullivan, eds, *States of Mind: Australia & New Zealand, 1901–2001*, Institute of Policy Studies, Victoria University of Wellington, Wellington, 2002.
3   My apologies to Stuart Macintyre upon whose description of Federation celebrations in Kalgoorlie this is loosely based. See Macintyre, *The Oxford History of Australia, vol.4, 1901–1942*, Oxford University Press, Melbourne, 1986, p.xviii.
4   Macintyre, *The Oxford History of Australia*, p.xviii.
5   Philippa Mein-Smith, 'New Zealand' in Helen Irving, ed, *The Centenary Companion to Australian Federation*, Cambridge University Press, Melbourne, 1999, pp.400–01.
6   Henry Parkes's Tenterfield speech, 1889, cited in Mein-Smith, 'New Zealand', p.402.
7   Swan River was a free colony from its foundation in 1829 until 1850. See Pamela Statham, 'Swan River Colony, 1829–1850', in C. T. Stannage, ed, *A New History of Western Australia*, University of Western Australia Press, Perth, 1981.
8   Federation Commission, *AJHR*, 1901, vol.1, p.xxii.
9   See John Chesterman and Brian Galligan, *Citizens Without Rights: Aborigines and Australian Citizenship*, Cambridge University Press, Melbourne, 1997, pp.85ff. See also Federation Commission, *AJHR*, 1901, p.x, for New Zealand's view of 'coloured labour' employed in Queensland as undesirable but necessary.
10 This policy was amended in 1920 to prescribe what some historians have called the 'undeclared White New Zealand policy'. Donald Denoon, Philippa Mein-Smith, Marivic Wyndham, *A History of Australia, New Zealand and the Pacific*, Blackwells, Oxford, 2000, p.211; on Maori councils, see Richard S. Hill, *State Authority, Indigenous Autonomy: Crown-Maori Relations in New Zealand/Aotearoa, 1900–1950*, Victoria University Press, Wellington, 2004, pp.50–51.
11 Manying Ip, *Dragons on the Long White Cloud*, Tandem Press, Auckland, 1996, pp.174–5. The comment is made about the idea of a New Zealand 'people', but is remarkably easily transferred.
12 Hill, *State Authority, Indigenous Autonomy*, p.19.
13 Hill, *State Authority, Indigenous Autonomy*, p.45.
14 Hill, *State Authority, Indigenous Autonomy*, pp.45, 46.

15 On New South Wales 'dispersal' policies, see Heather Goodall, *Invasion to Embassy: Land in Aboriginal Politics in New South Wales, 1770–1972*, Allen and Unwin, Sydney, 1996, chapter 11; on Victoria, see Richard Broome, *Aboriginal Victorians: A History since 1800*, Allen and Unwin, Sydney, 2005, pp.194–9.

16 Chesterman and Galligan, *Citizens Without Rights*, pp.38ff.

17 Geoffrey Bolton, 'Black and White after 1897', in Stannage, *A New History of Western Australia*, p.128.

18 Chesterman and Galligan, *Citizens Without Rights*, pp.38–9; Bolton, 'Black and White after 1897', pp.128–9.

19 http://www.idealcity.org.au/a_nation_needs-4-choosing_location.html accessed 10 June 2005.

20 http://www.idealcity.org.au/a_nation_needs-4-choosing_location.html accessed 10 June 2005.

21 http://www.idealcity.org.au/a_nation_needs-4-choosing_location.html accessed 10 June 2005.

22 Russel Ward, *The Australian Legend*, Oxford University Press, Melbourne (1958), 1988, pp.1–2.

23 The Nullarbor Plain and the Great Victoria Desert make up the approximately 2000 kilometres of desert that separate temperate Eastern Australia from the Western Australian coastal settlements.

24 www.netballnz.co.nz/thegame accessed 13 June 2005.

25 M.P.K. Sorrenson, 'Buck, Peter Henry', *Dictionary of New Zealand Biography*, www.dnzb.org.nz, 7 March 2005.

26 See Denoon et al, *A History of Australia*, p.312.

27 Bolton, 'Black and White after 1897', p.140.

28 Cited in Bolton, 'Black and White after 1897', p.133.

29 Bolton, 'Black and White after 1897', p.146.

30 Bolton, 'Black and White after 1897', p.147.

31 Bolton, 'Black and White after 1897', pp.148–9.

32 See for New Zealand in the 1920s and 1930s, Michael King, 'Between two worlds' in Geoffrey W. Rice, ed, *The Oxford History of New Zealand*, Oxford University Press, Auckland, 1992, pp.286–7; see for New South Wales, Heather Goodall, *Invasion to Embassy*, 1996 pp.115ff; for Victoria, see Richard Broome, *Aboriginal Victorians*, pp.183ff.

33 King, 'Between two worlds', p.287.

34 King, 'Between two worlds', p.288.

35 King, 'Between two worlds', p.293.

36 See Goodall, *Invasion to Embassy*, chapters 10 and 11.

37 For ongoing purchasing of Maori lands, see Hill, *State Authority, Indigenous Autonomy*, p.69; for 'using' their lands, see Hill, *State Authority, Indigenous Autonomy*, p.82.

38 Hill, *State Authority, Indigenous Autonomy*, p.66.

39 Bolton, 'Black and White after 1897', p.151.

40 The pavlova question has been explored by Jennifer Hillier, 'The pavlova and "the fate of nations"', in Grimes, Wevers and Sullivan, *States of Mind*.

41 Chesterman and Galligan, *Citizens Without Rights*, p.11.

42 Chesterman and Galligan, *Citizens Without Rights*, p.7.

Notes

5 What if the strikers at Waihi had triumphed?

1 See Erik Olssen, *The Red Feds: Revolutionary Industrial Unionism and the New Zealand Federation of Labour 1908–1914*, Oxford University Press, Auckland, 1988. For an account of the 1951 waterfront strike, see Michael Bassett, *Confrontation '51: The 1951 waterfront dispute*, Reed, Wellington, 1972.

2 It is true that the Liberal government appointed Cullen rather than Mitchell, but this was in part because of the opposition's strong preference. See Sherwood Young's essay on Mitchell and Richard S. Hill's on Cullen in Claudia Orange, ed, *The Dictionary of New Zealand Biography*, vol.3, *1901–1920*, Auckland University Press and the Department of Internal Affairs, Auckland, 1996, pp.125–7, 345.

3 The strike at the Blackball coal mine led to a decision against the miners' union by the arbitration court (which fined the union). This inflamed the miners and widened support for their cause among workers elsewhere. In the end the miners succeeded in defying the court, and the law under which it had been established, arousing greater worker solidarity while at the same time angering employers and farmers. See Olssen, *The Red Feds*, chapter 1: 'The Blackball Strike and the West Coast Miners'.

4 See E.J.B. Allen, *Labour and Politics*, Wellington, 1918 (with a foreword by Labour leader Harry Holland).

5 Workers were also in the process of being domesticated, as the Caversham team has shown in *Sites of Gender*: see Barbara Brookes, Annabel Cooper and Robin Law, eds, *Sites of Gender: women, men and modernity in Southern Dunedin, 1890–1939*, Auckland University Press, Auckland, 2003.

6 De Leon and his followers had been expelled from the IWW in 1905. Members of the IWW also came to be known as 'Wobblies' or 'Bummers', the latter from their unofficial anthem: 'Hallelluja I'm a Bum'.

7 Evans was a 'Red Fed' engine driver, killed in November 1912 as the Waihi strike came to a violent end, with fighting amongst police, workers and 'Red Feds'. See Olssen, *The Red Feds*, p.159.

8 *Tom Barker and the IWW*, recorded, edited and with an introduction by Eric Fry, Australian Society for the Study of Labour History, Canberra, 1965.

9 *Maoriland Worker* was a journal of industrial unionism, socialism and politics established by the shearers' union in 1910 but taken over and managed by the New Zealand Federation of Labour from February 1911 until the federation voted to end its existence in 1915.

10 See E.J.B. Allen, *Revolutionary Unionism*, London, 1909 and Auckland, 1913.

11 This would have been comparable to the situation that finally came to prevail in the 1940s except that the Labour movement—the Red Federation—would have had an influence on Reform governments comparable to that of the New Zealand Employers' Federation on Peter Fraser's Labour government.

6 What if New Zealand soldiers had never fought at Gallipoli?

1 Christopher Pugsley, *The ANZAC Experience: New Zealand, Australia and Empire in the First World War*, Reed, Auckland, 2004, p.64; and

Christopher Pugsley, *Gallipoli: The New Zealand Story*, revised edition, Reed, Auckland, 1998, p.363.

2   Ian McGibbon, ed, *The Oxford Companion to New Zealand Military History*, Oxford University Press, Auckland, 2000, pp.27–30, 198; Peter Dennis, Jeffrey Grey, Ewan Morris and Robin Prior, eds, *The Oxford Companion to Australian Military History*, Oxford University Press, Melbourne, 1995, pp.37–49.

3   See Pugsley, *The ANZAC Experience*, pp.20–21.

4   Pugsley, *The ANZAC Experience*, pp.71–3; Martin Gilbert, 'Churchill and Gallipoli', in Jenny Macleod ed, *Gallipoli: Making History*, Frank Cass, London and New York, 2004, pp.14–43; John Charmley, *Churchill: The End of Glory: A Political Biography*, Hodder and Stoughton, London, 1993, pp.104–25.

5   Gilbert, 'Churchill and Gallipoli', pp.14–43. Also see Charmley, *Churchill: The End of Glory*, pp.104–25. Jenny Macleod, *Reconsidering Gallipoli*, Manchester University Press, Manchester, 2004, p.2, argued that 'the [Gallipoli] strategy was initiated by First Lord of the Admiralty Winston Churchill. That it was accepted by the war council had much to do with, on the one side, Churchill's vigorous enthusiasm and, on the other, Secretary of State for War Kitchener's and Prime Minister Asquith's passivity.'

6   Charmley, *Churchill: The End of Glory*, p.110.

7   The Churchill Center website: '1895: Action This Day' (http://www.winstonchurchill.org/i4a/pages/index.cfm?pageid=174). Also see John Keegan, *Winston Churchill*, Viking Penguin, New York, 2002, pp.31–3.

8   Winston S. Churchill, *The River War: An Historical Account of the Reconquest of the Soudan*, Nelson, London, 1899, pp.331–74 (especially see pp.333–4, 346–56, 361, 373–4, 385–6); Keegan, *Winston Churchill*, pp.46–7; and Wikipedia, the free encyclopedia website: 'Battle of Omdurman' (http://en.wikipedia.org/wiki/Battle_of_Omdurman). Keegan, p.47, provides somewhat different numbers for the cavalry charge: 310 members of the 21st Lancers, charging 3000 infantry.

9   Churchill, *The River War*, p.385. Churchill does not specify the units to which these three war correspondents were attached.

10 Winston Spencer Churchill, *London to Ladysmith via Pretoria*, Longmans, London, 1900, pp.76–97; and The Churchill Center website: '1899: Action This Day' (http://www.winstonchurchill.org/i4a/pages/index. cfm?pageid=178). On 12 December 1899, after a month in captivity, Churchill escaped from a prisoner-of-war camp in Pretoria. He then travelled across Boer territory to safety in Delagoa Bay in Portuguese East Africa, from where he was given safe passage on a ship bound for Durban. Once back on territory controlled by British military forces, he quickly returned to the front lines to continue his reports on the war. (See Churchill, *London to Ladysmith*, pp.175–214).

11 The Churchill Center website: '1900: Action This Day' (http://www.winstonchurchill.org/i4a/pages/index.cfm?pageid=179). Also see Churchill, *London to Ladysmith*, pp.286–8, 307–12, 318–26, 329, 332–4, 470–71.

12 Pugsley, *The ANZAC Experience*, p.72; and Arthur Banks, *A Military Atlas of the First World War: A Map History of the War of 1914–18 on Land, at Sea and in the Air*, Leo Cooper, London, 1989, pp.110–17.

13 McGibbon, ed, *Oxford Companion*, p.174.

14 David L. Bullock, *Allenby's War: The Palestine-Arabian Campaigns, 1916–*

1918, Blandford Press, London, 1988, pp.9–10.

15 Bullock, *Allenby's War*, pp.13–14. Also see Rachel Simon, *Libya Between Ottomanism and Nationalism: The Ottoman Involvement in Libya during the War with Italy (1911–1919)*, Klaus Schwarz Verlag, Berlin, 1987, pp.68–9.

16 Bullock, *Allenby's War*, p.13; and Feroz Ahmad, *The Young Turks: The Committee of Union and Progress in Turkish Politics, 1908–1914*, Clarendon Press, London, 1969, p.145.

17 Iraj Bashiri, 'Enver Pasha', copyright 2000 (http://www.angelfire.com/rnb/bashiri/Enver/Enver.html); Ahmad Feroz, *The Young Turks*, pp.98, 164; and Dankwart A. Rustow, 'Enwer Pasha', in B. Lewis, Ch. Pellat and J. Schacht, eds, *The Encyclopaedia of Islam*, vol.II, 2nd edition, E.J. Brill, Leiden, 1965, p.698.

18 Stanley Sandler. ed, *Ground Warfare: An International Encyclopedia*, vol. II, ABC Clio, Santa Barbara, 2002, p.422.

19 Simon, *Libya Between Ottomanism and Nationalism*, including pp.360, 386, provides a number of references to works in German or Turkish which may clarify how closely Enver participated in the fighting in Libya.

20 Bernard Lewis, *The Emergence of Modern Turkey*, 3rd edition, Oxford University Press, New York and Oxford, 2002, pp.224–5; and Ahmad Feroz, *The Young Turks*, p.119.

21 McGibbon, ed, *Oxford Companion*, p.198.

22 As quoted in Gilbert, 'Churchill and Gallipoli', p.35.

23 My thanks to Aaron Fox, New Zealand Defence Force, for his suggestion of a detour to England in 1915 for extra training and re-equipping.

24 McGibbon, ed, *Oxford Companion*, pp.601–2. For the Australian casualty figures see Dennis, Grey, Morris and Prior, eds, *Oxford Companion*, pp.261–2, 654–5.

25 Pugsley, *Gallipoli*, p.363.

26 Dennis, Grey, Morris and Prior, eds, *Oxford Companion*, pp.654–5.

27 Compare Jenny Macleod, *Reconsidering Gallipoli*, pp.12–13, 238, who has argued that the relatively lower cost in casualties, and the timing of the campaign (before the horrors of the Battle of the Somme), have enabled British 'recollection of the Gallipoli campaign to be in a manner quite separate from that of the Western Front'. (The quote is from p.12).

28 For general comments by Winston Churchill to the British War Council on 26 February 1915 concerning the variety of possible roles, including combat operations, which Allied occupation troops may have undertaken, see Gilbert, 'Churchill and Gallipoli', p.35.

29 Pugsley, *The ANZAC Experience*, p.79, states that this Turkish fear of being stripped of 'Turkey in Europe' was accurate.

30 Gilbert, 'Churchill and Gallipoli', pp.39–40.

7 What if New Zealand had not gone to war in 1939?

1 For accounts of New Zealand's participation in the Second World War, see F.L.W. Wood, *The New Zealand People at War: Political and External Affairs*, Department of Internal Affairs, Wellington, 1971, in New Zealand's Official War Histories Series; and, for a more recent history, Ian McGibbon, *New Zealand and the Second World War: The people, the battles and the legacy*, Hodder Moa Beckett, Auckland, 2004.

2. For an account of New Zealand's relations with Australia during World War II, see Denis McLean, *The Prickly Pair, Making Nationalism in Australia and New Zealand*, Otago University Press, Dunedin, 2003; chapter 6, 'Rivalry in Patriotism', looks at Australian and New Zealand dealings with Britain during the war and chapter 7, 'Ties that Bind', covers relations with the United States and the efforts of the two regional countries to uphold their own interests and establish an ANZAC sphere of influence in the Pacific region.

8 What if Japan had invaded New Zealand?

1 I am grateful to John Crawford and Peter Cooke for commenting on this paper and for making a number of helpful suggestions.

2 On 10 May 1942 the German raider *Thor* intercepted and captured the merchant ship *Nankin* in the southern Indian Ocean. Although secret papers were destroyed before the Germans got aboard, a number of intelligence summaries prepared by the New Zealand authorities had been inadvertently included in the ordinary mail. These papers were eventually passed by the Germans to the Japanese authorities, who do not appear to have derived any benefit from them. Careful analysis might have allowed them to deduce that their signals traffic was being read by the Allies. Had they changed their codes before the Battle of Midway, Nimitz would have been deprived of a vital source of information about Japanese plans. However, the Germans would have had to hand over the papers to the Japanese almost immediately for such action to have been possible, since Midway began only twenty-five days later.

3 I have based my outline of a Japanese victory at Midway on Theodore F. Cook, Jr, 'Our Midway Disaster, Japan Springs a Trap, June 4, 1942', in Robert Cowley, ed, *What If? Military Historians Imagine What Might Have Been*, Pan Books, London, 2001, pp.311–40.

4 See Ian McGibbon, *Bluewater Rationale: The Naval Defence of New Zealand 1914–1942*, Government Printer, Wellington, 1981, pp.371–2.

5 The myth that Australia demanded its troops back immediately after Japan entered the war, in contrast to New Zealand's willingness to leave its division in the Middle East, is now deeply engrained in the New Zealand consciousness of the Second World War. In reality the divergence in the Australian and New Zealand positions occurred in late 1942, after the Allied victory at El Alamein, when Australia removed its remaining division and New Zealand, much to Australian Prime Minister John Curtin's ire, decided to leave its division in the theatre until the end of the North African campaign. But by this time the enemy was no longer at the gates, because the danger of invasion of either country had receded to virtually nil as a result of US naval victories. On this issue see Ian McGibbon, *New Zealand and the Second World War: The people, the battles and the legacy*, Hodder Moa Beckett, Auckland, 2004, pp.104–5, 139–40.

6 I am indebted to Peter Cooke for these figures.

7 The former quarantine station on Somes Island, in Wellington Harbour, was used by the New Zealand authorities during both world wars to intern enemy aliens.

8 In effect, I am suggesting that the Japanese would have adopted the same

approach as the Americans did in reality in Bougainville in November 1943. The object of the US landing on that island was to secure an area in which air bases could be built and protected in order to facilitate the drive on the main Japanese base in the region at Rabaul. No attempt was made to occupy the rest of the island, at least until Australian forces took over from the Americans in late 1944.

9 Featherston was, of course, the site of the camp in which Japanese prisoners of war from the Solomon Islands were held.

10 I have based Shannon's destruction on the awful fate that befell the French village of Oradour-sur-Glane on 10 July 1944. After their column was fired upon, Waffen-SS troops surrounded the village and killed every inhabitant they could find, including babies and the very old, before destroying the town. It remains today in the state they left it, a poignant memorial. To be sure, this atrocity was committed by Germans, but Japan's inglorious record of occupation in China and elsewhere suggests that such action by Japanese troops in New Zealand would have been entirely possible.

11 There would have been immense societal pressures against any social contact with a hated enemy. But relationships between local women and men of an occupying power are not uncommon, even when different races are involved. Contact between German women and black French troops in Germany after the First World War, for example, led to the birth of mixed-race children, who would suffer at the hands of the Nazis in the late 1930s. When they had the opportunity after the Second World War to meet Japanese on a personal level, New Zealanders often found that they liked them a lot, and about seventy members of Kayforce married Japanese women. In the event of relationships developing between Japanese soldiers or civilians in an occupied New Zealand, the women involved may well have decided that returning to Japan with their man was preferable to facing the judgment of a vengeful community, one so small that it would be impossible to hide. The humiliation meted out to French women who consorted with German soldiers, following France's liberation in 1944, is an indication of their probable fate.

9 What if the Manapouri power project had never been constructed?

1 This chapter—or at least its factual aspects—is based upon my doctoral thesis: Aaron P. Fox, 'The Power Game: The development of the Manapouri-Tiwai Point electro-industrial complex 1904–1969', department of history, University of Otago, Dunedin, unpublished doctoral thesis, 2001.

2 See, for instance, Michael King, *The Penguin History of New Zealand*, Penguin, Auckland, 2003, p.441.

3 Fox, 'The Power Game', p.142.

4 P.S. Hay, superintending engineer, public works department, Wellington, 'Report On New Zealand Water Powers Etc. 16 September 1904', *Appendix to the Journal of the House of Representatives*, Wellington, 1904, vol.II, D-1a, p.31.

5 *New Zealand Gazette*, 1904, vol.II, pp.2751–2.

6 See, for instance, A.H. Reed and A.W. Reed, *Farthest West Afoot and Afloat. Together with E.H. Wilmot's Journal of the Pioneer Survey of the Lake Manapouri-Dusky Sound Area*, A.H. and A.W. Reed, Wellington, 1950.

7   See, for instance, R. Graham, *The Aluminium Industry and The Third World: Multinational Corporations and Underdevelopment*, Zed Press, London, 1982.

8   Hamish Keith and William Main, *New Zealand Yesterdays: A look at our recent past*, Reader's Digest Services, Sydney, 1984, p.48.

9   John E. Martin, ed, *People, Politics and Power Stations: Electric Power Generation in New Zealand, 1880–1998*, 2nd edition, Electricity Corporation of New Zealand and Historical Branch, Department of Internal Affairs, Wellington, 1998, chapter 6, 'Planning for Demand'.

10 Fox, 'The Power Game', chapter 3: 'A New Era of Industry (1929–1936)', and chapter 4, 'White Gold (1936–1952)'.

11 Fox, 'The Power Game', p.108.

12 Fox, 'The Power Game', p.143.

13 J.R. Hanan, 'Financial Statement', *New Zealand Parliamentary Debates* [*NZPD*], Wellington, vol.287, 2 September 1949, p.1833.

14 *NZPD*, vol.305, 29 April 1955, pp.680–81.

15 Brian Carroll, *Potlines and People: A History of the Bell Bay Aluminium Smelter*, Comalco, Melbourne, 1980, p.45.

16 Matthew Paterson, *The Point at Issue: Petroleum energy politics in New Zealand 1955–90*, Collins, Auckland, 1991, pp.5–21; George Fraser, *Both Eyes Open: A Memoir*, Pauline Fraser and Graham Adams, eds, John McIndoe, Dunedin, 1990, pp.111–14.

17 Fox, 'The Power Game', pp.168–9, 174–5.

18 J.T. Salmon, *Heritage Destroyed: The Crisis in Scenery Preservation in New Zealand*, A.H. Reed and A.W. Reed, Wellington, 1960, p.100.

19 *The Nature Conservation Council 1962–1975*, Wellington, 1975, pp.8–11.

20 The 90 MW Aratiatia power station is located at the site of the Aratiatia Rapids on the Waikato River. The rapids remain a tourist attraction, having been permitted to run at set times each day since the power station commenced operation in 1964. The 540 MW Benmore power station, constructed between 1958 and 1965, is the largest hydroelectric station on the Waitaki River. Benmore consists of a gigantic earth dam and Lake Benmore, New Zealand's largest artificial lake. Martin, *People, Politics and Power Stations*, pp.168–70, 183–8.

21 R. J. Hogg, 'Energy, the Economy and the Environment: An Administrative View', in D. M. Adcock, ed, *Energy and the Environment*, New Zealand Institute of Public Administration, Wellington, 1974, pp.142–3.

22 It is interesting to note that the atomic power division of the Westinghouse Electric Corporation had previously approached the New Zealand government in September 1968 when the company was investigating suitable locations around the world for the establishment of facilities for the chemical processing of nuclear fuel. The magnitude of the proposal, which required between 2000 and 3000 MW, proved to be beyond the government's hydroelectric resources. See Fox, 'The Power Game', p.298.

23 See, for instance, Wolfgang Rosenberg, *A Guidebook to New Zealand's Future*, Caxton, Christchurch, 1968, pp.57–8.

24 Nicola Wheen, 'A History of New Zealand Environmental Law', in Eric Pawson and Tom Brooking, eds, *Environmental Histories of New Zealand*, Oxford University Press, Auckland, 2002, p.265.

25 See, for instance, Roger Wilson, *From Manapouri to Aramoana: The*

battle for New Zealand's environment, Earthworks Press, Auckland, 1982, pp.171–89.

26 Barry Gustafson, *His Way: A Biography of Robert Muldoon*, Auckland University Press, Auckland, 2000, pp.277–89.

27 Wilson, *From Manapouri to Aramoana*, p.48.

28 On 28 March 1979 the Three Mile Island Unit 2 nuclear reactor near Middleton, Pennsylvania, suffered a loss of coolant which led to a partial meltdown of the reactor core. The world watched for five days as the damaged plant was then rescued from the brink of disaster. See http://www.nrc.gov/ reading-rm/doc-collections/fact-sheets/3mile-isle.html; and Peter Pringle and James Spigelman, *The Nuclear Barons*, London, 1982, pp.422–3.

10 What if Muldoon's 'think big' energy projects had succeeded?

1 Nathan Small, '"Think Big" on Energy Independence', *The Herald Sun*, 9 June 2005; Tammy Baldwin, 'House Debate on Energy Legislation', 15 June 2004 (accessed from Congresswoman Baldwin's website); Carl Mortished, 'Big is Beautiful in a World of Scarce Energy', *Times Online*, 11 May 2005.

2 James D. Fearon, 'Counterfactuals and Hypothesis Testing in Political Science', *World Politics*, vol.43, no.2, January 1991, p.194.

3 Hon W.F. Birch, *Energy Strategy '79*, Parliament Buildings, Wellington, December 1979, p.14.

4 G.S. Harris, M. Ellis, G. Scott, J. Wood and P. Phillips, *Energy Scenarios for New Zealand*, Report no.19, March 1977, New Zealand Energy Research and Development Committee, p.43.

5 Birch, *Energy Strategy '79*.

6 Harris et al., *Energy Scenarios for New Zealand*, p.5.

7 Robert L. Hirsch, Roger Bezdek and Robert Wendling, 'Peaking of World Oil Production: Impacts, Mitigation, and Risk Management', February 2005: available from Cornell University Library's Open Access Depository at http://dspace.libary.cornell.edu/handle/1813/692?mode=full.

8 Chevron Corporation, 'Why Now?', http://www.willyoujoinus.com/ vision/.

9 P. Fraser, 'Economic Management in Retrospect: Old Wine in New Bottles? A View from 2004', Paper presented to the 2004 New Zealand Association of Economists' Conference, Wellington, p.20.

10 Hon Bill Birch, 'Natural Gas and Liquid Fuels', news release by the minister of energy, 13 September 1979.

11 See, for example, Tim Hazeldine, 'Why "Think Big" is "Think Bad"', *New Zealand Listener*, 28 February 1981; Aynsley Kellow, *Transforming Power: the Politics of Electricity Planning*, Cambridge University Press, Cambridge, 1996.

12 Jeanette Fitzsimons, 'Beyond Logic: The real reasons for synthetic petrol', *NZ Environment*, Winter 1982, p.22.

13 Simon Louisson, 'Engineering Triumph: But will Motonui prove worth it all?', *The Press*, 19 March 1986, p.19.

14 Michael Cullen, 'Appropriation Bill no.3: Financial Statement: Second Reading', 9 August 1990.

15 Hirsch et al., 'Peaking of World Oil Production'.

16 Fraser, 'Economic Management in Retrospect', p.26.

17 Roger Kerr, 'Energy Efficiency', address to the Gas Association of New Zealand Energy Symposium 2000, 28 August 2000.

18 Dick Cheney, full text of Dick Cheney's speech at the Institute of Petroleum autumn lunch, 1999, London Institute of Petroleum, 9 June 2004: available from http://web.archive/org/web.20000414054656/http:www.petroleum.co.uk/speeches.htm.

19 Harris et al., *Energy Scenarios for New Zealand*, p.43.

20 Helen Murdoch, 'Fuel-cost rise sinks fishing', *Press*, 29 June, 2005, Edition 2, p.6.

21 James Hamilton and Robert Kaufmann, 'Drilling for Broke?: Experts debate "Peak Oil"', *Wall Street Journal Online*, 3 August 2005.

22 Birch, *Energy Strategy '79*, p.8.

11 What if Brian Talboys had said 'yes' to the plotters in 1980?

1 So named after the colonels who ruled Greece in the early 1970s. Also involved as a numbers man was backbencher Geoff Thompson, who went on to become a parliamentary undersecretary under Muldoon, despite his disloyalty.

2 These influences are summarised in Colin James, *New Territory: The transformation of New Zealand, 1984–92*, Allen and Unwin, Wellington, 1992, pp.334–9.

3 I have a number of other 'what ifs' (quite apart from Nigel Roberts's topic) but this is the most sweeping in its potential implications. Others might be: (1) if Jim Anderton had stayed in the Labour Party instead of forming the breakaway New Labour Party in 1989, Labour might well have won the close-fought election of 1993 (perhaps with him as leader) because it would have lost fewer votes to its left and that would have blunted the economic reforms; (2) if the Christian Democrat half of the Christian Coalition in 1996 had fielded candidates in all its share of the seats instead of a mere handful, that might have pushed its vote over five per cent and established a moral conservative bridgehead, which had to wait until the Christian Democrats (renamed Future New Zealand) merged with United for the 2002 election; and (3) if Winston Peters had really *not* been a Maori, that might well have narrowed NZ First's appeal and reduced its influence in the late 1990s and mid-2000s.

4 For convenience, I use the term 'orthodox' to describe a version of Keynesian economic management applied in New Zealand from the 1940s. This relied on a high degree of internal regulation, and protection of local industry from imports, to part-insulate the domestic economy from external shocks. Among the instruments were a fixed exchange rate (changed by fiat by the finance minister), import quotas, consumer and industry subsidies and, from the mid-1970s, budget deficits (financed to a large degree by external borrowing) to maintain consumer welfare and employment.

5 Barry Gustafson, *The First 50 Years: A History of the National Party*, Reed Methuen, Auckland, 1986, p.125: 'One long-term woman activist remarked that before Muldoon became leader, "I could have gone into a room and known it was a National party gathering just by glancing around but [after] I'd go to the National party gatherings and think I was at the local football club . . . He brought a whole new group in."'

6   I shall use the phrase 'market-liberal' to encompass the range of economic ideological tendencies which go under various titles, including 'more-market', 'free-market', 'classical liberal', 'neoliberal', 'neoclassical' and 'new right'. Generally the phrase encompasses a preference for more reliance on market mechanisms and less on regulation, the transferral of government activities that might be described as 'businesses' into private hands, relatively low taxes and government spending, greater private provision and funding of social services (such as health and education), and targeted instead of universal social assistance.

7   Gustafson, *The First 50 Years*, p.139.

8   Don Brash's successful challenge to Bill English for the leadership of the National Party in October 1980 did not have a majority committed in advance and Brash expected to fall just short.

9   If Talboys had won, it is near-inconceivable that National could have won in 1984, whether under him or any other leader, in which case the actual-history post-1984 scenario kicks in, though it might not have been configured in exactly the same way, since Talboys might have averted the financial/currency crisis that gave Roger Douglas his initial impetus.

10 Indeed, he might even have wrested the prime ministership back off Talboys before the 1981 election. If so, actual history would have been put back on track, so that option needs no further exploration here.

12 What if the All Blacks had not won the final rugby test against the Springboks in 1981?

1   Warwick Roger, *Old Heroes: The 1956 Springbok Tour and the Lives Beyond*, Hodder and Stoughton, Auckland, 1991. By 1981 there was perhaps a degree of frustration among New Zealand rugby followers, as over the 1976–80 period the All Blacks had won 'only' seventeen of their twenty-seven tests (63 per cent), fewer wins than in any four-year period since World War II other than immediately after the war, from 1946–50, when they won seven out of fourteen. In 1976 there was some feeling that the All Blacks had lost the test series in South Africa because of biased hometown refereeing, with the referee in the final two tests (each won by the Springboks) telling the All Blacks following the final test, 'I have to live here'.

2   In fact the referee had allowed play to run several minutes into 'injury time', probably because there had been time out taken during the game when a low-flying plane dropped flour bombs onto the field, one of which hit an All Black player—not Allan Hewson (another potential 'what if'!).

3   The author acknowledges the advice and support of sportscaster Keith Quinn in selecting possible images to accompany this scenario.

4   All voting figures are from 'The General Election 1981', *Appendices to the Journals of the House of Representatives*, E9, Wellington, 1982.

5   In the actual election these three seats had the smallest winning margins for National—Taupo by 36 votes, Eden by 117 votes, and Gisborne by 150.

6   See Roger, *Old Heroes*.

13 **What if the fourth Labour government had allowed a visit by the USS Buchanan?**

1   For a fuller version of this author's interpretation of events, see John Henderson, 'The warrior peacenik: setting the record straight on ANZUS and the Fiji coup', in Margaret Clark, ed, *For the Record: Lange and the Fourth Labour Government*, Dunmore Press, Wellington, 2005, pp.136–43. This book also contains recollections from a number of other participants in the events covered in this chapter. For Lange's own view, see David Lange, *Nuclear Free: The New Zealand Way*, Penguin Books, Auckland, 1990.

14 **What if Ruth Richardson had never delivered the 'mother of all budgets'?**

1   See Colin James and Alan McRobie, *Turning Point: 1993 General Election and Beyond*, Bridget Williams, Wellington, 1993, pp.32–63.
2   See Jon Johansson, 'Past sins continue to haunt National's leader', *New Zealand Herald*, 16 July 2002; and Jon Johansson, 'Leadership and the Campaign,' in Jonathan Boston, Stephen Church, Stephen Levine, Elizabeth McLeay and Nigel Roberts, eds, *New Zealand Votes: The 2002 election*, Victoria University Press, Wellington, 2003.
3   I would extend this hypothesis to incorporate the 2002–05 period, during which first Bill English was replaced by the unlikely politician Dr Don Brash and then National—driven by its desperate political context—defected from the previous consensus around Treaty and race policy in the run-up to the 2005 election campaign, provoking division and souring race discourse.
4   James and McRobie, *Turning Point*, p.32.
5   See Niall Ferguson, *Virtual History: Alternatives and counterfactuals*, Macmillan, London, 1997, pp.6–7.
6   See Robert Cowley, *What If? Military Historians imagine what might have been*, Pan Books, London, 2003, p.xvi.
7   For instance, during the 2002 campaign, when Bill English was asked whether he wanted to offer a *mea culpa* for the Richardson era he struggled mightily throughout the campaign to construct a cogent response, saying variously that National had 'moved on', that it had taken 'it on the chin', or that he was 'only looking ahead'. When finally pinned down by John Campbell in the final *TV3* leaders' debate, English said that he wanted to 'turn his back on the dogmatic and narrow-minded attitude that came through in the policy and made New Zealanders feel threatened'.

15 **What if Winston Peters had chosen to go with Labour in 1996?**

1   Nigel S. Roberts, *One Network News Special*, Television New Zealand, 13 October 1996.
2   Jonathan Boston, 'Forming a government' in Raymond Miller, ed, *New Zealand Government and Politics*, Oxford University Press, Melbourne, 2001, p.122.
3   Boston. 'Forming a government', p.122.
4   Further details of the conference and Rein Taagepera's contribution to it are contained in Jørgen Elklit, ed, *Electoral Systems for Emerging Democracies*, Ministry of Foreign Affairs/Danida, Copenhagen, 1997.

Notes

5 Boston, 'Forming a government', p.124.

6 *The Dominion*, 6 December 1996, p.1.

7 Michael Laver and Kenneth Sheplse, *Making and Breaking Governments: Cabinets and legislatures in parliamentary democracies*, Cambridge University Press, Cambridge, 1996, p.54.

8 Gabriel Dekel, Survey Research Unit, Waikato University, 31 October 1996.

9 Raymond Miller, 'Coalition Government: The people's choice', in Jack Vowles, Peter Aimer, Susan Banducci, and Jeffrey Karp, eds, *Voters' Victory: New Zealand's first election under proportional representation*, Auckland University Press, Auckland, 1998, p.129.

10 Jonathan Boston and Elizabeth McLeay, 'Forming the First MMP Government: Theory, Practice and Prospects', in Jonathan Boston, Stephen Levine, Elizabeth McLeay, and Nigel S. Roberts, eds, *From Campaign to Coalition: New Zealand's first general election under proportional representation*, Dunmore Press, Palmerston North, 1997, p.215.

11 Boston and McLeay, 'Forming the First MMP Government', p.217.

12 Boston and McLeay, 'Forming the First MMP Government', p.209.

13 Jonathan Boston, 'The Cabinet and Policy Making Under the Fourth Labour Government', in Martin Holland and Jonathan Boston, eds, *The Fourth Labour Government: Politics and policy in New Zealand*, 2nd edition, Oxford University Press, Auckland, 1990, p.64.

14 See also Boston and McLeay, 'Forming the First MMP Government', p.215.

15 Again, see Boston and McLeay, 'Forming the First MMP Government', p.240, for further details in this regard.

16 Boston and McLeay, 'Forming the First MMP Government', p.237.

17 Coalition Agreement, 41.3 (d).

18 This has been well documented by Boston and McLeay in 'Forming the First MMP Government'. See especially p.239, which is where these quotes can be found.

19 Tizard was elected MP for Auckland Central in 1996, while Turia and Hobbs were elected on Labour's list. Although Dyson lost the Banks Peninsula seat in 1996, she was returned to parliament as a Labour list MP.

20 Helena Catt, 'Women, Maori and Minorities: Microrepresentation and MMP' in Jonathan Boston, Stephen Levine, Elizabeth McLeay, and Nigel S. Roberts, eds, *From Campaign to Coalition: New Zealand's first general election under proportional representation*, Dunmore Press, Palmerston North, 1997, p.200.

21 Boston and McLeay, 'Forming the First MMP Government', p.209.

22 Hunt was first elected to parliament in November 1966, and thus had 30 years of continuous parliamentary experience when he was elected speaker on Friday, 13 December 1996. Needless to say, Hunt had to endure opposition taunts about his election proving that it was, indeed, a Black Friday. These gibes were, in part, a result of the fact that the new government refused to re-elect National's Jim Gerard as deputy speaker, opting for Labour MP Geoff Braybrooke instead.

23 For further details both in this regard and with respect to the changes to parliament's standing orders, see Jonathan Boston, Stephen Levine, Elizabeth McLeay, and Nigel S. Roberts, *New Zealand Under MMP: A new politics?*, Auckland University Press, Auckland, 1996, pp.71–86.

24 See, for example, Stephen Levine and Nigel S. Roberts, 'Surveying the Snark: Voting behaviour in the 1996 general election', in Jonathan Boston, Stephen Levine, Elizabeth McLeay, and Nigel S. Roberts, eds, *From Campaign to Coalition: New Zealand's first general election under proportional representation,* Dunmore Press, Palmerston North, 1997, pp.191–3.

25 Even the *Women's Weekly* noted that 'Labour leader Helen Clark outshone her political opponents in the recent campaign . . . blitzing [them] in the TV debates.' See *New Zealand Women's Weekly,* 28 October 1996, pp.6–7.

26 It is believed that the source of this quote was Jonathan Elworthy, but I have been unable to confirm it: sadly, Elworthy died in mid-2005.

27 See Fiona Barker, 'Negotiating with New Zealand First: A Study of its coalition agreements', in Jonathan Boston, Stephen Levine, Elizabeth McLeay, and Nigel S. Roberts, eds, *From Campaign to Coalition: New Zealand's first general election under proportional representation,* Dunmore Press, Palmerston North,1997, pp.247–73.

28 See Barker, 'Negotiating With New Zealand First', p.250.

29 Barker, 'Negotiating With New Zealand First', p.264.

30 Barker, 'Negotiating With New Zealand First', p.268.

31 *Sunday News,* 9 March 1997, p.4.

32 See Bob Gregory, 'Political responsibility for bureaucratic incompetence: Tragedy at Cave Creek', *Public Administration,* vol.76, no.3, 1998, pp.519–38.

33 The Beehive is the widely used nickname for the executive wing of the New Zealand parliament.

34 Paul Perry and Alan Webster, *New Zealand Politics at the Turn of the Millennium: Attitudes and values about politics and government,* Alpha Publications, Auckland, 1999.

35 The Chief Electoral Officer, 'The General Election 1996', *Appendices to the Journals of the House of Representatives,* E9, Wellington, 1997, p.5.

36 Jon Johansson, 'The Rhetoric of Illusion', *Political Science,* vol.56, no.2, December 2004, p.127.

37 Johansson, 'The Rhetoric of Illusion', p.117.

38 Barker, 'Negotiating With New Zealand First', p.251.

39 See Barker, 'Negotiating With New Zealand First', p.271. Barker also points out that had NZ First chosen the National Party as its coalition partner, there would have been a referendum on a 'compulsory superannuation scheme . . . no later than the end of September 1997 for implementation on 1 July 1998'. In light of information from survey research into electors' attitudes towards altering New Zealand's superannuation policies, I would confidently predict that had it ever been held, the National–NZ First referendum would have been soundly defeated (but at the same time I concede that we will never really know what would have happened regarding a 'counterfactual' proposition like this). See Stephen Levine and Nigel S. Roberts, 'Elderly people and the political process', in Peggy Koopman-Boyden, *New Zealand's Ageing Society,* Daphne Brassell Associates Press, Wellington, 1993, pp.230–54, especially p.238.

40 Boston and McLeay, 'Forming the first MMP government', p.216.

41 The Taieri Plains are in Otago, south-west of Dunedin. They are renowned for heavy frosts during July and August, in particular, and the area also experiences fairly frequent floods.

42 In August 1990, in response to three rounds of questions to discern who

electors 'would vote for as prime minister', Mike Moore was supported by 56 per cent of those interviewed, compared with only 37 per cent support for Jim Bolger. See Stephen Levine and Nigel S. Roberts, 'National to Power: Voter choice in 1990', in Hyam Gold, ed, *New Zealand Politics in Perspective*, 3rd edition, Longman Paul, Auckland, 1992, p.497.

43 There is a good deal of evidence to suggest that the deputy prime minister knew of the planned coup in advance but did nothing to alert the prime minister to it.

44 Boston and McLeay, 'Forming the first MMP government', p.216.

45 For further details, see, for example, Michael Bassett, *Third Party Politics in New Zealand 1911–1931*, Historical Publications, Auckland, 1982).

46 Geoffrey Palmer and Matthew Palmer, *Bridled Power: New Zealand constitution and government*, 4th edition, Oxford University Press, Melbourne, 2004, p.57.

47 Caroline Morris, 'The Governor-General, the Reserve Powers, Parliament and MMP: A new era', *Victoria University of Wellington Law Review*, vol.25, 1995, p.345.

48 It is worth noting that Mike Moore was only the third New Zealander to have been prime minister on two separate occasions during the twentieth century. The other two were Joseph Ward (who was prime minister from 1906–12 and 1928–30) and Keith Holyoake (1957, and 1960–72). However, while Ward and Holyoake each had at least one substantial term in office, Moore had only two brief stints in power and is the only New Zealand prime minister ever to have lost two elections and won none.

49 For further details, see Stephen Levine and Nigel S. Roberts, 'The New Zealand Electoral Referendum of 1992', *Electoral Studies*, vol.12, no.2, June 1993, pp.158–67; as well as Boston, Levine, McLeay, and Roberts, *New Zealand under MMP*, p.21.

50 After the March 1996 census and the subsequent Maori option, the representation commission began drawing New Zealand's new electorate boundaries. However, because the representation commission's report had not been not promulgated by the time the 1997 election was held, the 1997 MMP election was based on the same boundaries as those used for the 1996 MMP election. There were, therefore, sixty-five electorate seats in the House of Representatives in both elections: sixteen South Island electorates, forty-four North Island electorates, and five Maori electorates.

51 Neither the 1956 Electoral Act nor the 1993 Electoral Act entrenched provisions for Maori representation, which meant that the former Maori seats could have been abolished at any time by a simple plurality vote in parliament. By way of contrast, however, section 249(b) of the 1998 Electoral Act, passed under National, stipulated that Maori electorates cannot be reintroduced without the support of either a 75 per cent vote of all the members of parliament or majority support in a referendum.

52 A final irony of the MMP era was that on 23 March 1998, five days prior to the second binding electoral reform referendum, the representation commission issued its provisional report regarding the *Proposed Electoral Districts 1998*, which detailed its suggested boundaries for sixty-seven MMP electorates— that is, increasing the number of North Island general electorates by one and the number of Maori electorates by one as well. The results of the 28 March 1998 referendum meant that the representation commission abandoned its provisional MMP proposals and began work instead on an entirely new set

of boundaries for New Zealand's new first-past-the-post system. The new electorate boundaries were promulgated on 22 February 1999 and were used in the next general election, which was held on Saturday, 14 October 2000. After the March 2001 census, the representation commission's next report was promulgated on 21 March 2002 and first used in the 11 October 2003 general election. Because there will not be time before the 2006 general election to redraw electorate boundaries after the March 2006 census, the boundaries promulgated in 2002 will still be in place for the 2006 general election, widely expected to be held on 25 November 2006 (symbolically returning to the day that was traditionally regarded as election day in New Zealand—namely, the last Saturday in November).

Epilogue

1   See Geoffrey Hawthorn, *Plausible Worlds: Possibility and understanding in history and the social sciences*, Cambridge University Press, Cambridge, 1991, p.121.

Acknowledgements

1   See C.P. Snow, 'Introduction' to Sir Arthur Conan Doyle, *The Case-Book of Sherlock Holmes*, John Murray and Jonathan Cape, London, first published 1927, introduction published 1974.

2   Nigel Roberts is no doubt the only contributor to the book to already be cited in the literature of political science for a daring counterfactual. One of political science's most distinguished practitioners, Professor Rein Taagepera, has written: 'The role of random events should not be underestimated. As Nigel Roberts asks regarding New Zealand: "What would have happened if David Lange had not made an inadvertent pledge during the 1987 election to hold a binding referendum on the question of electoral reform?" Except for this irretrievable slip of tongue, the ball may not have started rolling.' The quote is from Rein Taagapera, 'Designing Electoral Rules', in Andrew Reynolds, ed, *The Architecture of Democracy: Constitutional Design, Conflict Management, and Democracy*, Oxford University Press, Oxford, 2002, pp.250–51.

Contributors

Donald Anderson, a policy advisor for the New Zealand Defence Force, has a BA (Hons) in history from Victoria University of Wellington and an MA in history from the University of Canterbury. He has been a member of the Trade Union History Project Committee since November 2003 and is the author of 'Crime as protest and the 1913 general strike in Wellington', in Melanie Nolan, ed, *Revolution: The 1913 great strike in New Zealand*, Canterbury University Press, Christchurch, 2006.

Giselle Byrnes is a senior lecturer in the history programme at Victoria University of Wellington, where she teaches courses on Maori–Pakeha relations, comparative colonial history and the Treaty of Waitangi. She has published two books, *Boundary Markers: Land surveying and the colonisation of New Zealand*, Bridget Williams Books, Wellington, 2001, and *The Waitangi Tribunal and New Zealand History*, Oxford University Press, Auckland, 2003. Giselle Byrnes is currently editing a new general history of New Zealand, namely, *The New Oxford History of New Zealand*. In 2005 she was awarded the Fulbright Visiting Lecturer at Georgetown University Award, a distinguished appointment which she took up in mid-2006.

Aaron Fox received his PhD in history from the University of Otago for his study, 'The Power Game: The development of the Manapouri-Tiwai Point electro-industrial complex 1904–1969'. Dr Fox is assistant director of medals policy for the New Zealand Defence Force in Wellington. He is the co-editor of *Lenin's Legacy Down Under: New Zealand's Cold War*, University of Otago Press, Dunedin, 2003, a collection of essays offering a reassessment of New Zealand's Cold War experience.

Bob Gregory is an associate professor in the school of government, and in the political science and international relations programme, at Victoria University of Wellington. He has published widely on the politics of bureaucratic behaviour, state sector reform and public policy theory. He advises that he once had a strong interest in rugby but that this greatly diminished soon after the All Blacks became a commercial brand name rather than a sports team.

Janine Hayward is a senior lecturer in New Zealand politics at the University of Otago, where her research focuses on Treaty politics with particular interest in resource management and representation issues. She is the editor of *Local Government and the Treaty of Waitangi*, Oxford University Press, Auckland, 2003, and co-editor of *The Waitangi Tribunal: Te Roopu Whakamana i te Tiriti o Waitangi*, Bridget Williams Books, Wellington, 2004. In 2004 she became book review editor of *Political Science* and in 2005 she was appointed as founding book review editor for the Royal Society of New Zealand's newly established on-line social sciences journal, *Kotuitui*.

John Henderson is associate professor of political science at the University of Canterbury's school of political science and communication. His research and teaching spcialties include New Zealand politics, Pacific Islands politics, and the study of political leadership.During the 1980s he worked for New Zealand prime minister, David Lange, as chair of the prime minister's advisory group and as director of the prime minister's office.

Kathryn M. Hunter would have simply been migrating interstate when she came to Victoria University of Wellington in 1995 if New Zealand had joined the Commonwealth of Australia. As it was, after studying at the University of Melbourne, where she gained a PhD in history, she was appointed to the history programme at Victoria University and moved countries rather than states. Her research interests include women's and gender history, Australian history, and trans-Tasman comparison. She is the author of *Father's Right-Hand Man: Women on Australia's family farms in the age of federation*, Australian Scholarly Publishing, Melbourne, 2004.

Colin James is a political journalist of more than thirty years experience and is well known to anyone who has been following New Zealand politics at all closely over this period. He writes in the *New Zealand Herald* and in *Management Magazine* and is an occasional commentator on New Zealand radio and television. He has written, co-written or edited eight books about New Zealand on a variety of topics: political, economic and social change, elections, the state sector and the constitution, as well as numerous chapters in other books and several monographs. Colin James has held several university fellowships and has contributed to academic seminars in the United States, Japan, the United Kingdom and Australia.

Jon Johansson has a PhD in political science and is a lecturer in the political science and international relations programme at Victoria University of Wellington. In 2005 he edited a special issue of the journal, *Political Science*, devoted to 'leadership in New Zealand'. His book, *Two Titans: Muldoon, Lange and leadership*, was published in 2005. Dr Johansson is a frequent commentator on New Zealand politics on television, radio and in the press, and has teaching and research interests in leadership, rhetoric, New Zealand politics and political psychology.

Stephen Levine is a professor of political science at Victoria University of Wellington and was the founding head of the university's school of history, philosophy, political science and international relations. His teaching includes responsibility for the parliamentary internship programme and he has written extensively about New Zealand's politics, elections and international relations. Professor Levine has served several terms as editor of *Political Science* and in 2005 he was appointed founding co-editor of the Royal Society of New Zealand's new social science journal, *Kotuitui*. In July 2005 his 'what if' article—'what if Winston Peters was made minister of foreign affairs' after the September 2005 election—was published in the *Dominion Post*.

Ian McGibbon has a PhD in history and is the general editor (war history) in New Zealand's ministry for culture and heritage. He has written extensively on New Zealand's involvement in the Second World War and his *New Zealand and the Second World War: The people, the battles and the legacy* was published in 2004. His other publications include a two-volume history of New Zealand's involvement in the Korean War as well as guidebooks to New Zealand's Western Front and Gallipoli battlefields. Ian McGibbon also edited *The Oxford Companion to New Zealand Military History*, published in 2000.

Denis McLean is a graduate of Victoria University of Wellington and of Oxford University. A member of the New Zealand foreign service for over twenty years, he served as secretary of defence in Wellington for nine years and was New Zealand's ambassador to the United States from 1991 to 1994. He has been a visiting fellow at the Woodrow Wilson International Center for Scholars, at the Carnegie Endowment for International Peace, and at the United States Institute of Peace. From 1995 to 1998 he was the Warburg professor of international relations at Simmons College in Boston. His commentary on New Zealand–Australia relations, *The Prickly Pair: Making nationalism in Australia and New Zealand*, was published by the University of Otago Press in 2004.

Erik Olssen is emeritus professor of history at the University of Otago. He has published extensively on aspects of US history and comparative social history as well as New Zealand history. His *The Red Feds: Revolutionary industrial unionism and the New Zealand Federation of Labour 1908–1914* was published by Oxford University Press in 1988. In 2004 Professor Olssen was the recipient of a prestigious Distinguished Visitor's Award from the Fulbright Foundation.

Nigel S. Roberts is an associate professor of political science at Victoria University of Wellington. He will be familiar to New Zealanders as one of Television New Zealand's election-night commentators since 1987, and he was a Radio New Zealand election-night commentator from 1975 to 1984. He has written extensively on New Zealand politics and elections, and has co-edited books about each of New Zealand's elections under MMP. He has won four Wallace Awards from New Zealand's electoral commission for his contribution to the analysis and understanding of New Zealand elections.

John Wilson holds a PhD from the University of Auckland and has taught in the political science and international relations programme at Victoria University of Wellington over a period of years. His courses at Victoria university focus on the politics of the environment and on the impact of globalisation on the state and its economic management. He is also a research analyst for the parliamentary library in Wellington, where he is responsible for providing statistics, research and analysis in the areas of New Zealand politics, trade, international relations and crime. He is also the editor of the parliamentary library's foreign affairs bulletin.